'Finally a book about abuse that blazes a path through the complex dynamics of domestic violence and helps the one who is being hurt to look at herself – with compassion and tough love. To be strategic and smart. To choose herself.

'This fairy tale busting, no-bullshit, no judgement gem of a book brings together the collaborative genius of a brilliant therapist and a courageous survivor of abuse and offers stories, strategies and solutions to one of the most misunderstood and intractable of human predicaments: when a woman loves a man who hurts her. This book will save lives.'

- JOANNE FEDLER, INTERNATIONAL BEST-SELLING AUTHOR AND WOMEN'S RIGHTS ACTIVIST

First published by MFBooks Joburg, an imprint of
Jacana Media (Pty) Ltd.
South Africa

ISBN - 10: 1512270083
ISBN - 13: 9781512270082

Cover design by Shawn Paikin

When Loving Him Hurts

Recovery from an
abusive relationship

Sue Hickey
and
Philippa Sklaar

We dedicate this book to every woman:
who smiled while she wept inside, who kept going
when she thought she couldn't and who cared
about the woman alongside her.
We wish you all the strength and insight
for the journey ahead.

Contents

Preface

*It's embarrassing to go home to a man who has hurt
and humiliated you. It's even more embarrassing to
want to and most of the time you do.*

Abuse is not just part and parcel of the plight of the poor. It hovers in the shadows and secrets of many middle- and upper-class marriages and relationships. It is not as simple as covering up a bruise with make-up or fabricating how you walked into the door, pre-occupied and careless. It is not confined to angry voices in the night, thuds and falls and restraining orders. Abuse includes words that cut like knives and humour that's sugar-coated arsenic. It's also about sexual wounding, humiliation, financial manipulation, threats of rejection, and alienation from all that makes you secure.

We all know that the workplace, family and friendship circles have their fair share of abusive elements, but the love relationship stands unrivalled in its ability to damage us. It is the most difficult place to flex our muscles against disempowerment. This book offers women ways to understand and manage ourselves and our relationships differently.

Did you know?
- Most abused women don't heed the signs of abuse because they don't know what they are.

- Most people think abuse is purely physical.
- Unless a woman has been raped or assaulted she cannot report it.
- Despite it seeming logical to the concerned outsider, an abused woman usually cannot just up and leave. The responsibility of children, rent and the effects of disempowerment that come with systematic abuse need to be overcome.

So, why doesn't she just leave?

In answering this most fundamental question, why doesn't she just leave, we've divided the book into three parts, each dealing with an important aspect of the answer to this question. We discuss how you can begin to heal yourself by examining your own answers and developing your understanding of the abusive pattern, developing the skills required to manage yourself in a relationship and beginning the journey of healing.

- Because she doesn't understand the abusive pattern, the profile of the abuser or her own co-dependency (Part 1)
- Because she doesn't have the skills required to manage herself or her relationship (Part 2)
- Because she is in survival mode and has not begun the journey of healing (Part 3)

When Loving Him Hurts breaks open victim-based myths on domestic abuse. The book includes a series of 'reflections' for you, the reader, to work through as you read the book. Should you wish to receive individual feedback and support, you are welcome to go online and register for our online counselling course at www.whenlovinghimhurts.com. If you prefer not to submit the reflections, we suggest that you do them anyway. Acquiring insight and skills is no easy feat and it helps to work with the information instead of just reading it.

Throughout the book you will find extracts from the letters we received and stories from women who agreed to have their stories told. Please be aware that the patterns of abuse are often very similar and so if someone's story sounds familiar it will be familiar to many abusive relationships. Many of the women whose stories we share have asked for their identities to be protected. The book also includes blogs from our website www.whenlovinghimhurts.com.

It is the combined insights of a therapist, a survivor and the women who offered up their stories to be retold to those who needed to hear them. We hope this book will be marked, written in, dog-eared and tattered from use. Like *The Velveteen Rabbit* it should look worn from being depended upon.

Acknowledgements

We would like to express our gratitude:

To Melinda from MFBooks Joburg who believed in the newcomers and fought to bring this book to print. Without you and Bridget, from Jacana Media, this manuscript would have collected dust in a box.

Megan, who managed to edit our material in such a relaxed and elegant way – while planning a wedding!

Anna, who nagged me until the book was well under way, and the women who agreed to share their stories so that other women don't feel so alone.

Philippa and I thank everyone who engaged with the website www.whenlovinghimhurts.com.

From Sue:

Thank you to my daughter, Jade, for never commenting on my unavailability, my sisters for their constant encouragement, and Pat for her discerning eye.

From Philippa:

In everyone's life a multitude of opportunities arrive and so often we don't recognise them for what they are. Sue, your offer to assist in the writing of this book was one of those opportunities. "Thank you" seems so inadequate to express my gratitude. What an inspirational journey this has been. Each of your insights delivers an 'Aha Moment' … they are pearls of wisdom that nourish the soul and comfort the psyche. I sincerely hope our readers experience this book as one of those opportunities.

Introduction

*In the beginning I thought it was impossible. Then
I began to understand and that too was difficult.
It was only because of Sue's guidance, through her
powerful and inspirational words, that I finally began
to heal. The dawn broke, the light slowly leaked
into my life. But in the fullness of time, I found
serenity and hope was mine again.*

My name is Sue Hickey and I have been a therapist in private practice for over twenty-five years. I started my practice in my late twenties and many of my clients were women who were desperately unhappy in their marriages and had husbands who were unwilling to attend marriage counselling. Some husbands claimed to be too busy and others simply denied their contribution to their wife's unhappiness in  any way. Some of those women claimed they were suffering from depression or anxiety. All suffered from a lack of self-confidence and many believed that they were the reason for the unhappiness in their marriage.

When we see a doctor about a medical problem, we explain our symptoms and hope for an accurate diagnosis from which will come a specific form of treatment designed to attend to our specific symptoms. However, when we arrive we usually have some idea of what is wrong with us. Beginning therapy is not that different. We arrive with what is called the presenting problem. For example, "I feel depressed all the time and I think my husband has fallen out of love with me. I am anxious and have no idea what to do". Unlike a medical session, the process is much slower and the client is required to explain what their lives look like and feel like. They tell their story. In this telling many things become clearer and patterns come to light that are often difficult to see unless the whole story is told.

Often those stories are about men treating their wives and partners in a way that is clearly unacceptable. I used to think that it sounded as though there was one man out there married to all these women because their stories had so many similarities. They were narcissistic men, insensitive men and serial womanisers, and these women struggled to understand why they were being treated the way they were. They were struggling to salvage their crumbling self-esteem from an onslaught of criticism and cruelty.

One day one of my clients phoned me to say she had found a book called *Men Who Hate Women and the Women Who Love Them* by Dr Susan Forward. She bought me a copy and I read it, and promptly bought five more copies for other clients. I confess that I didn't like the title because, while they qualified as the worst husbands on the planet, I never had the impression that they hated their wives. Dr Susan Forward, whose book I highly recommend, explained that these men were misogynists. By dictionary definition a misogynist is a man who hates women – and clearly their behaviour is hateful – but I don't think they hate their wives or women in general. They do, however, create abusive relationships, and the patterns of abuse are startlingly similar.

Let's call the client who found the book and bought it for me Anna. It's not her name but she is the reason that this book is in existence. When I told Anna how many other clients I had given the book to she suggested a support group. I talked to the others and they all agreed. So we began a support group for these women and encouraged newcomers to join us. A few months later I received a call from a radio station asking if we would be prepared to participate in a radio talk show. I discussed the invitation with the group and they all agreed that Anna and I would go on the show. Anna, of course, was to remain anonymous. The radio talk show was a huge success and we were very pleased with the outcome.

Then the letters began to arrive at the radio station. There were hundreds of them and my phone rang off the hook for weeks. There were so many women asking for help and identifying themselves finally as abused women in abusive relationships. We were, of course, completely unprepared for this and frankly had no idea of what to do or how to handle it and so we did nothing.

I got married and had a child. Our support group came to an end and life continued, and over time I have wondered what happened to them. I saw one of them in an exam hall and it delighted me to see her there. Of course, Anna was on my mind often as she had been so instrumental in the creation of the support group. Earlier this year I ran into her by chance in a coffee shop and we arranged to meet and talk. She is one of the women who decided to stay in her marriage and I needed to ask her if she was glad of that decision after all these years. I wanted to know if he had ever changed and if it had been worth it. She will give you her own answers in her introduction a little further on in this book.

Once again she has been instrumental in getting me to start something. Now, much has changed in the last twenty-five years, not least of which is the internet, so this time, instead of a support group for ten or so women, we decided to take it to the internet and see if we could assist more women. We have both been painfully aware of how we had neglected to attend to the bag of letters and the barrage of appeals we had received.

That support group twenty-five years ago was one of the most powerful learning experiences of my career. It gave those involved the sure knowledge that they were not in it alone. It was not their fault. Their shame and humiliation at being treated the way they were was not theirs alone. Just turning up every week was an act of assertion. Many lied about where they were and endured many rows and punishment for their attendance but they still came. They were given the opportunity to tell their story to other women who had endured the same problems. Their despair and loneliness was respected. No one said stupid things like, "So why don't you just leave" as though it was as easy as changing your socks. They came to really understand that it was not their fault and not as a result of their inadequacy.

At times I was afraid of the anger they seemed to unleash. They began to fight back and I remember feeling fearful for them and afraid that I would be responsible if anything awful happened to one of them. They began to understand that it was their decision to stay or go and if they decided to stay, they had to stay differently. They needed to understand the abuser and the abusive patterns. They needed to fight back but also be safe. They needed to rebuild their self-confidence despite the constant criticism and ridicule that they endured.

Each one of them is one of my unsung heroes. They go out there every day and survive in some form or another. Many of them appear to the world to be one of the privileged few, well-heeled and fortunate, but they aren't. I dedicate this book to each of them who arrived every week and taught me how painful it can be when love hurts and how strong one needs to be in order to survive.

We all know that there are abusive parents, abusive bosses and abusive friends. When we ran the support group, a man applied to join the group as he was being abused by his wife, although we elected not to include him at the time.

This book does not consider the full range of abusive situations that people find themselves in. The intimate relationship has its own particular dynamic and so this book applies only to women who are in emotionally abusive relationships with a husband or romantic partner. The purpose of it is to guide you through the process of healing yourself.

My name is Philippa Sklaar. I was born and raised in South Africa, and wrecked most of my life there. In 2001 I boarded a plane to the United States to start my life afresh. At the time I told myself and anyone who asked that I was immigrating because America was the 'land of dreams' to me like it was for so many others. I intended  to create an opportunity for my sons to immigrate. I did what so many people do – I attempted a geographical escape, thinking I could leave my problems behind me. I knew that I needed to change my relationships but the fundamental truth was that I had taken myself with all my problems and relocated us to the US.

With the benefit of hindsight I think the truth is that I fled from South Africa. I had just endured a second failed marriage. The abuse that I experienced at his hands made me damaged in places I never knew existed. I was more devastated and ashamed than I was prepared to acknowledge even to myself. With my bravest face and fearful heart I arrived in the US determined to rectify my life. I was well aware that I had in some ways contributed to the failure of my life. I had selected not one man but two who had treated me appallingly. Twice I had believed that marriage would transform a difficult and hurtful relationship into a 'happily ever after'. Twice I had believed that if I loved the Beast well enough, he would become Prince Charming and I would live the life of a Princess.

Intellectually I was well aware of the fact that I had much reflection as well as hard work ahead of me. I needed to work on building my life from scratch as well as changing my thought patterns. I realised that in some way I was part of the problem and I resolved to be hyper vigilant in the future. It constantly amazes me that you can tell yourself something rational and sane over and over but it's only when you are able to act on it that you know you are finally healed.

I moved to Los Angeles and settled myself in with aplomb, despite my fear and loneliness about my uncertain future. After a few months I met a man who I was convinced was completely different from the men I had married in South Africa. Well, I was wrong, and it took a third, and very damaging, relationship for me to finally re-look at myself, my thoughts, patterns and insights.

Sue had been my therapist in South Africa and in the grief and devastation of my third failed marriage I called her. She talked me through that divorce over long-distance telephone calls and emails. I needed to speak to someone who had known me for a long time. Sue had warned me against my second marriage and had patiently picked up the pieces throughout its collapse. I needed someone who knew my whole story and everything about abusive relationships. It was she who could help me identify the pattern yet again – the abusive relationship I couldn't see coming. We have become close friends in the process.

> *When I could no longer stand the person I was,*
> *I began to heal. It was a painful beginning*
> *and a magnificent journey.*

Ever since I arrived in the US I have been inviting Sue to visit. She and I see one another from time to time when I am in South Africa and we talk on the phone. Sue is what I call a 'reluctant traveller'. In April 2014 I moved to the Berkshires and as I walked into the house and saw a panorama of trees and a hummingbird on the ledge I just knew she would love it. I picked up my phone there and then and called her, described my vision and reissued my invitation. I find it remarkable that after all these years in which I have issued invitation after invitation, it was on this occasion that Sue's life circumstances made it possible for her to accept. She told me that she had Googled the Berkshires and the photograph was of the trees in the fall. It was the trees that did it. Thank heavens it was summer – it was impossible to get her to come inside. She was completely captivated by the view of the ski slopes (of which there are none in South Africa), the trees and the hummingbirds. That got us talking about nature's perfect understanding of timing. The Universe is no less skilled and we are both excited and in awe of the perfect timing that has made this project possible.

While Sue was with me she told me that she was working on a book for women in abused relationships. She told me about the bag of unanswered letters after the talk show that had sat heavily on her conscience. I have always known Sue to be a fan of AA as the best support system for any alcoholic. The reason, she claims, is that no matter how hard you study an issue, the nuances are always best understood by 'someone who has been there'. She believes that a recovering alcoholic gains more confidence from seeing someone who has actually 'done it' than from the person who explains why and how it should be done. And so, with that in mind, Sue invited me to assist her in the writing of this book on healing yourself in the abusive relationship. Like the recovered alcoholic has much to offer, she believes that I do too. I was so excited to be a part of this project and, with heartfelt appreciation of her offer, I accepted.

As my guest we spent many hours trawling through the work she had already done, drinking copious amounts of coffee. She asked me to go back and remember those times. We analysed and dissected incidents as we did so often in the past. However, in the past I was distraught most of the time; I just wanted her to tell me what to do next. Now my whole life is different and I can look back with quiet reflection, not static with hurt and regret, but able to observe what was going on. Sue calls that the 'reflection of the enlightened witness'.

Sue explains 'enlightened witness' like this: There comes a time when you are able to look back on your life with the serenity of a witness, not a participant. Memories no longer elicit embarrassment, hurt or anger. You no longer relive the memory. The enlightened witness doesn't recall who said what to who, when and where – she sees through the detail to the truth. She sees how insecurity is masked as anger and how fear creates begging and that need feels like love. She sees the misunderstanding not the incident.

The time that we spent together was incredibly valuable to me because, among other things, I had a real opportunity to see how much has changed for me. I no longer just *think* differently. Those thoughts are a part of me now. I have actually transformed – not just changed my thinking. Sue has had some resistance from some women who haven't wanted to 'go back and look again' but for me it was easy and we spent much time in bittersweet laughter about the things I had done. At the time I was too ashamed to tell even her what I was really doing half the time. Not telling is a form of denial because it allows us to not fully interrogate our behaviour. The most valuable realisation I have had during this time is that I really am like the recovered alcoholic not the dry drunk. I finally know that I do actually have much to offer and more importantly that I *want* to offer it. I want to assist women who, like me, felt misunderstood and ashamed of our inability to let go of a relationship that was killing us. It's like wanting to hug a shark – why on earth would you do that? I understand because I have been there, emerged damaged and broken from there, and then – heaven forbid – I went back! I know what it feels like to yearn for the love of a man who pulled out your hair, spat in your face and tried to choke you. I know what it feels like to tell people you are back there and watch their faces and see them thinking, 'then you deserve what you get'.

I also know what an absolutely inspirational walk it is when you are through the first few steps of really healing yourself. There is a place past managing yourself in an abusive relationship and that is the exciting part – healing from the inside out, not from the outside in. It is an honour and a privilege for me to be a part of this project. I know that I needed a helping hand through my darkest times and Sue has been that hand. Now I would like to hold your hand while you begin this journey.

Many women have left and returned to abusive relationships. Some left and found themselves inexplicably in other abusive relationships. Others left and regretted it and some experienced real liberation from the abusive cycle. Our recommendation is that unless you are in a physically abusive relationship, staying can be, but isn't always, a legitimate option. This book empowers women no matter whether they decide to stay or leave. Anna, introduced earlier, was one of the women who attended the original support group. She elected to stay and this is what she has to stay about that decision.

ANNA'S STORY

I am the woman Sue calls Anna. I have lived in an abusive marriage for over fifty years and I am still married. When Sue and I talked about writing this book I was eager but also reluctant to go back to those dark years and dredge up memories that have long since been buried. I was part of that first support group so many years ago and much happened before and after that time of my life. After so many years, and at this stage of my life, I have the benefit of hindsight and I really hope that it is in some way helpful to those of you who are still struggling daily with the challenges of your relationship.

I stayed in my marriage for several reasons and over the years those reasons have changed. Very simply, initially I stayed because it seemed too difficult to raise two children on my own with no money. In those days the thinking was very much that children were more stable when the parental unit was not broken down. When I was much younger staying in a bad marriage was something to be proud of and I am sincerely glad that this is no longer the case. The truth is that there have been repercussions because of that decision. Both my sons are very verbal about their belief that I made the wrong decision and they both still feel neglected by their father. Of course, he was a neglectful father. He was so preoccupied with himself that he barely noticed them unless they were bringing him glory. When they needed his understanding he was angry and critical and blamed me for their shortcomings. Even now if they are critical of him, he blames me for mollycoddling them and shouts at me because he demands more respect from them than they are prepared to give. It is all my fault – they blame me and he blames me. I sometimes feel like running into a field and just screaming.

But other than the financial reasons, I also stayed because for many years I was obsessed with him. Apart from being a misogynist he was also a serial womaniser and I spent years following him, stalking him and wishing he would love me enough not to find it necessary to seek the company and sexual favours of other women. I blamed myself and thought I wasn't good enough. He never asked me for a divorce. Perhaps if he had I might have agreed to it because the truth is that being married to him was painful beyond your imagination. I was in agony for years and years until I thankfully sought counselling.

After many years he is still critical, rude, insensitive and demeaning to me. But I changed and my life changed. I began to make money and become a person in my own right. Bit by bit I reclaimed parts of myself and then I stayed with him because I had found ways to live with him. When Sue and I met for coffee she asked me if I was glad I had stayed with him for all these years.

My answer is yes. I have made peace with my decision. It was a slow process but it happened. I must make it clear that my marriage was hell for me but it was not a physically abusive marriage. I don't wish to give the impression that staying in any relationship that threatens your physical wellbeing or that of your children is an option. It absolutely isn't. I also caution you against using finances as an excuse under these circumstances. I am a person who places high value on financial security because I have been painfully and humiliatingly poor, but poverty is not reason enough to place your life at risk.

I am elderly now and over the years I have seen many things change, but not so much beneath the surface. One of those is that so many modern women still want to be wives. In my case it wasn't beneath the surface – it defined my life the way it did the lives of so many women of my generation.

I have seen many women scurry away from an abusive marriage only to find themselves in the next one. I hope younger women will enter marriage with care and caution despite the fact that we can all sometimes throw caution to the wind when we are in love. Marriage isn't something to be rushed into with relief and gratitude. On the other hand, leaving a marriage should be done with no less caution. A hasty exit is not always the solution. It took me years to understand how ill I really was and, unless you heal yourself, you have solved nothing by leaving.

I am glad I stayed married because I don't believe I could have chosen well a second time. Now that I am older, I am able to say that I am glad he comes home every night. I am not saying the nights are easy. Often they aren't. He shouts at me for giving him mushrooms at night – "Don't you know I never eat mushrooms at night?" I didn't know but I do know next week there will be something else he doesn't eat at night. Next week I will again apologise for feeding him the wrong thing when the truth is that I care for him like he is a baby. The difference is that I simply know that it is like this and it no longer bothers me and I no longer engage in conversations with him about it.

He apologised to me a few years ago. He had surgery and I slept next to his bedside all night in case he needed anything. In the morning he took me in his arms and apologised. He didn't say he was apologising for the years of abuse and to this day I am not even sure which he meant. I don't think he even knows what he did for all those years and what he still does. However, I was as gracious as I could be in the moment although inside me I felt a sad and bitter laugh.

Of course, I look back at my life and there is some sadness about my marriage. He has never been my companion in any real sense. Sometimes he is just disinterested in me and often he is like a predator, watching and waiting for me to make a mistake so he can attack me. I have been hurt beyond words by his womanising. Making peace with my decision to stay married, however, has allowed me not to get hooked by those things. In the support group we used to talk about those hooks and how to recognise and avoid them and I do. When he blames me for our sons' failures to recognise him I don't try to engage with that conversation because I see ahead of time that it will be pointless.

At some point in my marriage I got a job that suited me and I began to do well. In the beginning the importance of that job was not about my success at all. I went to an office and people were nice to me. They listened when I spoke, they told me that I looked nice. I started to feel like I had some worth. I think my success grew from feeling worthy in that environment. So for a few hours a day I could pack away my hurt and anxiety and go somewhere where people liked me and smiled at me. As my success grew so I was able to reclaim my self-esteem.

My achievements did nothing to boost me in his eyes and the other day Sue reminded me of the occasion when I won an award. We were on our way to the event and as we were getting into the car he said, "You know I hate the way you breathe." All the way through the presentation I was painfully self-conscious of how I was breathing. There were thousands of those hurtful encounters. However, now I understand that he is the one with the problem. I understand clearly – the problem is not me.

Ironically it's precisely because I have lived in an abusive relationship that I am the success I am today. My work became so precious to me because that environment was my sanity. I believe that I am so much wiser than I would otherwise have been. I understand that all people have their challenges, even those apparently well off. I have come to really understand that if you can't change your circumstances you can change your reaction to them. I know those words are easy to say and difficult to do but I have done it.

Once I started working I no longer needed my husband financially. The truth is that I no longer love him. Love does not have that level of endurance. I live with a man I have lived with and shared a bed with for fifty years. I am a wife but inside of me I don't feel like I have had a husband in any real sense except in name.

My marriage hurt me. Whenever I felt overwhelmed by depression and when I saw myself as useless and inadequate, I used the mantra, "I don't care to care". It was my defence against the constant criticism and rejection I was subjected to. It took a long, long time. Of course, I do care about him. Often I am very proud of his achievements. However, when he is being abusive I can easily not care about that behaviour. I don't absorb it anymore.

The greatest irony of my life is that I fought with everything I have – and believe me I dug deep – to stay a wife, only to find that I was married to a man incapable of being a husband. On the upside, we travel together and I have enjoyed that despite the challenges of being with him for extended periods of time. I have a home and my children and grandchildren visit and I like the simplicity of not having divided homes. I am glad I didn't get divorced – not because he improved, but because I did. Finally I feel comfortable in my skin – not so much in my life but in my skin. I have worked with many women for many years and I know how often one can divorce one man and then find another who is scarily similar or who has other problems that are equally horrendous to live with. I really believe that staying in the abusive marriage is a legitimate option and not one to be ashamed of.

However, just 'staying' will destroy you. You will become broken and bitter and depressed beyond your wildest imagination. If you elect to stay you need assistance. Without therapy I would have died inside if not outside. In fact, I am not convinced that I could have lived in the indescribable pain that was my life.

It took me years of practice and failing and trying again, and even now there are days when I call Sue just to have a sounding board. She reminds me of all that I have learnt and all the skills now in my possession.

I wish every one of you the very best with this challenge. You have nothing to be ashamed of. The problem is not you, it's him.

PART 1

Understanding the abusive relationship

Introduction

Relationships are inherently difficult. Two adults from different backgrounds with different personalities and different needs are attempting to build a life together. They are expected to occupy the same space over an extended period of time and remain committed to one another despite the fact that they are also supposed to grow and evolve and therefore change. Both parties often feel that the other has changed so much that he or she isn't the person they married. Of course that person has changed. Life happens and we mature and develop. Not changing was the demise of the dinosaurs. Relationships are, alongside the joy and security and sense of belonging, also opportunities to grow. Relationships go through periods when we feel in harmony and happy with each other, there are times of boredom and restlessness, and times when we feel challenged beyond our capacity to cope. We often struggle to see those times as opportunities for growth. There are realistically also the deal breakers in relationships – when we no longer feel willing or able to remain committed under the circumstances.

Feeling abused does not necessarily mean that we are in an abusive relationship. We feel abused when our needs are unseen or ignored. We feel abused when we are neglected and taken advantage of. We feel abused when we think we have been unfairly criticised or when we are perceived in a negative light. Sometimes we feel abused when we are tired or negative or just filled with self-pity. However, an abusive relationship has a format, an exact pattern with characteristics that I will help you to identify later in the chapter so you can rate your relationship against that format.

When a relationship is going through a difficult phase, we often feel abused. During those times we usually argue. We say unkind things and shout obscenities. We deny the legitimate feelings of our partner, we sulk or behave badly. We act out and refuse to make dinner or keep arrangements or embarrass our partners at social functions.

There are times in everyone's life that we have been an abuser in some form or another. We have loomed over our young children and shouted in their faces. So many behaviours qualify as abusive. Silence, for example, can be nothing other than quiet contemplation or it can be a cold vacuum designed to make you afraid and insecure. It can be a reprimand and a rejection when used to intentionally hurt the other person. So silence can mean nothing or it can be abusive. Kind, generous people can brood and sulk and, sometimes, they can feel angry and shout. That does not make the relationship abusive.

An abusive relationship is a constant pattern of demeaning and controlling the other person, with intention. It is important to distinguish between an abusive incident and a constant pattern of abuse. If I drop a glass once a month, so what? If I drop a glass and a plate and crack the mirror and tear my shirt and lose my bank card and yours in a month then there is a problem. There is a pattern of carelessness that suggests I need assistance. It happens too often to pretend that 'accidents happen'.

Sometimes abuse is so quiet that it remains invisible and unrecognised for years. The result is an insidious but relentless diminishment of the woman who lives in it.

Physical abuse

Violence has a distinct energy that you usually sense before you see it – a whiff, a gut feeling, or the chilly hand of fear. Some relationships 'progress' to violence after months and even years of abusive foreplay. In others, the violent episodes start even during the so-called honeymoon phase and are notched up to passion and occasional heavy drinking.

If you are being physically assaulted, you know you are being abused. If you have been slapped, pushed, punched, kicked, burnt and even pinched, you are being assaulted. Often your abuser has raped you. You know you are being abused because you have the bruises and welts and burn marks and scars to prove it. You can look in the mirror and your body is the canvas of that abuse. You should plan to leave as soon as possible, despite the challenges involved in leaving a marriage – your life is at risk. If your partner is physically or sexually abusing the children, you need to make plans to leave as soon as possible

Emotional abuse

Sticks and stones can break my bones,
but words can never harm me.

We all probably remember this childhood rhyme, but clearly it is a long, long way from being the truth.

Emotional abuse is more difficult to diagnose and, almost without exception, the women who have consulted with me have not 'diagnosed' their relationships as abusive. They have usually blamed themselves for the problem. Often they believe they suffer from depression, anxiety and self-esteem issues, but seldom see those as a consequence of an abusive relationship.

The pattern of abuse is so uniform that it is shocking and we will give you a checklist, which we call the Bully Barometer, to mark. If at least twelve of those characteristics apply to your relationship, it qualifies as abusive. At its very core an emotionally abusive relationship is about controlling the other partner consistently and relentlessly. The best way to do so is to damage their self-esteem and destroy their support network.

Reading this book will prove invaluable in clarifying the problem, in teaching you skills and in assisting you to heal yourself. Re-reading it helps even more and submitting the assignments will be the most helpful. For those readers who require assistance in working with the suggested assignments in the book, please register online at www.whenlovinghimhurts.com. A tutor will be allocated to you and assignments will receive personal and confidential feedback.

What is an abusive relationship?

If roses are the flowers of love,
should the thorns not warn us?

The abusive relationship is astonishingly uniform and will follow a predictable pattern. Despite differences in financial status, intelligence and life circumstances, the abuse will follow a particular pattern, not unlike that of a disease. We have loosely referred to the person who abuses you as simply an abuser or a misogynist. I prefer the term abuser because technically a misogynist is a man who 'hates women' but I have seen too many men fight to keep their wives to believe that they actually hate them. I agree, however, that the behaviour qualifies as being hateful. The narcissist is also an abuser. He is totally pre-occupied with himself and demands that you act as his mirror of self-love, and the slightest criticism or discomfort that he feels will be your fault or your problem.

The abused woman finds herself under siege from every direction. Her self-confidence and her sense of safety in the world is assaulted and vandalised. The abuser does not inflict this abuse with deliberate calculation. It is his lens and not his intention. When it is intentional, in his perception there was a legitimate reason. He is in the clutches of his own demons, which we will explore at length later in this book. However, with unerring accuracy he will target every area of your life that allows you to feel safe and confident. The checklist, which we like to call the 'Bully Barometer', will give you the clues as to what areas are likely to be under attack.

He will attack your self-confidence with constant criticism and name calling. You will be labelled negatively at every turn. A mistake is not a mistake – it will turn into a character assassination and a barrage of insults. An incident that seems small and seemingly incidental will be amplified into something that is not even recognisable to you. Anecdotal humour will always be at your expense, and while others are laughing you will find yourself also trying to laugh in order to hide the hurt.

Money is a source of security to all of us and so the abuse will find its way easily and readily into financial issues. You will be manipulated around money in various ways which we explain in the discussion on abuse and money later in this chapter.

Our intimate relationship should be a source of security for us and the abuser makes that relationship anything but secure. He does this by making any resolution of the problem virtually impossible. He takes responsibility for nothing that goes wrong, and the name, blame and shame game is his speciality. You will be named as the person in the wrong, blamed for whatever goes wrong, and forgiveness will come only once you have exhibited sufficient remorse and shame.

With an abuser, your feelings will never get the respect they deserve in a loving relationship. If you say you feel unhappy or insecure, you will be called paranoid, mad, premenstrual and any number of other labels. In other words, your inner world will be dismissed and regarded as unreasonable, unstable and unimportant.

You are also enabled by your friendships, acquaintances and colleagues. These relationships are your props and nurture you in healthy and sustainable ways. These will be under attack in a variety of ways that make sustaining any honest and meaningful relationship very difficult.

Your family is a safe haven. Unfortunately, abused women do often have 'family issues' to begin with, which is why some find themselves in these relationships anyway. Regardless of that, the family for many people remains an anchor. The abuser will not allow that to stand unchallenged and family relations end up as fraught as the marriage and fail to act as the anchor we need them to be.

Sexual intimacy is another area for target practice. The abused woman will find that this part of her life is not the sacred and cherished aspect of her marriage that she hoped it would be. Many abusers are serial womanisers and it goes without saying what a challenge that is to a marriage and to love itself. Others expect sex on demand with no acknowledgement of his wife's needs, wants and circumstances. He will demand participation in sexual acts that she finds demeaning and he intends that she feels demeaned. He also withholds sex as a form of punishment.

The abuser threatens to leave or to have her leave. That is his solution to any marital problem until that game fails to elicit a response, after which it is seldom mentioned.

Physical abuse happens when the rage has reached another level. Once a man has found his fists, you need to find the door and leave. We need to reiterate the initial warning here. Staying in an emotionally abusive relationship is a legitimate option under certain circumstances. There are ways to manage yourself in that relationship and ways to heal yourself from the inside out. It is a journey of learning strategies and skills that will allow you to regain your confidence and resurrect your life. However, once he has begun to beat you, your life is at risk. The beatings are going to continue and they will escalate so please do not make the mistake of minimising the problem or denying its severity. We strongly advise that you attend to escaping from that relationship as soon as possible, and we do not propose that staying is a viable option under those circumstances. The abuse has reached proportions that are unlikely to be managed.

We will now examine in more detail the areas of abuse.

Control by criticism

The very core of an abusive relationship is that one party controls the other relentlessly and there is no balance of power. In any functional relationship there is some level of power-sharing, with one person having more authority in certain areas than the other. Generally speaking men have more authority when it comes to organising the financial affairs of the family, for example. They make decisions regarding life, car and home insurance. They are responsible for decisions on pension planning and the final word when it comes to discipline. Women usually have more authority when it comes to home affairs and child management. They usually oversee the nutritional needs (and shopping) and the social calendar of the family. This doesn't mean that women have nothing to do with family finances or that men have nothing to do with the home. It means that when there is a dispute, there is a 'captain of the ship'. In a well-balanced relationship both parties participate in most things but there is a tacit understanding that the final decision in the face of a dispute will lie with the captain of the ship. Important decisions like where the children will attend school are generally managed by consensus.

In other relationships roles are determined by skills levels. If a woman is a skilled financial manager or accomplished in this field, this will become, by mutual agreement, her ship to captain. It is in that difficult first year that many of these decisions need to be mediated. Women buy gifts unless men are particularly good at it. Men attend to car repairs unless perhaps she had a brother who is a mechanic. Bit by bit these understandings are reached. In an abusive relationship, one party has no ship. The disempowered person is never the second in command – she is merely the deckhand. The abuser micro-manages everything or does virtually nothing but criticise everything.

Not only does she have no authority at all, she can do nothing right. Quite simply a woman with almost no self-confidence is easier to control than one with some self-esteem. The abuser/misogynist will criticise everything from what she wears to how she walks, how she pronounces certain words and how she cooks. Eileen (not her real name), who attended the support group all those years ago, told us a story about how on the nights of the support group she always made a huge effort with dinner because she felt so guilty about going out. That particular night she had done the same. He ate well and she was delighted, thinking that finally she had produced a meal that was up to scratch. When she asked him if he had enjoyed it he said no, he hadn't. It was too salty. He was scratching in his briefcase when he said it and she says she has no idea what came over her but that night it was enough. She slammed the briefcase down on his hands until he was wailing in pain and then walked out. We were all afraid for her when it was time to leave the meeting that night.

That support group became a breeding ground for acts of defiance in the face of that relentless criticism. One of the women had a husband we called The Captain. The Captain liked to snack after dinner and so she dutifully provided the snacks he asked for – peanuts, chips, dried fruit and a decent variety from which to choose. If she had peanuts, he wanted peanuts with raisins. If there were salted chips, he wanted barbecue flavour. If there was dried mango, he wanted peaches and if there was both, he wanted prunes. Night after night he played this game of cat and mouse with her not being able to produce the snack he wanted. Every night after dinner she was afraid of what he would ask for, knowing in advance that she was unlikely to be able to produce it. When she failed he would shake his head and say, "Pathetic! Just pathetic! Can't even get this right." So she went out and bought peanuts – with and without raisins, salted and plain, with red skins and without. She bought cashew nuts (raw and roasted), Brazil nuts and almonds. She bought chips – salt and vinegar, tomato, Mexican chilli, barbecue, plain salted, biltong, chives and sour cream, cheese and onion, and others. She bought dried apples, apricots, peaches, prunes, mangoes and figs. It cost a fortune and one night the same ugly ritual played out and she went to the pantry and produced this enormous garbage bag of snacks that she poured on his lap and over his head. At the support group, we were all afraid underneath our laughter. I was especially afraid because I felt that I would in some way be responsible when this backfired. Over a period of time I came to understand that those acts of defiance were the beginning of a sacred "NO". Every person has to have a sacred no. We are allowed to say no. We have to say no, no, no!

Many abusive men hide their criticism behind humour. They ridicule by making jokes at your expense and if you confront them or say you are hurt the fall-back position is always, "You know I was just joking." The problem with this style is that it goes down so well socially that it is almost impossible to be sure that you aren't taking yourself too seriously. If something is funny it doesn't hurt, so if his humour hurts, it's intended to. These misogynists select social situations in which to exact their most poisonous barbs.

Constant criticism is like an acid drip. It is corrosive to our self-esteem. Bit by bit we begin to feel more stupid, more worthless, more broken and more defeated. We feel more grateful that someone will have us, more convinced that no one else will and more sure that we are 'in the wrong'.

Every healthy woman needs to own a firm "NO".
Most women attend to good shoes instead.

Using money as a weapon

Money may not buy you happiness but it certainly contributes significantly to feelings of security. It may not guarantee success for your children, but it ensures that the opportunities are paid for. People constantly quote the limitations of money and the dangers of greed but the abuser knows only too well the power of threats of poverty to keep his woman well ensconced at his side.

The misogynist uses money as a way of controlling you. It is important to him that you don't have much money of your own because that would make you feel secure and a woman who feels more secure is more difficult to control. Please read that sentence again because it is the essence of emotional abuse using money. He will not allow you to have money because it will make you feel secure and confident. Secure, confident women are more difficult to control.

There are so many ways to abuse a woman using money, and the most obvious one is to limit her access to money independently of you, to make her spend it or to insist that she spends it on you.

To illustrate how abusers use money to control women, I am simply going to tell you some of the stories or reproduce many of the letters we received. I have changed the identifying details in the letters to preserve the confidentiality of the writers, and where I have had permission I have simply reproduced the letter. However, as I said earlier, please be aware that the pattern of abuse is often very similar so if you know someone whose story sounds like one of these it could also be one of hundreds who tell a very similar story. Many of these stories are told by women who may seem wealthier than you are but that is only because they are gleaned mainly from a private practice where therapy is only possible for those with either medical insurance or who have some means – it does not presuppose that misogynists are on average wealthier than the norm.

ASANDA'S STORY

My husband is a wealthy man. I am not wealthy. Every day he tells me or shows me that he is rich and I am a pauper. People come to my house and they think I am lucky but it's a huge lie. I feel like I live in a lunatic asylum. I love the garden – it's the only place I feel at peace and I work really hard at making it beautiful. One day he came home early and found me working in the garden in my gardening clothes and went mad. He says that should someone turn up I will be seen looking like that and so I am to garden in decent clothes or not at all. No one turns up at our house because he is so rude to everyone.

Anyway the point is that when he feels like it he tells me I am not allowed to put on the irrigation because he isn't paying the water bills anymore. It is as though he waits for me to get excited about the garden and then declares that I can't water it. I sit on a bench

13

under the tree and watch the garden die and feel like dying myself.

My sister gets angry with me and tells me to just put it on and he won't even notice but he does. He checks. Although he has a really important job I think he waits all day just to come home and feel if the soil is dry enough. I'm scared to just put it on. What is wrong with me?

$

SARAH'S STORY

I stood on a street corner waiting for the bus and had a miscarriage. The doctor said it was from malnutrition. My husband was playing golf while that all happened. I don't know if I blame him or myself. I was so unhappy I hardly ate and he didn't notice. But I also hardly ate because I wanted him to have everything he wanted so that he would love me, so I saved the money from my own food.

$

RITA'S STORY

Rita tells me that when she met (let's call him) Scrooge, she was young and pregnant and deserted by the father of her unborn child. Her own father had deserted the family when she herself was a young child and her mother was an alcoholic and barely coped with her own life. Rita found a saviour in Scrooge who accepted her, 'pregnant and all'. He had a car but she didn't. She walked to and from work because her meagre salary made no allowance for transport of any description. Towards the end of her pregnancy the people at work all collected money to buy her a coat because they couldn't stand watching her walk to and from work in her clearly unsuitable clothes. She remembers how many people went out of their way to take her home but it never occurred to her that Scrooge had failed to make a similar offer. He did, however, charge her half the rent despite the fact that he earned three times as much as she did.

By the time she came to see me, her child was already three

years old and she was still with Scrooge who had been refusing to marry her or postponing the marriage at every opportunity. She had worked hard and had several promotions, but relied on loan after loan so that she could continue to live with him. She now paid two-thirds of the rent and electricity and internet. She paid two-thirds of the food because there were, after all, three of them now. Her uncle paid for her counselling as she was up to her neck in debt, but she never told Scrooge because he would accuse her of being incompetent. She was afraid he would use it as another excuse to refuse to marry her. When she first arrived she used to tell me that she was grateful to him for teaching her how to sit like a lady and how to eat in a restaurant. They usually went out on the day she got paid and she paid for it. His money was spent on body-building supplements and if she objected he would get furious and accuse her of not loving him enough to go to gym herself.

Finally Rita grew tired of the constant 'lessons' on how to sit and how to pronounce words and began to see that Scrooge was just a guarantee of ongoing poverty and criticism. However, her debt is significant.

$

MEG'S STORY

If I make my husband angry (and sometimes I don't even know what I did), he takes my car keys to work with him so that I have no transport. Sometimes I have plans to meet friends for coffee or lunch and I have to cancel. I am too embarrassed to tell them that I have no car or that I didn't get enough money today to even pay for a latte. The car is in his name. He leaves money for me on the dressing table when he goes to work. Sometimes it's a lot and sometimes it's almost nothing.

If we have to attend a function he likes me to be the best dressed woman there but there are other days when I have to ask for even a hundred rand. I have tried saving money but it seems so pointless. I once went to a lawyer to find out what my position would be should I want a divorce. After about a year of saving I had nowhere near what I needed to pay as a down payment for legal representation.

I feel like a Barbie doll – he pays for my clothes and hair and new breasts and new teeth and then I go back into the box until he feels like playing again. I look at people who drive more ordinary cars and wonder if I would drive one if I could own it and use it whenever I like. Maybe I am just too lazy and greedy to leave him

$

JOAN'S STORY

This story speaks volumes on how the abuser uses money and any opportunity he can to gain power in the relationship.

Joan tells me that her sister has cerebral palsy and the family is in need of assistance. When she first met the man she is currently married to he was very supportive of the family predicament and paid for many of the additional treatments that her sister required. When she married him and fell pregnant he declared that their priorities must now change and with that he cut off all assistance and began to be very disparaging of her father – calling him a loser and 'useless and pathetic'. A few years later her father died and the family position worsened. By then she had had a second child and both were at school.

Joan wanted to get a part-time job to assist her own family, but her husband made it impossible. Initially he insisted that she was useless and unemployable, that she couldn't even earn enough to pay the petrol to get to work and back. Despite his lack of support, she did get a job and one that she wanted in an industry that she was interested in. She was excited and used her savings to buy a decent working wardrobe despite the fact that he claimed that her desire to work was the equivalent of neglecting the children, even though the job was a mornings-only position.

But then working became a nightmare. If one test result on a school report was less than perfect he blamed her. He insisted that the children stay home from school if they had even a slight cold, which meant that she had to stay home from work too. He phoned her constantly at work to hassle her about something that wasn't right at home. Finally, he booked a school holiday vacation for three weeks knowing that she was not eligible for leave and insisted on taking the children. They phoned constantly, crying and wanting to come home. All these led her to resign. She felt guilty about not doing enough for her mother and sister. She felt guilty about leaving the children while she went to work. She explained that she became a complete shrew. She was so afraid that their school marks would drop and she would be blamed that she was impossible about their projects and tests and damaged her relationship with them. She has resigned herself to never being able to work again.

$

ZINTA'S STORY

My husband insists that I transfer my whole salary into his account. He then gives me money and he calls it pocket money! I have tried to talk to him about arranging it differently. I am really happy to contribute to our joint expenses but I would like to manage the rest of my money. He flatly refuses to talk about it properly. He tells me how stupid I am and how we would have nothing if he didn't organise it. He accuses me of not trusting him and that makes him wild. He refuses to discuss finances with me at all and if I ask for extra 'pocket money' you would swear I was asking for the crown jewels. Ever since I asked him not to call it pocket money because it makes me feel like a child, he insists on talking about my 'allowance' and he thinks that hugely funny. I hate him.

A misogynist is not an easy man to divorce and that is the truth. They are willing to fight and will fight hard. Many women elect to stay in an abusive relationship and manage themselves differently simply because they are unable to sustain themselves and their children outside of the relationship. If you are unable to sustain yourself, then you should seriously consider changing how you manage yourself in the relationship instead of electing to leave. There is no loss of self-respect or dignity in this decision. However, if your partner is making you increasingly more poverty stricken, you need to seriously consider leaving while you can.

A friend and colleague once told me that he always asked about the financial arrangements in a relationship because how a man treats his partner financially will tell you a great deal about how he loves her.

Some questions to consider:

1. How are you treated financially?
2. Would you know where to invest some emergency funds? Whose advice could you get?
3. Can you access bank accounts and marriage certificates and life insurance funds? If you can then do so.
4. How can you stop him from spending your money?
5. Are you trying to buy his love and approval?
6. Do you feel guilty because he keeps telling you how hard he works for you and the family?

Goals:

1. Stop acting as though the finances are not your business and find out everything you can about your financial status.
2. Start building an emergency fund.
3. Educate yourself about money and investments – slowly but surely you can find out if you ask and pay attention.
4. Understand that you make a valuable contribution to the family and that your marriage is a partnership. He may contribute the money but you contribute the labour so you have the right to refuse to feel guilty and beholden to him.

For the most part money can only buy three things – status, security and power. Most of what you are buying, outside of the necessities like groceries and petrol for your car, will be one of those three things. All of us relate strongly to one of those three, then comes the second and the third barely exists.

Abusive men usually have the profile of buying power first. When you buy a Rolex you are the status type. If you buy a Fossil watch instead, you are the security type and when you buy another person a Rolex you have just bought yourself power. Abusive men understand the power of money extremely well and abused women (in fact most women) are under no illusions about who runs the show. The Golden Rule is well known in most homes ("I have the money so I make the rule"), but is shoved down the throat of abused women. A financially unsuccessful abuser (and there are many) manipulates a woman by expecting her to use her money on his status symbols and on the holidays of his choice.

The favourite game is the birthday present that is always declared inadequate and in its 'inadequacy' lies the proof that she does not love him enough. That so-called fact causes women weeks of misery after the birthday.

$

SHELLEY'S STORY

Shelley is a person who definitely links money to security and is very cautious with money. She loves having a savings account and takes pleasure in those deposits. She decided that having been in deep trouble for four years for failing to produce an adequate birthday present, she would break with her norm and splash out. Having little confidence in her taste she consulted several friends and even their husbands to check the 'correctness' of this gift. It apparently ticked all the boxes and she bought it. For good measure she booked a table at a restaurant with an impeccable reputation (for her account). This took at least five months of savings, by the way. The day of the birthday dawned and for the first time in years she was excited instead of apprehensive. This time she was sure she had it right. But, apparently not. His response to his leather jacket was lukewarm at best. The restaurant booking was given to him as a beautifully made invitation. While she was getting ready for work he walked in snarling. He shoved it in her face and said, "As you can get nothing right, please do nothing – it's less painful for me."

Shelley sat in her car with oil pooling on the ground underneath it from a leak she hadn't yet had repaired, crying. Her relationship was costing her money she could ill afford and yet she didn't seem able to break away. Why was she trying harder instead of leaving? Why had she given in to his demand and made his birthday more important than her car repair? What was she to say to her friends when they phoned to ask if he had 'loved' his present? Why was she going to lie and say he had been amazing?

Sex as a form of punishment

It is not unusual for the marital bed to become the marital torture chamber where guilt and need vie for attention. Giving, taking and trading favours replace mutual desire. Gender differences make the sexual relationship a minefield of difficulties in many relationships that are in no way abusive. Men use sex to relax and women need to be relaxed to enjoy sex. Men are visually stimulated for sex and women are emotionally stimulated so they like to feel loved to make love. Many women are guiltily uncomfortable about casual sex and men are clear on the differences between making love and 'sex for sport'. Many men suffer from erectile dysfunction around which they are very uncomfortable. Couples struggle with differences in levels of libido. So the existence of sexual problems in a relationship is in no way indicative that a relationship is abusive.

A loving, respectful intimate relationship is one of the gifts that healthy couples give each other. It is undeniably difficult to sustain this relationship for a lifetime and is one of the real challenges of marriage. Children render mothers exhausted and fathers feel excluded and unimportant. Beautiful bodies are changed for women and the burden of support grows heavier for men. Child-rearing is often a bone of contention for couples, the marital bed is invaded and young children make even a substantial conversation a rare event. Career stress, financial burdens and just the passage of time dampens sexual sparks and often couples find their sexual relationship more mundane and erratic than they imagined at the beginning of the relationship.

However, the misogynist has his own brand of sexual abuse. It can take many forms but its purpose is always to control and subjugate his partner through fear, humiliation, and physical and emotional abuse.

The most common forms of abuse are:

- Withholding sex as a form of punishment to express his displeasure.
- Demanding sex constantly as a way of dealing with the stress of day-to-day living.
- Demeaning his partner in the sexual arena.

Let's elaborate briefly on each of these.

Withholding sex as a form of punishment to express his displeasure

When Victoria came to see me she announced with considerable pride that she had "never, ever, ever refused her husband sexually". She saw that as the fulfilment of one of her wifely duties. I asked what happened if she was tired or busy or just in the mood to watch a movie on TV instead. She didn't have an answer. It just simply wasn't the way this arrangement worked and she seemed surprised that I was less impressed by that than she thought I should be. In time it became clear that Rufus was a man who withheld sex for long periods of time to express his displeasure. To make matters worse he had also had several longstanding extra-marital affairs for which he blamed her. So if he initiated sex it was always a huge relief to her because it meant that he wasn't angry with her. It also suggested that just possibly she was going to be 'woman enough to keep him out of another woman's bed'. Victoria never thought of refusing to have sex with her husband because she was so grateful for the opportunity to be in his good books. She pulled out all the stops to try to out-perform her competitors.

Demanding sex constantly as a way of dealing with the stress of day-to-day living

These men use sex as a way to relax in the same way that other men use alcohol. If this type of man is also a misogynist, he is unable to accept that his partner will not always accommodate him. He will punish her by demanding sex at inappropriate times and settings. Her willingness to accommodate him is proof of her love for him and, of course, it stands to reason that refusing is proof of her failure to love him. He cannot accept her needs and desires as something separate from his own or the fact that the negotiation of needs is an ongoing process in any relationship. His needs and desires are all important and the failure to meet those instantly will be a declaration of war.

Demeaning his partner in the sexual arena

The misogynist will insist on sexual acts that his partner has specifically stated that make her uncomfortable. It is his way of telling her who is in control in this relationship. It is his way of controlling her.

Tracey told me her husband had joined a swinging club despite the fact that she had told him she has no intention of participating. She told him repeatedly that the very idea was abhorrent to her and his response had been that he didn't see his way clear to stay with someone with such inhibitions. This implied threat is a common feature of the abusive relationship. She was so distressed she asked me to see him to try to explain the ways in which this situation was unacceptable to her and actually very hurtful. When I discussed it with him he told me that "Everybody does it." Clearly the statement is blatantly untrue but more importantly what he was saying was that his wife's distress and discomfort were of absolutely no significance to him. Sacrificing the experience (even one less dramatic than this) out of respect for her and the marriage was not an option for him. Ultimately he slung his jacket over his arm, declared that he was not paying for a session that had "achieved nothing" and walked out. Tracey was initially unable to respect her own discomfort enough to stick with her refusal and tried the swinging club once. That was not enough for him.

I am pleased to report that she was young and childless and so it was easier for her to extricate herself from the marriage and fortunately she did so.

I can write example after example but the core remains the same. The abuser uses sex to humiliate and subjugate his partner with the express purpose of increasing his control over her. Her feelings, sexual needs, opinions and preferences are incidental. Her body is his playpen and the sexual relationship is not a precious part of their life together. The abused woman often ends up feeling frigid, unattractive, unworthy of saying no or initiating sex and increasingly depressed about her relationship and herself. It is just another place where she can't get anything right.

Destroying your support network

I have friends who always take my side and I love
them for that. I have other friends who help me see
life more reasonably and I love them for that too.

Your support network is made up of friends, acquaintances and colleagues. These are the people you turn to for support. Your friends are a sounding board and provide you with the opportunity to gain perspective when life feels overwhelming. They are the people that like you and accept and enjoy you as you are, and as a result they give you confidence. Often we have known them for a long time and so they understand us. Friendships can be cosy or challenging but they have much, often underrated, importance. People with good longstanding friendships are happier and safer in the world than those without.

Our colleagues often provide more value than we give them credit for. Many of them help us and are helped by us. Every morning they smile and say "Good morning" to us. I know that it feels like just another day but ask anyone who has retired or who is without that and they will tell you that they miss it more than they imagined. We do projects together or we endure work together but we have company and those colleagues have the same issues as us. There is a measure of togetherness that provides us with support.

Acquaintances are often people we enjoy without the intimacy of a friendship. They too have value. We discuss current affairs and we learn or we teach. We debate ideas and entertain each other.

All of these people are your support network and the abuser subconsciously knows that. He is, despite the bravado, an incredibly insecure man. He does not want you to have that support network. Quite simply it threatens him. It gives you a place to go where you will feel strengthened and supported. That support network will give you the very thing he doesn't want you to have – your self-confidence.

The attack on your support network is corrosive but often indirect and subtle. He will tell you that your friends are a 'bad influence' on you and that you change in ways he doesn't like when you are around them. He will often criticise them and tell you that he thinks very little of them – by implication you go down in his estimation for having friends who are less than impressive. Initially you would have been excited to have him meet your friends and they will probably be excited for you that you have met such a wonderful man. After a while he will begin to behave badly around your friends. He may be aggressive or provocative to such a degree that you feel like the proverbial piggy-in-the-middle – feeling like you should support him but his views and behaviour make it difficult to do that.

One of the favourite games of the abuser is to tell stories about you. They are done with humour but each of these stories manages to demean you in some way. Your friends feel uncomfortable. They know they are supposed to laugh at the funny anecdote but they are starting to realise that there are too many amusing anecdotes at your expense. If they refuse to laugh, he will be furious and you will be uncomfortable. If they oblige, you will begin to feel like they are letting you down as a friend. It's a lose-lose scenario for you every time.

Another popular abuser game is to flirt with your friends. After the event he will tell you how attractive he thinks a particular friend of yours is. Why on earth would you like to invite the competition around again? Often they will compliment one of your friends to such a degree that you end up being so threatened by her that it is easier to just see less of her.

Philippa's story below shows how accurate this depiction of the abuser can be.

Sue describes the stories abusers tell at our expense that are meant to demean us. It's exactly what my second husband did at our wedding. I couldn't wait to hear what he had prepared for his speech. I have heard men talk in glowing terms about the woman they are about to marry and I really wanted to hear that said publicly. Soon after he began, I felt the onset of a panic attack. His speech was crammed with facetious quotes on marriage he had gotten off the Internet, like "The secret of a happy marriage remains a secret" and "A good marriage would be between a blind wife and a deaf husband" and "Marriage is a three-ring circus: engagement ring, wedding ring, and suffering".

I forced myself to laugh along with everyone else until he came to the part about how he would allow me to cook for him and his girlfriends when he had affairs. A strange sequence of thoughts raced through my head. He was only saying it to be funny, wasn't he? Surely he would never do it to me again? The last time he did it, I broke off our first engagement and he begged me to forgive him. This is our wedding, he can't possibly be serious. Well, of course, he isn't serious because everyone is laughing. He'll do anything to raise a laugh. He really is a brilliant speaker. Look at how everyone is laughing and enjoying his speech. It is remarkable how proficient I was at denial and lying to myself. Each time I was faced with another unbearable incident I found a way to rationalise it. Normalising the abnormal was how Sue described it.

With time you tell your friends what has been going on and they have correctly advised you to leave him. Often when you are angry you have agreed that this is the right thing to do – but you don't. You go back to him over and over again and eventually your friends become frustrated and exasperated with you. They don't understand and neither do you (so you can't explain) why it seems so impossible to leave him. Friendships get strained to breaking point because of your relationship that makes no sense to anyone and they feel helpless and unable to understand or assist you.

Philippa talked candidly about the dilemmas she had around her friends.

All my damaged relationships damaged my friendships as well as me. It was such a confusing time for me. Part of me wanted my friends to like him and above all to be impressed by him. Women feel proud when their friends think highly of their partner. Why wouldn't you? On the other hand, a friendship is an intimate relationship and we share our feelings and tell each other what is going on in our lives. If I told them what actually went on, then naturally they could not possibly be impressed by him. That would have made me unhappy and ashamed. It is one thing to complain that your husband doesn't help with the dishes but something altogether different when he aims those dishes at your face. It's one thing to say that he doesn't pay attention when you talk because he is reading the paper but it's totally different when the truth is that he kicked you, punched you and threw you into the garage. Somehow you aren't one of them anymore. Your problem isn't like theirs and so it's hard to talk about it. It's isolating and you feel lonely.

To make things more complicated my second husband was very intent on creating the impression that our relationship was perfect. In public he was flirtatious and charming in the beginning and I just played along with it. Actually, those were good times for me. He was amusing. I laughed along with the jokes as though I had never heard them. I pretended alongside him that we were crazily and passionately in love. Had I been watching us from the outside I would have been envious and like him I wanted people to think that everything was fantastic. It gave me hope that this façade might be real and that we could recreate that privately. That didn't happen. It made me lonelier because I was lying to my friends.

He made it impossible for me to sustain that lie himself. If he thought someone was impressed with him he would 'perform' for them. He had a very charming routine that he could deliver at a moment's notice. However, there were others who were less gullible. When they visited he wouldn't even bother to come out of the bedroom or he fell asleep in their company. If we had guests he just disappeared and I would find that he had gone to bed without even saying goodnight to anyone. It was very embarrassing. He only ever liked people who applauded him in some way. There was no single other characteristic that defined his affection for anyone. He could never find anyone interesting or amusing. They either applauded and he liked them or they didn't and he wanted absolutely nothing more to do with them.

On reflection, the most difficult part is looking at my own role in all that. I actually damaged my friendships by pretending and lying, and then it was very difficult for me to speak the truth because I had acted the lie so enthusiastically. I accept that we 'don't hang our dirty laundry in public' and that there are circumstances under which we all pretend that everything on the domestic front is fine when it isn't. It was a ball-faced lie because I wanted people to envy us. I wanted to impress, but we couldn't be what we wanted people to think we were.

Our pretence was on many levels. It was about privacy and dignity because I needed to protect myself from the shame and humiliation. The effort that went into living this lie drained everything out of me. I was pretending to myself that I was in a glamorous relationship, and pretending to my friends that everything was fine while I was dying inside. At home I was walking on eggshells, and anticipating his needs to show how indispensable I was to avoid his wrath. It felt like I was fielding a war on all fronts. I worked so hard at pretending that the lines were blurred between lies and truth for me too.

Abuse is such an embarrassing subject that some friends who did know pretended along with me. The ones who didn't became openly hostile towards him and I had to keep them away.

The day we got back together after another breakup, we went to look for a house to buy. He had a few drinks before we went. The estate agent was thrilled to see us and showed us around the home. We were in the kitchen and she went out for a minute. There were some eggs on the counter. He took one and threw it at me. I jumped out of the way and it landed on the floor. He laughed. He walked out and, of course, I scrambled to find paper towels to clean it up. Just then the agent came in and I explained laughing that he only did it because he was so excited that we were back together. She laughed along and I was relieved I could explain it as cute. Wasn't he adorable?

I think it should be said how easily women buy into the façade of 'happily ever after' no matter what. We are brilliant at lying to ourselves and each other. "You're getting married?" women enthuse. "You are so lucky." Yes, to a beast.

I was so desperate for his affirmation that I would manipulate my friends into liking him so that he would like them. I knew he only liked people who applauded and complimented him so I encouraged them to do that. I wanted him to think I had nice friends – that would mean that I was worthy. There was no way that I could honour the honesty and intimacy required of a friendship.

I also have to say at this stage that even if you have the gift of good friendships, there is real merit in using a therapist as a sounding board instead of your friends. Once they know what is going on, the sensible advice they give is to leave and it's incredibly difficult to understand why you can't. If they are angry with him, you will be in trouble – both with him and with yourself. I agree that friendship is a wonderful part of life but when it comes to abusive relationships I see no way to sustain them effectively unless you separate your friendships from your marriage as much as possible.

I met and married my last abuser in the United States where I had no longstanding friendships. In some ways it was harder because initially he was my only close friend. In other ways it was easier because I didn't need to try to live the lie. When you are in an abusive relationship you feel so alone anyway that actually being alone isn't more difficult.

Your friendships are going to be challenged but it's worth working to sustain them because they are the support you need during and, in the event the marriage terminates, after. Friendships need to be protected from the relationship.

Philippa explains the pre-occupation of the co-dependent with the relationship.

My abusive partner used to compliment me into staying away from my friends and family. He used to tell me not to leave the house because he had a difficult day ahead of him and may need me. Well, I didn't leave the house. The need to be needed was so powerful that I would cancel an arrangement with a friend at short notice 'in case I was needed'. I wanted to see myself as indispensable. I wanted him to see me as indispensable and at the time I really had no idea how unhealthy that was. I was well aware of the fact that I was becoming increasingly isolated and it made me feel fine – it was him and me against the world – just the two of us. I liked that he was jealous of the people in my life. It made me feel powerful and loved and much more secure.

My second husband had a serious drug and alcohol problem. If he arrived home and passed out, I sat vigil. I was proud of being the person whose job it was to protect him. I was indeed a co-conspirator when it came to damaging my own support network.

A healthy relationship co-exists easily with friendship. An unhealthy relationship demands an unhealthy amount of space that leaves no room for friends.

Your relationships with your colleagues are also under siege. The abuser often acts as though he is highly protective. If you tell him about a skirmish at work he will support you fully and tell you how you are being taken advantage of. He will feed your resentment every time until what was an irritation has been whipped up into a fury that will damage, not heal, the relationship. Initially you are allowed to feel self-righteous and supported but you are losing sight of the long view which is that these are your colleagues and a pleasant and congenial working relationship is much more beneficial to you than being furious.

Destroying your family support network

Patricia Taylor, the mother of Oscar Pistorius's former girlfriend Samantha, has written a book called *An Accident Waiting to Happen*. She describes the 18-month relationship that "almost killed her daughter". She describes how he "went on the offensive against her daughter", trashed her name and reputation and used his friends to threaten her friends and family. Initially she found herself wanting to mother the young man who had lost his mother at an early age and had shown such bravery and determination in his life. However, his moodiness, constant lies, anti-social behaviour and rages soured his relationship with the family completely.

There is no doubt that Oscar Pistorius is an abuser. He abused Samantha and killed Reeva Steenkamp. But Oscar still has a girlfriend! Clearly there is yet another woman out there who believes that it will be different with her. She will make him see the light. She believes she will love him enough to curb his rage. Patricia Taylors say, "I wish I had told my story earlier. Perhaps Oscar might have sought assistance and things may have turned out differently." Unfortunately, Mrs Taylor, I suspect that it would not and will not. Until domestic violence is better understood in all its complexity and nuances, some women will continue to believe that their particular breed of loving is the answer. These women are at risk, no less than Reeva was when she began her idyllic romance with the hero of the track.

Our families are probably the most grounded support system we have. They are the people who should take us in when we have nowhere to go and they are the people who only want what is best for us. The abuser removes the family as a support system for the same reason he removes friends – because he is afraid they will strengthen you and support you against him. Initially the relationship will be one he nurtures in order to gain control over you, seduce you and own you.

Let me tell you the story of Thomas who controlled the family of the woman he loved.

THOMAS'S STORY

Thomas employed his girlfriend's mother, who was for the most part fairly unskilled and unlikely to easily find employment elsewhere. When she and Thomas fought he threatened to fire her mother, who incidentally liked her job and was more than relieved to have one. They had a huge celebration one New Year's eve and he had sex with her sister. I am not for a moment excusing the sister here but I did ask him why he had done it. It was because he didn't like the sister's attitude and he wanted to show her that at the end of the day all women are the same – give them enough alcohol and compliments and they will go with anybody. That was the end of her relationship with her sister. Of course she was angry and devastated but she also felt threatened that she might lose him to her sister, so she clung more tightly and more desperately instead of walking away.

He organised for the father to attend a strip club 'with the boys' and encouraged him to drink and ordered one lap dance after another. I don't know the details but I assure you the father would prefer to hide them. Thomas has a weapon and no compunction when it comes to using it. The result was obvious. The family was no longer able to provide their daughter with any safety without threatening their own. She was unable to seek it without placing them at risk.

Philippa's family was never financially dependent on her abusive relationships but her mother had her own reasons for failing to provide her with the support she needed. In her opinion marriage gave a woman status and acceptance and a marriage to a man regarded as a very eligible bachelor provided exactly the level of status she required. In this way she too was dependent on the relationship and was unwilling to threaten it and was therefore unable to support her daughter.

My mother was well aware that my relationship was physically abusive. I phoned her one morning at about 5am, crying, and told her how I had been beaten for most of the night. She arrived at our house with my father's gun and banged on the door, demanding that he explain exactly what he had done to me. I was so relieved that finally I had someone on my side. I left with my mother. The next day he phoned and my mother and I both went to his house and listened to his earnest apology. Together we accepted it and six weeks later I got married. My mother was delighted with the union. It is only now, when I look back, that I realise that my mother needed the status of my marriage more than the desire for my safety. It also brings into sharp focus the absolute failure to understand the nature of the beast. In what fantasy land were we living that we believed that an apology was the solution? We didn't believe it. We ignored what we knew to be the truth because we both had a huge vested interest in this marriage taking place.

Many abused women are in the unfortunate position of managing not only themselves in an abusive relationship but also their children from a previous marriage. The divorce statistics show that many non-abusive marriages falter and fail because of what the literature charmingly refers to as 'one's previous commitments' – by this they mean your children and presumably your ex-husband or maybe the family dog. However, children are a very serious consideration in trying to decide to stay or leave.

Philippa was one of the women who tried to manage both the

relationship and her sons in the relationship. Here is what she has to say.

I understand that adding children into the mix in a marriage is difficult at the best of times. Doing this in an abusive marriage is terrible and to this day I suffer the deepest regrets that I subjected my sons to the experiences they had. I have two sons and it stands to reason that they will defend me against any attack and in so doing place themselves at risk.

I didn't give my sons a happy mother who loved life. I was tense, unhappy and trying desperately to be the image of the cheerful newlywed. It was a dismal failure and the lies between my sons and me grew daily. They knew something was very wrong and I was intent on hiding the abuse for my own reasons. I wanted them to like him. I wanted us to be a family but was so consumed by my misery that I had no idea how to convert this group of people into a family.

I should have realised that we were doomed on the wedding day. My husband threw my son into the swimming pool fully clothed. It was clearly a sub-conscious statement that he made appear as a joke, but it wasn't. He told us everything that day. "Stand in my way at all and see what will happen to you." Like Anna's children, mine also pleaded with me to leave and had much difficulty understanding and forgiving my decisions. I can't blame them.

A very similar event occurred in the US. My husband invited my son to come and live with us. I was so incredibly happy. He had children from a previous marriage so it was not as though he had no idea what living with young adults is all about. No sooner had he arrived than the trouble started. He was incredibly jealous of any time I spent with my son. He was angry because I was excited about seeing him and planned his room and prepared for his arrival like a child waiting for a birthday party. My husband offered him a job and with that an opportunity to live and immigrate to the US. I was overwhelmed with gratitude and excitement. Before long it all changed and he retracted that offer. It was excruciatingly painful to me but also catapulted me towards seeing the demise of the marriage. He had made me an offer to be with my son and then snatched it away. I agree with Anna – sometimes there are actually no words to describe how debilitating it actually is and that was one of those times.

Conflict management = war

If you want to be heard, whisper don't shout.

'Conflict management' and 'joint decision-making' are skills that healthy couples learn. Often they have had good role models in their parents and so they emulate the conflict management they witnessed as children. There is a constructive way to have an argument but not a formula, unfortunately.

Most arguments fail to achieve much because the mind-set of both people arguing is what I call 'lawyer mentality'. This means they are trying to establish who is right and who is wrong – the outcome is intended to be a verdict. A more healthy and constructive approach to conflict management is to intend to make yourself understood and to intend to understand the other. The fact that there is a dispute of some nature is perfectly natural and disputes can easily be resolved if the situation is managed as a misunderstanding.

Here is a list of what *not* to do in an argument:

1. Don't raise your voice. The other person hears and reacts to the volume and not the content.
2. Don't start sentences with YOU. 'You' is a word that acts like a big finger. It is an accusation. For example, "YOU never let me finish a sentence because YOU know I'm right." Instead a sentence could begin with something like "In my opinion..." or "The way I see it...". This qualifies as your opinion and not a fact, and doesn't sound like an accusation.

3. An argument must be contained to the issue at hand and is not a licence to dig up every other bone you remembered burying. Remember that your mind-set should be that you would like to resolve *this* particular problem and not provide an arena for every other offence you feel sensitive about.

4. The past is relevant only in so far as it holds an example to verify your point. If your issue is that your partner speaks to you disrespectfully and in a tone that ridicules, he may argue that he didn't and you have misunderstood the tone. Then it becomes relevant to quote what he said last week and two nights ago. The point you are making is that this is not an isolated incident and so even if today you were hypersensitive the issue remains a problem.

5. Name-calling is an absolute NO-NO. If he starts calling you names, you end the conversation/argument by saying that this is completely unnecessary and unconstructive and you can revisit this conversation when this stops. Obviously, the same rule applies to you.

6. Time-out is a valuable conflict management tool. Sometimes we can feel ourselves losing our temper and we know that we are going to unhelpful and unconstructive places. However, this is only helpful if used to assist the argument and not as a punitive measure. Most people struggle when the other party leaves the house or even the room. Storming out of the house, wheels spinning and leaving behind a dust storm is not time-out. It is aimed to make the other person feel abandoned and anxious. Women often capitulate at this point and men get even more incensed. Time-out is telling your partner that your temper is fraying and suggesting that you make coffee or walk in the garden for ten minutes to collect yourself to avoid being destructive.

7. Ask for clarity. If you don't agree it's just possible that you don't understand what the issue is. A popular issue with men in general, but particularly abusive men, is that when

35

they met their partners they were very attracted to how sexy they were. Once married, however, he wants you to tone down your appearance. The problem is that he doesn't say that. He accuses you of wanting the attention of other men and calls you a whore and a slut. It is worth having the conversation about the changes men expect and feel when their girlfriends become their wives. You don't have to agree, but constructive conflict management always requires that you listen with an open heart and attempt to understand. They often misconstrue casual friendly conversation in a social setting as flirtation and women are very offended because it was never their intention to flirt and they feel wrongly accused. These issues are potentially a minefield but can be managed with the right skills.

8. Don't respond to an accusation with retaliation. It is pointless and takes the dispute into the sewer instantly. I understand that you feel wrongly accused but remember that people do see situations through different lenses and often it is the lens of their damaged psyche. It is worth trying to understand what that lens is.

These general guidelines on how to constructively manage conflict are worth studying and practising because managing conflict well is a life skill that will serve you well wherever you are.

One of the characteristics of abusive relationships is that these couples are particularly poor at conflict management. Abusive men suffer from arrogance and so they almost never enter a confrontational situation with the mind-set that they would like to understand the situation and the other person's perspective better. They have no intention of understanding – they are going to win and draw blood if they have to. They are completely convinced of the 'correctness of their position'.

CAROL AND SIMON'S STORY

Carol and Simon saw me together for couples counselling. We addressed the issue of conflict management early in the sessions because the reason they came for counselling was that the fighting was out of control and constant. I asked Simon what behaviour he thought he could change to make the arguments less destructive. As far as he was concerned the solution was simple: "She must shut up when I tell her to and do as I say." He actually wasn't joking. He thought he had a perfectly simple solution to the problem. The misogynist really does not place that much value on the feelings of his partner and that outrageous sentence was not even remotely problematic to him.

The women from the support group and in my practice all report the same pattern with respect to conflict management:

1. They are called "mad and insane".
2. He denies what actually happened as though she wasn't there.
3. He will never take responsibility for anything that goes wrong and always blames her or someone else for the problem.
4. He is completely unwilling to negotiate when it comes to solutions that partially meet the needs of both parties.
5. He dismisses her feeling as pre-menstrual, post-menstrual or menopausal. No feelings that she may have about an issue are ever seen as valid.
6. Just "shut up and do as you are told" is the short version of what I hear from all these women. Even when they have proof of what happened that proof will be negated and ignored.

The truth is that nobody can manage conflict well if they are trying to do it alone. A conflict involves two parties and both need to play by the rules, so to speak.

Managing conflict is about managing yourself.
Do it well and no matter what the
outcome you are a winner.

The Bully Barometer Checklist

This is a useful checklist to evaluate whether or not your relationship qualifies as abusive. If you say yes to twelve or more of the items in this list, your relationship qualifies as abusive.

1. Does he criticise you constantly and no matter how hard you try to please him it isn't good enough?
2. Does he constantly blame you for all his problems or anything that goes wrong for him?
3. Does he ridicule you when you are alone and in public, even if that ridicule is hidden in humour?
4. Does he refuse to discuss problems, accuse you of being unstable or making things up if you try to force the conversation?
5. Does he undermine your opinions and your feelings and undervalue your achievements?
6. Does he constantly criticise your friends and try to prevent you from seeing them?

7. Have you given up important activities such as hobbies or sports or people to please him?

8. Does he flirt with your friends or tell you how much better they are than you in order to make you feel insecure and unwilling to see them?

9. Does he constantly criticise your family and try to prevent you from having contact with them?

10. Does he constantly accuse you of flirting or having inappropriate contact with other men?

11. Does he manipulate you with money by withholding it or making you spend your money on him?

12. Does he constantly demand sex when you are unwilling and accuse you of not loving him if you do not have sex with him?

13. Does he try to force you to do sexual acts that you are uncomfortable with?

14. Does he withhold sex to punish you for making him angry?

15. Does he threaten to leave you if you displease him?

16. Does he have affairs with other women?

If your relationship scores 12 or more out of 16 you are in an abusive relationship. Read this list again and again. It is a very painful realisation to find yourself in an abusive relationship and one that you would prefer to deny than acknowledge.

If you continue to deny it you will never find ways to deal with it. It is an accurate diagnosis and the result will be a helpful treatment.

LARA'S STORY

Sue asked me to read a book after I had been in counselling with her for a while. I had it in my handbag, covered in brown paper so that no one would know what I was reading. I read my marriage. Everything I was struggling with was in that book. It was so painful to me that I opened the car window and threw it into the Emmarentia Dam while I was driving over the bridge. I stopped going to counselling for months after that because I was too embarrassed to tell her that I had hurled her book out of the car window. More importantly, I was a strong, professional woman and the thought that I was in an abusive marriage was more painful than I was up for. I hated those words. I hated that thought.

> *Denial is like cheap booze – it serves its purpose for the night, but in the morning what was true before the drink is still true but harder to face.*

The Jekyll and Hyde problem

In the novel, *The Strange Case of Dr Jekyll and Mr Hyde*, Dr Jekyll invents a potion, under the influence of which he transforms into the violent and debauched Mr Hyde. With time Mr Hyde grows more powerful and dominates the amiable Dr Jekyll and eventually he commits murder. For the abuser that potion will be insecurity, anger or just tiredness, and the charming Dr Jekyll will transform into the violent, unpredictable Mr Hyde. The potion did not create Mr Hyde – it merely released him in the same way that alcohol often does. Abused women have met the Mr Hyde of their husband's personality and live in constant anxiety of what will release him from the shadows of his former self.

Living in an abusive relationship sounds awful doesn't it? Who would do that? Why would you put yourself through this?

For a start, the abuser isn't always abusive. Sometimes he is charming and complimentary. Sometimes he has your back and having a tiger in your corner is comforting. When he is in full fight and it's not with you, he sounds strong and he makes you feel secure. He can protect you from this intimidating world.

Sometimes he tells you how different you are from his first wife or last girlfriend, or mother, who, according to him, were liars and manipulators – so they encourage you to feel different and proud and important. Please remember that you may well become that last significant other about whom nothing nice is ever said. When a man takes no responsibility for why a previous relationship failed, your alarm bells should start ringing. Our ego stops us from being properly alert to the ways in which these narratives are unbalanced.

No one stays with someone who is always awful. These men start off with incidents that are very troubling, but we ignore these early warning signs. We rationalise them away:

- He is very stressed.
- He has been badly hurt and these are the wounds that I will attend to.
- Maybe it was funny and I was being hyper-sensitive.
- I must be grateful for the ways he is helping me be better.

All of these are examples of denying and lying to ourselves.

Reflection

Introduce yourself

We advise that you read Part 1 completely before you start on this reflection. If you choose to write your story down and share it with your counsellor it should be no less than five typed pages, to allow you to be as thorough as possible.

This reflection is a long one and serves several important purposes:

1. When you tell your story it serves as a very personal introduction to your counsellor as you would do if you went for a therapy session. The role of your personal counsellor is to give you specific feedback on both the material you share, if you choose to share it, but also how that pertains to your particular story. You are not a student with a number – you are a person with a story and we would like to know that story. Everything you say will be treated with the same strict confidentiality that applies to any therapeutic intervention. You can submit your story to www.whenlovinghimhurts.com.

2. Telling your story will provide you with the opportunity to see the links between your childhood issues and your current choices and those links will be the ones you will be attending to during Part 3: Healing Yourself.

3. You are free to tell your story any way that you would like to. However, if you prefer structure, there is a suggested outline for a story that you can use as a guide for this reflection.

4. Should you have any questions about this reflection, please e-mail us at whenlovinghimhurts@gmail.com if you have registered to do the online counselling course.

Suggested outline to tell your story:

1. Identifying data: What is your name and age? How long you have been married or in a relationship and do you have any children? What are your current life circumstances? (What job do you do? Are you anxious, depressed, on medication, seeing a therapist, having problems with your kids, etc.).

2. Describe your parents' marriage: Was there abuse, alcoholism, drug abuse, gambling and infidelity? Did you have a good relationship with either parent and why? With whom did you have a poor relationship and why? Who was the person who damaged your self-esteem and who built it and how?
3. Describe yourself as a person: What are your best and worst qualities?

Profile of the abused woman: co-dependency

Who are the women in abusive relationships and why are they there? Most literature focuses on the abuser and portrays the women as passive victims. The relationship is, by implication, an unfortunate accident. It's simply not true. The abusive relationship is the coming together of two people whose pathologies find a perfect fit. Every woman in an abusive relationship can remember at least one incident, but usually many, that indicated to her that he was abusive but she married him anyway. Why?

Usually (although not always) women in abusive relationships are co-dependents. This means that the meaning of their lives is derived from saving someone else's. As a result a typically co-dependent woman is attracted to men who she perceives as needing to be saved. Stable men fail to provide her with the purpose she seeks out in her love relationships. She has poor self-esteem and as a result the insults and dismissive behaviour don't strike her as outrageous or unacceptable. She is quick to blame herself and to resolve to work harder to gain the recognition she craves. Unlike the person with a healthy self-esteem, she is inclined to be apologetic and is prepared to work inordinately hard for the love she believes she must earn to receive. Typically she will have an exaggerated sense of responsibility and will consistently do more than her share in a relationship.

Philippa's story below shows how co-dependency will play out in the abused woman.

I met Sue in 1992 when a friend of mine recommended that I see her. I was in a relationship with an alcoholic and drug addict and was desperate for a quick fix. Never having been exposed to alcoholism I was confused, bewildered, angry and filled with resentment. When I heard that Sue was not only a brilliant therapist but an expert on addiction, I couldn't wait to see her for counselling.

I left my first session filled with enormous relief. She knew so much about addiction and abuse she could well have lived in the house with us. She described the madness, the pain, the brutality and the trauma so succinctly I burst into tears. But more than knowing, she had a way of delivering sentences that comforted me like a cozy sweater. I no longer felt like I was going crazy, that what I was feeling was real and, most importantly, that I wasn't worthless. It was in that first session that Sue planted the seed, but I was a really slow and obstinate learner, and the seed burrowed underground for a very long time.

It goes without saying that the relationship was unsuccessful and during that time I went to hell and back, over and over again. My usual pattern of working like a maniac for the love and approval of this man who was clearly unworthy was by now well established. Sue was by my side throughout the whole process. She would explain to me over and over again that when I thought he had fallen in love with someone else he was in fact creating a smoke screen for his relapse.

"Phil, he's not fallen in love with someone else. He is with someone who is tolerating his substance abuse. It is never about the other woman. That's his way of diverting your attention off the real issue, which is the drugs and alcohol. He doesn't want to see you not because he doesn't *want* to see you but because you are not going to 'give him permission' to relapse." She explained to me over and over again that I would never be his number one. His real love was his substances.

I held onto these words and took comfort from them. But those words provided comfort for five minutes and then the fear and need to be his number one would resurrect itself. Sometimes I used to think that Sue would be annoyed but I've learned that nobody learns anything without repetition. It was a comfort to me to know that in that space I could make as many mistakes as I needed to without ever being criticised or rejected. This is not to say that she agreed with any of my decisions – in fact, it was usually the contrary.

I phoned Sue from all over the world. I remember calling her from Disney World with my two sons. That sounds like fun but it was torture. I know I sound spoilt but I would have given anything not to be there feeling like I was. I phoned Sue and made notes on napkins and on programmes from the theme park. Inside I was screaming. I sat on benches waiting for the kids to finish their rides and I watched people who were couples and yearned to be one of them. I imagine if you had seen me you would have had no idea of how badly I wished to be somebody else.

Happily, and at last, I 'fell in love' again. On our first date I took him to an AA meeting. I was delighted with the fact that I had pulled off getting him to attend AA so early in our relationship. By now I was an expert in substance abuse and completely convinced that I could 'cure him'. Of course, I knew about once an alcoholic always an alcoholic but I was well versed in the language of sobriety. However, the reality of alcoholism still eluded me.

Sue was less impressed with me than I was. I was very happy to have fallen in love and I must admit I was a bit disgruntled at her lack of enthusiasm. According to her this was more of the same except with a different name. Because I liked Sue a lot I thought I would stay in therapy and prove her wrong. She would eventually see that I had in fact learned very well from the previous relationship. I would show her that I was an expert. How could she not be impressed because I had already managed to organise his first AA meeting? This relationship was fraught with chaos, anguish, and gut-wrenching pain, but that did not prevent me from marrying him, my second husband.

Sue reminded me what I proudly announced one day, "We are going to marry S." She screeched and said, "Not we. You are in this all by yourself. Trust me when I tell you this is a disaster." I knew Sue was wrong and I knew that she would eventually have to come round and see that.

I worked like a slave to create the most gorgeous wedding. Sue attended. I was glad to have the opportunity to show her how I had it all under control. Being a true all-star co-dependent I needed to execute this entire wedding single-handedly. That would surely have earned me the accolades that I deserved. I did all the cooking, the flowers, the tables, arranged white bird cages filled with white birds. I organised fish in bowls on each table and ice moulds on the buffet tables. I also sewed strands of ivy onto the banquette skirts, searched for the perfect candles to fill the garden and hung lanterns from the trees. I had already re-done the garden and house in preparation for the wedding. I worked like a Trojan for weeks.

For years I believed that I worked this hard for his approval and the security of being indispensable. It was only in recent years that I have come to understand it is a long way from the whole truth.

The truth is just a little bit of a co-dependent –
she works and works despite being ignored and
disregarded. It took me years to befriend truth
and there is no greater friend.

The real truth is that as a co-dependent I needed to work, to obsess and to be consumed. It was the very essence of my pathology and he was the perfect foil.

S started drinking before the ceremony and was drunk by the end of the night. He ignored me under the chuppah and seemed to be struggling to stay awake. His wedding speech was filled with references to him having affairs and jokes about how he would expect me to provide food for them. He then sexually propositioned my sister and several of my closest friends. Before the end of the evening he stumbled off to bed, but not before planting a salacious kiss on our housekeeper and throwing my son into the swimming pool fully clothed. The next day he laughed as he had no memory of any of it including the setup, the food, the flowers or the wedding cake.

The most interesting part of this has happened right now. Sue and I are sitting at my dining room table in the Berkshires laughing while comparing memories of that night.

"That was not your finest moment," she commented.

"No, it *was*. In my mind I had won the prize. I denied the horror of the wedding. Despite all that happened I was The One. He had chosen me and committed himself publically to me. It was indeed my finest moment and I could flick those things aside like irritating flies."

I spent a lot of time on Sue's couch during that marriage. Before this my mother had begun to refer to her as the fortune teller. It irritated me at times that it was true, but once I started healing I knew that whatever she said should be taken seriously. Had I done so in the first place it would have saved me years of aggravation and hurt. While we can laugh now, that marriage almost destroyed me. I was physically assaulted repeatedly for seven years. I was often in physiotherapy without any real recollection of what happened the night before. He criticised me constantly. Stupid, paranoid, jealous, crazy, know it all. He swore at me all the time. My self-esteem was at an all-time low during the time I spent with him. The sexual manipulations were never ending. In public he pretended we had a wonderful sexual relationship and as soon as we got home, he rejected and ignored me. Although he was a wealthy man I was never allowed to spend anything without his permission. When I felt brave and rebellious I would find the most expensive designer item I could and leave it on the bed for him to see.

Co-dependents have bales of last straws.

Eventually I left because I could no longer stand who I was as a result of living with him. His lying, cheating and physical abuse had become untenable. I knew that he would kill me. I left him and South Africa. I was broken and desperately hoped that America would offer me a better future. As usual my plan B didn't exist and plan A was barely formulated. My fall-back position was always that I could get married again.

I did meet and marry a man who I thought was different in every way. Firstly, there were no signs of substance abuse. Secondly, he seemed able to discuss his feelings, which I mistook to be signs of intimacy. Thirdly, he gave me all the approval I was desperately seeking. I remember that a few days after meeting him we spent almost an entire day on the phone talking about his divorce. He hung onto my every word and my need to be needed was satiated. It was a very familiar and comfortable place for me. It would take time for me to recognise how dangerous that actually was. When a co-dependent feels that this is a familiar space her alarm bells should be shrieking. I lacked the insight and so my bells didn't even ping. I sailed forth into the future full of confidence that I had finally found the man that I needed. The very things that I initially found attractive I grew to find repulsive. His neediness and miserliness drove me to the brink of insanity. It was, however, his sexual aberrations that would force me out of the house and out of the marriage.

I cannot even begin to describe my disappointment and anger when this relationship also failed. Like most co-dependents I often felt that the most recent incident was the last straw. Co-dependents have bales of last straws. Among those many hurtful incidents was that he asked my son to immigrate and offered him a partnership and sponsorship. Once he was here, having left his life behind in South Africa, he reneged on that deal. I wish I could say that it was the last, last straw but as I sit here I cannot remember what the last straw was.

This marriage was the same series of disappointments but this time there were no substances for either of us to hide behind. The divorce was bitter and acrimonious.

We fight so hard about so little because we fail
to see that the problem is who we are and
what we have become.

For the first time in my life I have been single now for a prolonged period of time. When I invited Sue to visit me in the Berkshires, I suspect I still had a residue of co-dependence that compelled me to prove to her that I had finally listened and I wanted to show off how her seeds finally took root. Sue taught me to love gardening and I wanted to show her how her lotus flower had finally emerged from the muck and mire of my life.

So we find ourselves among the forests of the Berkshires and this time we are working together to create this book. Sue was my guide dog and I have given myself the title of Poster Child for Recovery. I am the proof of how Sue's wisdom, insights and patience gave me a life I didn't know I could dream of.

Why me? – co-dependency is born in childhood

The safest children are those with a healthy
self-esteem. There is no greater gift you can
give your children.

Women who are in abusive relationships, in the majority of cases, have a poor self-esteem and it is often as a consequence of their upbringing. Many have had at least one abusive parent and many have watched the pattern of abuse being played out throughout their childhood. Many of them have been sexually abused and have had mothers who failed to protect them from abusive fathers or stepfathers. If not abused, they may have been severely neglected by mothers who suffered from depression or substance abuse or narcissism.

You may ask why the effects seem to have been so permanently scarring. These are often intelligent women who must surely be able to grasp that their childhoods were dysfunctional. Surely they are even more alert to signs of abuse and thus able to avoid them? Sadly self-esteem develops slowly and methodically over many years and much of the damage is done in a time we refer to as 'pre-cognition'. Older children and young adults are able to assess a situation and easily see that it is unacceptable. They are capable of judgement that is reasonable. Toddlers and young children have poor judgement skills and usually nothing against which to compare a situation. If they are shouted at they assume that they were wrong, stupid or annoying. When they are treated badly they assume that the parent is right and that they are wrong. When they are continually shouted at and insulted, they assume that they are worthless. Those labels 'stupid, worthless, annoying, unwanted, etc.' build up like layers until they become a part of your assumption about yourself. In the same way that a person with self-esteem assumes that they are fine without giving it much thought, a person with a low self-esteem assumes that they aren't without giving it much thought. It's an almost sub-conscious understanding about yourself. Every healthy childhood should carry the gift of a positive self-esteem.

Anna describes her childhood as follows:

ANNA'S STORY
My mother was mad. She was so beautiful and charming that people allowed her to do what she liked. She was hysterical all the time and my brother and I were so afraid of her. She was always screaming at us until we were too terrified to breathe. She never loved us – of that I am sure. Then my younger brother was born and for some reason she loved him. I don't know what was different but she definitely loved him and you won't believe the difference between him and us.

Anna often uses the word 'mad' to describe her mother and maybe she did have a psychiatric condition but it is also possible that she was a narcissist. A narcissist is a type of personality disorder in which the person thinks of themselves in grandiose ways. Clearly her grandiose thoughts were reinforced by her great beauty. Narcissists need constant admiration and when the world appears to function in ways that don't suit them, they experience levels of fury that are out of all proportion to the event that has just taken place. They act as though they are a law unto themselves because they are more special than other people. The narcissist has no empathy at all and usually makes a terrible parent. They are demeaning and neglectful. Her two oldest children must surely have thought themselves unlovable and unimportant. Their feelings would never have been addressed as though they were important and clearly their opinions were worthless unless they reinforced the mother's self-importance.

The term comes from Greek mythology in which the god Narcissus was on a life journey and caught sight of himself in a pool of water. He was so captivated by himself that he was unable to continue his life journey for fear of losing sight of his own reflection. His obsession with himself prevented him from entering relationships or having a normal life. He eventually drowned in the pond in which he gazed so lovingly at himself. The mythology leaves no doubt as to the outcome of such self-obsession.

Anna says with such certainty that her mother was mad. Narcissism is a form of madness. I am almost sure her mother was a narcissist because Anna then married one. When she got married she was completely selfless, worthless and ready to be impressed. As a child she had been programmed to be a perfect fit for a narcissist. She was what he needed and he was all she understood love to be. She was accustomed to being with someone who treated her as a second-class citizen – it was all she ever knew. She was used to being made to look up in admiration. She was used to never expressing her opinion or assuming it was incorrect – she had been perfectly trained to be the wife of the narcissist.

REBECCA'S STORY

In another example, Rebecca (not her real name) was sexually abused by her father over many years. As a young adult she started attending counselling and after a few years found the strength to totally reject her father as well as her mother for not protecting her from it. She also divorced her abusive husband. For about fifteen years she raised her son alone, working hard, and coped with a difficult life. She says she was lonely but also too tired and often too broke to have much of a life.

Her son left for university and she decided to try internet dating. Within a short period of time she met 'a lovely guy' who just seemed to really want to take care of her. She admits to being tired and wanting a safe harbour and she thought she had found that in his arms. With relief, she handed in her resignation and moved in and married him within a few months of meeting him.

Well guess what – she finds herself back in an abusive relationship. He is physically, verbally and psychologically abusive. Rebecca had divorced her first husband and had rejected her parents and she had avoided all relationships until she met the 'lovely guy'. As a result she was unaware that she still didn't have healthy boundaries. She didn't have alarm bells that went off when behaviour was offensive. She had fixed the situation but had not healed herself. She is a perfect example of what Anna talked about; she left one relationship but failed to address the problems and so went headlong into another in her gratitude at being a wife again.

Co-dependency is not simply about a low self-esteem. A co-dependent person is a person who seeks meaning as a passenger in someone else's life. A co-dependent is characterised by high levels of responsibility, guilt and a need to control. She seeks recognition and affirmation that usually doesn't come and that triggers her compulsion to work even harder.

In the following story Philippa explains those co-dependent impulses.

The underbelly of my beast

Last night Sue was going up the stairs to the guest bedroom when I announced that I was to blame for the abuse.

"What do you mean?" she asked, shocked, as she sat on the steps not sure what to do with either the coffee or the information.

"I chose every single one of them. I had lots of opportunities to leave when the abuse started but I needed that abuse. I needed his pathology to fit in with my mine. My pathology was that love was an obsession not dissimilar to an addiction. I was no different to a drug addict. I was consumed with him. I needed my fix the way a drug addict needs his."

Sue was confused so I tried to explain by describing my day-to-day life.

"The focus of my day was my labours of love. What errands I could run, what food I could make, what outfits I could wear and what I could do to earn the applause and approval when he came home. How could I show him how indispensable I was? And that was another example of my manipulations.

"The business of my day began when he woke up. I had buttered his toast to the edges the way I was sure no one else would have done. Not only had the toast been buttered to perfection but the timing around the delivery of the toast and coffee had become an art form too. Having successfully achieved breakfast on time it was now time for wardrobe consultation. I was smug in the knowledge that I was The One. Don't for a minute forget that affairs are the norm. The abuser always manipulates with other women. The hidden truth was that my manipulations were no less deceitful."

"How so?" Sue asked.

"In lots of ways. Firstly, I manipulated him to take me to every single event and function so that my presence in his life was as public as possible. I dressed to the nines and I lauded it over other women. In my mind I had the prize and I shamelessly showed off. I was a bigger liar than he was. He showed me exactly who he was. He was an addict, an abuser and a cheat. I pretended to be something that I wasn't. I was anything he wanted me to be."

"Had he given you everything you wanted, as in appreciation, kindness and consideration, would you have stayed?" Sue asked.

"No, I would have been bored stiff. Decent men didn't supply enough drama to justify being consumed. That's why I wasn't a victim. I chose him and he performed perfectly."

"It still sounds like a difficult and painful way to live."

"I have learned that there is always a payoff for destructive behaviour. Mine was that as long as I was focused and consumed by his life I never had to do anything worthwhile with my own. He was the perfect camouflage for the fact that I was doing nothing with my life."

The profile of an abuser: why does he abuse me?

Damaged people damage people

There never was a winter that was not followed by a spring – no matter how bitter the winter.

As I mentioned in my introduction, I am not convinced that all abusers are necessarily misogynists (men who dislike women). Some abusers are narcissists and others are general destroyers but actually that is just semantics. At the core, the abusive relationship hinges on excessive, pathological and relentless control.

The abuser doesn't necessarily understand what he is doing and more often than not he is living semi-consciously. He has not planned this coldly. He isn't aware that his behaviour is abusive unless he has received some counselling and that's unlikely – unlikely that he attended and unlikely that he conceded that his behaviour is abusive. More likely he felt misunderstood and ganged up on. More often than not he will tell you that he loves his wife and will fight hard to keep her. The chances are that should she attempt to leave or divorce him, he will put up a grim and bitter fight and promise the earth to keep her. These are not signs of a man that hates her and yet his behaviour is hateful. It is no wonder the abused are confused.

The following three stories of Adam, Brett and Clive illustrate some of the ways in which a man becomes an abuser. Adam, Brett and Clive are not just three people, they are also three *types* of abusers. I have selected their stories because they typify the circumstances, given a certain personality, that will create abusive men. There are many Adams, Bretts and Clives, and if you are in an abusive relationship you might recognise one of these three as your own husband.

1. Adam: His mother's love was untrustworthy. She was either an abuser or a neglectful mother. This abuser cannot trust love and so he attempts to keep it by controlling his partner excessively and in ways that destroy her and her love for him. He achieves the very thing he has been trying to avoid.
2. Brett: His father was an abuser and he has learnt his role (as we all do) from him. He has witnessed and mimicked the relationships his parents taught him.
3. Clive: He has an enmeshed mother who has over-parented him.

You can't bake a cake or make
a marriage work with a rotten
egg no matter how skilled you are.

Let me introduce you to my closest friend of almost two decades and a man who is definitely a misogynist. I will call him Adam. He has no idea what he is doing to the women he has loved so much and so destructively. Because I have known him for such a long time and he has appealed to me so often to assist him with his failing relationships I know his insides and how he feels and why he feels as he does.

ADAM'S STORY

Adam grew up poor and I introduce that fact because he sees it as relevant with the passage of time. His mother was a bitter, angry woman who had a tough life that she never stopped reminding them of. She was also fanatically religious and her family attended church almost all day every Sunday of their lives. She had an angry, spiteful God and she threatened her children with that angry God all the time. She would tell them menacingly that God was watching them and that He knew their thoughts were evil and unclean. She told them about hell and how easy it was to end up there. A few unclean thoughts was all it would take and her God never allowed a moment of privacy. Not only did she have a powerful ally in this angry God, she was herself physically abusive to the degree that welfare services should have been called in. She would beat her children until they were literally bloodied and unable to walk.

Adam's father was a travelling salesman and was away for weeks at a time. However, when he was there he never intervened to assist the children at all. He would spend the majority of his time in the garage and never responded to the cries and screams of his kids. When he saw them limping or the welts on their legs he never made any comment. His father was Scottish and his face was always slightly red from the South African sun and his eyes watery as though he was crying. At the end of his life he was incontinent and Adam told me that he deserved nothing better because he had always been 'such a baby'.

However, the most damming part of that unpleasant childhood was that his mother had affairs with other men when her husband was away – which was almost constantly. Adam would arrive home from school and the curtains of the house would be drawn and then he knew he wasn't allowed inside. He would wait and watch and then the man would leave and he would go in and he said the house "just stank of her and sex". He could never understand why she wasn't afraid of God, who surely knew what she was doing and surely understood how wrong it was.

As a result of all this, Adam learned that women could never be trusted. Even the most God-fearing were fatally flawed and destined to be unfaithful whores unless they were watched all the time and checked up on all the time.

Try to imagine a little boy, the oldest of five children, trying in vain to protect his siblings from a vitriolic, violent mother, a weak father and a God who not only lacked compassion but had double standards. The mother is the primary caregiver from whom we learn most about love. She was bitter and brutal and her legacy was ultimately a man who could never love or respect women. He could never trust love and above all else he could never believe that he was lovable or worthy of love. He used to tell me that in his mind he called women 'Delilah' – the woman who betrayed Samson in the Bible by telling the Roman soldiers that his strength lay in his hair.

At this stage of the story, do you feel empathy for Adam?

In time Adam created abusive relationships with any woman with whom he had a romantic/sexual relationship but he could never see it that way. The relationships were so painful to him that he could never stand back and evaluate his behaviour objectively or from the point of view of his partner. The first time he married he was still struggling financially. His young wife was subjected to excessive control over what she wore and how she conducted herself. He would have had her dress like a nun and the arguments were frequent and often became violent. Despite the fact that they needed the money he flatly refused to allow her to work.

In many respects she was the blueprint of the woman the abuser marries. She was young and had no siblings. He met her in Durban and relocated her to Johannesburg where she knew no one. She had been sexually abused by her father and Adam used this to cut off all ties with her biological family. Quite simply, she was too young to have any real confidence; she had no money, no support system and no function outside of being there for him. She had almost no reflection of herself from the world. There was no one to tell her she looked good today or that she had done a good job at something. Her self-esteem lay almost entirely in the hands of a man who was afraid and damaged and angry with the women he loved.

A few years after they got married his business began to flourish and he decided to take her on a cruise. The cruise was important to him because it signified that he could now belong to a social sphere that he had only previously dreamed of. The cruise was a disaster. He failed to anticipate the social cues that indicate whether one belongs somewhere or not. There was too much cutlery on the table and his wife befriended the young staff not the other passengers – all of which was a massive disappointment to him. One night he had been drinking excessively and went to the cabin early. When he woke up she wasn't there and he scoured the ship for hours looking for her. She arrived later and claimed that she had gone with her friends (the staff) to their quarters when they were off duty because she was lonely and bored. He was convinced that she had been 'whoring around' and nothing she said could convince him otherwise. He beat her almost senseless and they were asked to leave the cruise liner at the next stopover. For years the destruction continued and she eventually did leave him for another man, but only after years of physical and emotional abuse.

Adam had two other significant relationships and the pattern was exactly the same. He refused to allow them to work. Initially it was not a direct refusal and he talked about wanting them to have a break from the burdens of the past struggles. He talked about needing them in the business and how much he would value their feedback – except they never actually got there. Adam promised that as soon as he had time he would purchase a business for them and he never did. When he was happy he was generous. He always knew how much money was in his wallet and he often counted it in the morning.

Adam was tormented if he called and his partner didn't answer. He would call me and fret and fume and no reasonable assurance could satisfy him. I would tell him that maybe she was having her nails done and her phone was in her handbag, but he would leave work and go home to investigate. By the time he was halfway home he was convinced that he had been betrayed and before she could even explain he would let loose a torrent of rage that cannot be repaired with an apology. It didn't matter how often he was proved wrong. He could not hold the idea that there was, in all likelihood, a reasonable explanation for what was happening. He 'bought' the family by employing at least one family member and making the family financially dependent on him. It was his security that they could never support their daughter without placing themselves at risk for unemployment. Money was power and he used it to secure her commitment, which never felt safe to him.

Nothing could ever satisfy his relentless insecurity. She was expected to get up before him and make breakfast and almost invariably he found the breakfast unsatisfactory. It was not that he was just being difficult for the sake of it. The breakfast was a sign that she loved him enough or was sufficiently grateful to him. A woman's gratitude made him feel safe because he reasoned that if she was grateful she would stay with him. He could never believe that she could just love him and so want to stay. Gratitude was a huge issue for him.

The truth is that we all see through a lens of our beliefs. If you think no one really loves you then that is what you see. A faulty fried egg becomes the proof that you are not loved. He made the women completely financially dependent on him and then accused them of only being there 'for the money'. The truth is that his behaviour was hateful. No – he didn't hate those women. He was simply sure that he would lose them. He controlled and abused from fear – not hatred. Then he lost them, which confirmed his deepest fears.

One holiday he drove down to Durban with a woman with whom he was in a relationship and claimed to love. They stopped at a popular tourist destination that is the smallest church in the country. It is between Harrismith and Sani Pass that goes into KwaZulu-Natal. It was built by a man in honour of his wife who pre-deceased him and is very charming. It has lovely stained-glass windows and an aura of love and respect. In the surrounding gardens are a few gravestones and the lawns are lovingly maintained. He insisted that she have sex with him in that church. She refused initially and finally conceded. Adam has no idea why he did that. Even when I gently tried to reason that out with him his only response was, "Please don't make me feel guilty." He doesn't know why he did it. My guess is that hurt, angry little boy was giving the finger to a

God who watched his mother do the same and, according to her, stayed on her side.

Adam would get up in the early hours of the morning and go through his partner's phone. He would phone and ask me how you find deleted items. "I don't know. You know I am no good at technology. I'm sure they are somewhere in the ether but don't ask me where. More importantly, however, do you see that this is a gross invasion of her privacy?" Too late – the moment had already mowed him down. He couldn't see reason. All he knew was that she was cheating and he needed to find the deleted proof.

Even in a relationship that had not yet become important, his behaviour was abusive. He told me he had met someone new and she had previously been a runner. He was impressed by that. I remember that we were having coffee, sitting in the sun and just relaxing. I gently warned him that this might not be much of an advantage given that athletes usually have strong feelings about smoking and alcohol and he both smoked and had bouts of excessive episodic drinking. They went to Sun City and she asked him to please not smoke in the bedroom. He lost his temper and threw her out of the bedroom in her pyjamas with a pillow and blanket. Despite being warned of the likelihood of this issue being raised and the fact that under the circumstances it was completely reasonable, he had been unable to contain his anger. With reflection he says that he wanted her to be grateful to him for taking her to Sun City and her comment was indicative of her lack of respect and appreciation.

He can see how unreasonable he is with hindsight but the moment is always too powerful and he cannot control himself. No amount of flowers was enough and fortunately for her she didn't return his calls. It stands to reason that a successful athlete has too much self-esteem for this relationship and predictably it ended almost before it had begun.

Adam was a good friend – even a great one – but friendship doesn't provoke him. It doesn't trigger his 'stuff'.

All of those important women, as well as his wife, have left him. One was hospitalised for depression. Initially the psychiatrist said

Adam wasn't allowed to visit. In her absence he showed signs of some insight into how damaging his behaviour was to her. After a while he insisted that as he was paying the bill he was entitled to access to her. Within days he began to suspect that she was too familiar with the male patients in the hospital. His was a hot, violent anger. Others have a cold and cruel anger but it is worth remembering that the anger is born of hurt. Its roots lie in damage from the past and in his own inability to master himself.

- Now how do you feel about Adam and has it changed since the first time you answered that question?
- Do you think that you could love him better?
- Do you think that if you lived with total transparency you could gain his trust?
- Do you think that if you showed him constantly that you love him he could believe in love again?

If you have answered yes to any of these you would be wrong.

BRETT'S STORY

I will now introduce you to Brett and I name him that because it sounds closest to 'brat' which is what he looks like from the outside. Brett looks like one of those golden boys that you see in the Hollywood movies who invariably lack character as a result of having life too easy. He is good looking and eloquent. He has been schooled in the most elite establishments in the country. He was schooled for success and has succeeded superbly. He is a popular choice for dinner parties because he is a social asset and can hold conversations with anyone about anything. He is almost obnoxious but not quite.

Brett's father was an abuser. He also held a high status position and thought it his obligation or purpose in life to improve people and in so doing to leave them under no illusion as to how sorely lacking they were. His children had to call him 'sir'. Their relationship with him constituted showing him their school achievements, which were always declared to be inadequate. Dinner times were silent and broody and then he would pounce on one of them and say, "So what clever question did you ask your teacher today?"

Brett was the school bully. He appeared confident and was well-spoken and so he taunted and ridiculed the other kids. He was acting out at school exactly what his home life was. He was ridiculed and taunted at home and so he did the same to others at school. Not only was his father unkind to the children, he was brutal to his wife. On the weekends he sat in his study and drank alone. When his drink was finished and he wanted a refill, he would bang his glass on his desk until his defeated wife heard him and rushed in to refill the glass – notwithstanding the bottle was on the desk with an ice bucket and tongs. He was surrounded by slaves. He never stopped telling his children what their education cost him despite the fact that it was he who insisted on these schools. He constantly told his wife in front of the children that she was "a manipulative bitch". One of his strictest rules was that no one *ever* spoke of the family unless they did so in glowing terms. Brett never had the opportunity to talk to his friends about his parents or what was happening in the family. Even the siblings were not allowed to speak between themselves about what was going on. 'Loyalty' was above all else.

The truth is that there was no real loyalty or respect. It was a regimented pretence that taught the boys that appearance was everything but you could do exactly as you pleased provided that no one knew. As long as you spoke well of your wife you were being respectful and loyal. You could treat her anyway you liked as long as it was not in public. He taught his sons that it was their job to improve their wives – the Professor Higgins of *My Fair Lady*. He taught them to ridicule the world and to know that they were superior – but not good enough for his love or approval.

Brett rules with an iron fist. He is impossible to please. He is irritable to the point that is wife is afraid as soon as he gets home. She is afraid that the washing machine noise will irritate him or that she has parked her car too far over to this side. She worries that she is reading a book that is socially unacceptable or not reading a book at all. She is afraid that she has not attended to the 'nutritional needs of the family' (direct quote from him). If the children do badly at school he holds her DNA responsible.

He has role-modelled himself on his father. He has mimicked his behaviour. He has taken on his attitude to women. He has continued the cycle of abuse.

Do I think he is hurting? Certainly! In the same way that he was not good enough, nothing in life is good enough. It is his lens and through it he will see all that is not good enough and it will upset and hurt him. Had he been allowed to be good enough, clever enough and successful enough, he could have given that gift to his family. But he doesn't have it to give.

In essence, misogynistic behaviour looks spiteful, bullying, sadistic and cruel – and it is. However, the person who is doing it is often a victim of abuse, neglect and cruelty himself. This, in no way, justifies the behaviour – it serves only to clarify what has confused so many women over the years. "I am the king of the castle. If you behave you can be the queen" is the general sentiment for these kinds of people.

CLIVE'S STORY

Clive is the product of an enmeshed mother. The emotionally enmeshed mother is the woman who has made her maternal role a sacred one. She has no identity outside that of being 'mother'. Her whole life revolves around her children and she finds it necessary to inform everyone of that fact. Invariably these women don't work but take up positions in parent bodies at their children's school or extra mural activities. If their children perform poorly or are even average, they declare the schooling system to be inadequate and the teaching poor. They hover when their children play with friends, always on high alert to intervene at any moment that is potentially difficult. As the children get older they are increasingly expected to reciprocate this level of engagement. Adolescents need space – physical and emotional space and privacy. They are moving towards independence. They spend a lot of time out of the home or secluded in their rooms. They often appear secretive, surly and uncommunicative. Their skills often lag behind their need for independence and many parents despair at how much independence they 'demand' while exhibiting quite poor survival skills. Quite simply they take the space we are reluctant to give them.

The enmeshed mother cannot tolerate this process. Instead of being irritated, she tries harder and serves them more diligently. She attempts to stay in their favour by being more conscious of their wants (not needs) and applying herself to meeting them constantly. The enmeshed mother sees this natural pulling away as rejection and abandonment. Her behaviour becomes more and more inappropriate.

Clive's parents were divorced and he lived with his mother. She would wait up for him after he had been on a date and ask him all the details but was particularly interested in any sexual activity that might have taken place. Her favourite sentence was, "I can't keep secrets from you ..." and would then proceed to tell him the most intimate details of her own relationships. This invasion of privacy is often gift wrapped as being open-minded and the relationship is declared as 'very close'.

Boundaries in all relationships are important. They are not boundaries to loving or to intimacy. They are a refusal to be invaded and having space does not mean loving less. For the enmeshed mother, no boundary will exist unchallenged. Clive's mother thought she could enter the bathroom without knocking and was comfortable for him to be in the bathroom when she was in the bath when he was well into his twenties. She was flirtatious with him and competitive with any woman he introduced to her. She either discouraged Clive from having any meaningful relationship or allowed it but then invaded it by forming inappropriately close links to his girlfriends. She would, for example, inform his girlfriend that the sheets indicated that he had had a wet dream the night before.

Clive's mother has taught him that:

1. If a woman loves you she has no needs other than to meet yours.
2. You are too special and extraordinary to ever feel stressed and uncomfortable.

3. You are the centre of the Universe and your needs are more important than anyone else's.

4. You are always right and if other people don't agree, they have misunderstood you but your mother won't.

Clive is pathologically unable to remain calm in the face of any kind of discomfort and he uses sex to calm himself down. If his wife dares to refuse to have sex with him whenever and wherever he requires it the marriage is declared to be a disaster. "If my mother doesn't like you – beware" is what Clive used to say.

Loving hurts – inevitably
19 January 2015 Blog post from
www.whenlovinghimhurts.com

Given the particular dynamics of a co-dependent woman and the abuser, it is inevitable that what was usually a 'big love' initially is doomed to fail. Neither the co-dependent nor the abuser actually understands the concept of love. Dependency and fear will be the undoing of their relationship.

When we begin a love relationship it offers the promise of a 'happily ever after'. We feel excited, safe, strong, beautiful and intellectually ready for the challenges of the relationship. We expect the challenges to come from the outside and that together and united we will overcome whatever life demands of us.

All not true. Most often the challenges will come from each other and from the bond that will often feel more like a chain.

Love offers us opportunities to grow and develop. We are challenged to remain committed when all we crave is liberation. We will be forced to face the differences between dependency and love. Dependency breeds fear and fear breeds resentment and resentment is love's enemy. It is a formula that is worth learning.

Love, on the other hand, heals. It makes us stronger. We grow and change and stay when we don't want to and answer patiently when we feel like screaming. Love faces challenges with grace and fortitude. Dependency faces challenges with anger and disbelief.

The offer of safety from a real life has been betrayed. Both the misogynist and the co-dependent have issues with dependency.

The misogynist offers his own type of challenge. He cannot trust love and so he must control whoever he loves to the extent that she cannot leave and to do so he must diminish her. Slowly and corrosively, and most often without intent, he will corrode her confidence, her support network, her access to financial independence, and finally her love for him. He will create dependency because he cannot believe she will stay unless she is dependent. He will break her to keep her and then often he loses respect for her once he has. Ultimately he will prove himself right – love will not endure.

The woman who fails to understand co-dependency will continue to respond to his problems by doubling her efforts to prove both that she is worthy and that love is worthy. She is completely dependent on being needed and ultimately broken. She wants the very dependency that he hates so much. They are in a dance of dependency and fear and resentment and ultimately hatred for each other.

Neither the co-dependent nor the misogynist understands the difference between love and dependency. Couples often feel comfortable with their dependency on each other and dispute that love and dependency are not the same thing. However, they fail to recognise that we may have a healthy dependency on each other's roles. Women depend on their husbands as primary breadwinners and men on their wives to bring up children and nurture the family's emotional needs. This is a functional dependency that is often healthy and provides opportunities for mutual respect and recognition. The nuclear family is small and unstable and works most efficiently when both parties do their job well and can depend on each other to perform effectively and reliably most of the time.

The co-dependent depends on the misogynist to be overly jealous and demanding. She depends on the drama to prove that love is real and she has something to work for. He depends on her to keep working and to need to stay even though he is excessively controlling, dismissive and disrespectful. He wants her to prove that love will survive anything – and it won't. She needs to try and will fail.

Dependency breeds fear, fear breeds resentment and resentment is love's enemy. Help yourself and learn the formula – it will help more than the periodic table you learned when you knew nothing of love and life.

Find the lens

*Your life will look the way you feel. If you feel
defeated you will see all that you can't overcome.
If you feel brave you will view those
obstacles as opportunities.*

Every person has a lens through which he or she sees the world.
Everyone! You will see what you expect to see.

People with a healthy self-esteem see the world with positive
anticipation even when their lives are challenging. Let's call the lens
'realistically optimistic'. For Adam the lens was that love/women
can never be trusted. What he found was proof of that everywhere
and he could never see that in fact he created it more often than he
found it. For Brett the lens was that no one was ever good enough
and that was all he could see. Had he been able to feel good enough
himself he would have been able to see all the wonderful qualities
in the people he loved instead of their failings. People with a low
self-esteem see the world through a lens of fear and dread. They
expect to find themselves inadequate to meet the challenges of life
and inadvertently they will experience just that. Clive had been so
over-protected that any healthy space meant abandonment and he
had to resolve that with sex. Because sex was a temporary solution,
his need for sex was constant.

When we get to the section on the skills that you need to develop to help you to manage this relationship we will attend to finding your lens and changing it. As soon as you can identify the lens through which you see the world, you have the opportunity to make adjustments to that through diligent training of yourself.

Once upon a time ... happily ever after!

I would like to return to a question I asked you about Adam. Do you think that if you loved him with total transparency, dedication and honesty he could be healed? The real question is, do you think if you kiss a frog he could become a prince and do you think that if you loved the beast as well as you could, he would become a prince?

Most of us were raised on the same fairy tales that have survived the ages. They were *Cinderella*, *Snow White*, *Rapunzel*, *Sleeping Beauty*, *Thumbelina*, *The Princess and the Frog* and my all-time favourite *Beauty and the Beast*. They all have a very similar theme. In all cases the main female character is in a predicament of some sort. Cinderella is dominated by a wicked stepmother and two equally mean stepsisters and she is given the status of a servant girl who fails to get an invitation to the Ball. Snow White barely escapes with her life as a result of the jealousy of her stepmother and is also a servant to seven dwarfs. Rapunzel is trapped in a tower in the woods because her father fails to keep her safe. Sleeping Beauty is cursed to sleep for one hundred years by a witch who isn't invited to the party and Thumbelina is almost forced to marry a mole and live underground forever. In every case the heroine is saved by a prince and in every case the story ends as she meets him and is followed by "and they lived happily ever after".

By obvious association we are brought up to believe that we can be 'saved' from our difficult lives by a prince of some description and as soon as we meet him we can expect to live 'happily ever after'. I need to point out that in almost every case the female in the story does or can do very little to change her situation and that she is wholly dependent on the idea that love saves. Deep down, and in many cases not so deep down, we would like to be saved. The abuser often has an uncanny sense of this underlying fantasy.

TANYA'S STORY

I fell for Brett (I am going to call that type of abuser Brett from here on) *because he was so different from other men. I am so tired of this idea that women want to get married and men don't and somehow we have to persuade them or trick them into marrying us. The idea is that they do us a favour by marrying us and giving us the status of a married woman. Brett was so different. Early in our relationship he painted these pictures for me about what a married life with him would look like. My father is a wealthy man and so I was accustomed to an easy life financially but he was a difficult man and we always struggled to please him. Brett seemed to understand that I lived in a gold-plated cage. Although I was technically an adult, my father was highly critical of me all the time. I still felt like a child in an adult body with an adult career and the feelings of a child. Brett was eloquent and strong and full of self-confidence (or so I thought). He could deal with my father. He thought I was good enough and he was going to take me away from it all. He talked about designing our dream house, about travelling and even about how we would raise our children. I saw that temper but by then those children were so real to me. He had talked them real. I could almost see them and feel them. It was so picture perfect and he seemed like the answer to all my problems.*

The terrible irony was that he was actually prepared to deliver on those promises, but it was intolerable. That dream house became a nightmare of my failings to do anything properly. He would come home and get that measuring thing and declare that the wall was not straight and any fool could see that. I would have to tell the builder to take it down again and again. Before that house was even finished I ran away – back to my father, who thankfully could deal with Brett. It was terrible from then onwards.

One night Brett came around to make a bid to try to work on the marriage. They were like two stags trying to kill each other. It took me a long time to run away from both of them.

Beauty and the Beast is a fairy tale about a young girl who lands up living with a Beast because her father promised her in error. (It is interesting how often the fathers of these girls are responsible for their predicament and I think very true. However, that is a reflection for another time). Over time the lovingness of Beauty transforms the Beast into what he really was – a prince. The idea here is that love heals. Love does heal many ills and pains for many people. It would be a lie to say that it does not. However, romantic love is probably the least healing type of love because it is so closely tied to our ego and our insecurities. It is so closely linked to obsession and more often than not we love because of how we hope someone will make us feel about ourselves.

I would like to tell you another story that is more likely to save you than any of the fairy tales of your childhood.

Once upon a time a scorpion decided that he was to go on the journey that would be his life. He set off excited and pleased with his decision to explore the world. However, after a few days' journey he reached the river and could see no way across. He was so upset and walked around and around in distress. A frog saw him and approached the distressed scorpion who explained his problem to the frog. "Don't worry," said the frog, "this is a gentle river and I can easily carry you across. Get onto my back and hold tight." The scorpion did that and in no time he was safely across the river. As he got off the frog's back the scorpion stung the frog. The frog lay dying at the river bank and asked the scorpion, "Why did you do that? I just helped you." The scorpion answered, "Because I am a scorpion."

Now I am not saying that people have a blueprint that cannot be changed in the same way that a scorpion has. People can change and they do. However, the abuser is a dangerous and destructive man to have in your life and you will be hurt, often and usually without just cause. Somewhere between the prince and the scorpion is the reality and it is that reality that you need to face sooner rather than later.

Why is love not enough to make him change?

Love has healing qualities. It is the balm for fear and loneliness and loving in the true sense is the equivalent of growing. It is other-person-focused and is gentle, generous, kind and forgiving. However, in an abusive relationship it isn't going to be enough and it isn't going to heal because it isn't love. The abuser doesn't love when he is abusing and the abused doesn't love when she is obsessing and fearful. The dance of abuse is about power, anger, obsession, fear, yearning and need. It is not the dance of love.

The abuser is created by the coming together of three factors: an inherent personality, with a destructive childhood pattern, within a certain social milieu. An inherent personality is obstinately intractable. It is the proverbial leopard that doesn't change his spots. Behaviour can change with diligent work but a personality seldom does and the core of the problem here is one of personality and not behaviour. A destructive childhood creates beliefs and worldviews that require scrupulous honesty to unearth and change. The core personality of the abuser is one of arrogance and thus a reluctance to view the situation from anyone else's point of view.

That arrogance is an obstacle to learning and changing. The social milieu is becoming more critical of abusive behaviour but most abusers gift wrap the abuse as something else.

Two boys can be brought up in the same family and one will become an abuser but not the other. Certain personality types are more prone to mimic the abusive behaviour they witness than others. It is also true that no two childhoods are the same despite the fact that they are brought up by the same people and witness the same marriage. Firstly, parents behave differently towards their children. One child may be favoured or may provoke a parent just because personality is linked to inherent compatibility. First-born children are treated differently to the others and last-born children are either ignored and neglected or babied long after it is appropriate. No two childhoods are the same. Middle children often report feeling invisible. Some children have a special relationship with a grandparent who salvages their failing self-esteem and provides intelligent nurturing.

What is intelligent nurturing? Parents need to meet the needs of their children in order to create functional, well-balanced adults. Meeting the needs of children is not the same as meeting their wants. Children may want the latest computer games but need to spend less time on electronic gadgets and more time communicating with the family. Refusing to buy that game is meeting the needs of the child despite the fact that your popularity will diminish substantially. Teaching children to understand the consequences of their behaviour often requires punishing them by withholding what they value. This meets the needs of the child.

Allowing a child to struggle with a friendship dilemma instead of intervening immediately improves a child's life skills. However, there are times when failing to intervene is the equivalent of neglecting the child. A child who is being bullied needs parental intervention. These decisions are often difficult and we get them wrong from time to time. Sometimes we err knowing that we are doing so but we are too tired to get through the conflict that will accompany a "no". Sometimes we say "no" because we are tired or upset about something else in our lives and we just feel negative about life in general. Sometimes we make decisions with insufficient thought and sometimes we think carefully and it backfires anyway.

Intelligent nurturing is not about being word perfect – it is about getting it right more often than not. We allow children to struggle on their own to a point and then we assist. We change how we handle them as they grow older and their skills levels change. We trust them but not so much that they are unsafe or abandoned. We have enough fortitude to support our "no". We encourage, discourage, step back, intervene, guide, insist and apologise. We are spontaneous, disciplined, resolute, flexible, consistent, gentle, strong, compassionate, trusting, suspicious, and so it goes on endlessly.

The bottom line is that there is really no helpful guide to effective parenting because it requires dozens of decisions every day for decades despite any number of complicating factors such as money, health, marital relations and work pressures.

Quite simply there is no way to be an effective parent unless you are an integrated adult personality. Inadequate adults make poor parents. Abusers usually had poor parenting.

This is not intended to excuse their behaviour but merely to assist you in understanding it. You cannot love him enough to heal him or change him – you cannot change anyone unless they want that change. It's difficult and we need to remain committed to doing the hard work required to bring about the newness in ourselves.

In almost every case, abusive men are surprised to hear that they are abusive. They don't think they are. They aren't committed to change because as far as they are concerned they don't need to.

Change is about evolution –
don't resist it unless you
crave your own extinction.

Reflection

Explore your relationship

In this reflection you will continue to tell your story but this time the focus is on your abusive relationship instead of your background. The purpose of this exercise is that in part it will assist you in breaking through the denial and misdiagnosis that plagues most abused women. If you choose to write your story down and share it with your counsellor, it should be no less than five typed pages, to allow you to be as thorough as possible, and it can be as long as you like.

1. Describe your relationship before you got married and what appealed to you about your husband.
2. What parts of the Bully Barometer Checklist (on page 38) apply to your marriage and in which ways do you feel most abused?
3. What parts of your marriage remind you of your parents' or do you think are a consequence of your childhood?
4. Did reading about the types of abusers provide any new insights as to the origins of your husband's abusive behaviour? Which profile fits your abuser best?
5. Think about any new insights you have gained from reading Part 1 and how they have affected or influenced your thinking about your own situation.

If you wish to share your story, you can submit it to www.whenlovinghimhurts.com.

Conclusion

Change in one part of a system reverberates through the system. Throwing a pebble into a lake will cause a ripple effect and if all you can do is cause a ripple, it may be worth more than it seems. Ripples are quiet but they are still there.

It is also true that counting someone else's faults does not make you a saint. You really cannot change your partner's behaviour despite the fact that he would be improved by those changes. You can, however, change your own – not because you are the problem but because you are the solution. Study the conflict management skills and use them. Parts 2 and 3 attend more heartily to managing yourself in the relationship and how to heal yourself.

PART 2

Managing yourself in the abusive relationship

Introduction

Just staying will destroy you. You will become
bitter, broken and depressed beyond your wildest
imagination. If you elect to stay you will need help.
If you elect to go you will need help. Therapy was
my lifeline through the darkest of times.

I am going to repeat some of what I discussed in the introduction of this book to emphasise its importance. I deliberately repeat things because learning anything requires repetition. If you are being physically abused you need to consider very carefully and very seriously the option to leave this partnership. Your life is at risk and the abuse is not going to stop. You are risking your children both psychologically and physically.

I draw your attention to a matter that found its way to the headlines and press recently. Ray Rice (an American football player) beat his then girlfriend Janay almost senseless. A video tape was released to the press which showed a violent episode before they got married and all those charges against him had been dropped. Despite that clear warning sign that this was a dangerous relationship Janay married him anyway. This is precisely the point we have made in Part 1 of the book. We all had warning signs that we were unable to respond to as alarm bells. Every woman in an abusive relationship can recall incidents that should have alerted her. For several reasons that are difficult to understand, those incidents were ignored. I guarantee you that the Ray Rice video was an incident that became public but was by no means the only incident. Regardless of that history of physical abuse, she married him and the general public and private conversations all point a direct finger at her for this error of judgement. Why indeed would a woman who was aware of the problem be so reckless as to marry him anyway? Why indeed? There isn't a succinct answer, but the following story sheds some light on the dynamic.

I make reference to Ray Rice not because he is in any way exceptional but just because at the time of writing this book he was the most recent case in a long line of celebrities who have been the perpetrators or victims of abuse. Janay Rice has publicly apologised and defended her husband. Many people will fail to understand this and without doubt Janay has lost public sympathy. She is making herself the poster child for 'first time a victim, second time a volunteer'. Janay Rice has been hooked again. Philippa, who has done the same, attempts to explain her behaviour.

When we side with the abuser we feel special. It's us against the world. We glow in the admiration he has for us when we take his side. We are special because we understand him and you don't. We bask in his acknowledgment of us. We are a team and we are the exclusive members. I have done the same to the exasperation of my family, my friends (who were growing tired of me) and my therapist, Sue, who was more compassionate and understanding. The truth is that I failed to understand much of the time. I felt like I loved him and in those days it felt like love was enough. I had never seriously evaluated what love actually looked like and the difference between obsession and love. I didn't know that love was not enough. I didn't know that assault had to be the deal breaker. It is for healthy people but it isn't for co-dependents. It is in some awful way an opportunity to be the only one on his side. In a very sick way, it is an opportunity for intimacy. His apology will be profound (even though dozens of equally profound ones

have been issued in the past). His confessions of love feel real.
One hopes for 'real' insight this time.

What is, however, crystal clear is that *it is not her fault*. This
appears to be so difficult to understand that even one of my clients
who is herself in an abusive relationship actually said the words,
"I wonder what she did." I asked her what she meant by that.
"Well, maybe she was flirting with another man," is the reply I
got. This conversation must draw our attention to a very serious
problem, which is that women who are in abusive relationships are
subliminally being held responsible for their abuse. They go home
to the abuser and so the assumption exists that they are in some
way handing themselves up for the abuse. They sacrifice themselves
willingly and knowingly and, therefore, can be blamed for being
abused. What on earth could this woman have done to justify a
beating? One understands an argument, a separation, a divorce if
the conflicts can't be resolved, but a beating?

Before they got married, but after the first physical assault that
became public knowledge, Janay Rice is quoted to say that she
"deeply regretted her role in the incident that took place that night".
For the public that just serves to confirm what they were thinking –
"What did she do?" Well who cares what she did? The woman was
beaten. This is gender-based violence and women are being beaten
and killed over and over again. Society claims to refuse to tolerate
domestic abuse and legislation is passed confirming that it is illegal
to beat your wife (or anyone else for that matter). Notwithstanding
all these protections, domestic violence remains rampant.

> *There is a careless little quote that gets trotted
> out conveniently in these domestic violence
> circumstances, as mentioned earlier: "First time a
> victim, second time a volunteer."*

No woman in a violent, abusive relationship is a volunteer. There
are very complicated dynamics that make going back easier
than leaving. Many abused women have emerged from abusive

backgrounds or narcissistic parents and as a result they feel grateful for any love they receive. They lack the confidence to evaluate the quality of the so-called 'love'. They seek affirmation constantly and they have an unhealthy fear of abandonment. For them, leaving feels worse than dying. There are very serious financial considerations that are easy to toss aside if they aren't yours. There is the issue of the opportunities that can be provided for children when there is a father in the house relative to those that can be provided by single mothers. Those are not to be taken lightly by mothers who are painfully aware of the value they hold for their children's future. Then there is the nature of the beast. Getting divorced is painful under the best of circumstances but trying to divorce an abusive partner is getting divorced under the worst circumstances. These men are prepared to fight with everything they have and many of them have considerable amounts. An abusive relationship is a corrosive one. It corrodes your confidence. It damages your support network of friends and family and it leaves you scared and isolated.

Feeling worthless and afraid in the world is often not obvious – not to us and not to anyone else. A true feeling of worth is most easily ascertained by the decisions people make and not by how they appear. Philippa appears to be the epitome of self-confidence. When she arrives in the room she has the X-Factor. People know she is there. Hidden somewhere in that well-heeled appearance lurked a truth that was not obvious until you looked at the decisions she took in her life. She felt worthless. She felt she was not good enough and as a result she was grateful to have a man in her life. She felt safe in a partnership and afraid as a single woman.

Taking a stand means challenging yourself to do the very thing you don't want. It will mean losing a man you think you love and hope loves you. You will need to belong to a group of women that you may not respect and don't want to be part of – divorcees. The moral high ground is easy when the problem isn't yours. It is easy to talk about leaving when you aren't the one trying to leave.

It is easy for other people to tell you that you should leave. Actually, you sometimes wish you could and at other times are grateful to be married. An abusive relationship is confusing.

Initially it is episodic and there are times when he is wonderful and you know exactly why you are still with him. Like most conditions, if not attended to, it will get worse not better without any intervention. The good times will get fewer and the bad times will come more often and with increasing brutality.

Philippa explains the pendulum nature of the abusive relationship. It is like the gambler who is winning less often but often enough to go back "just in case tonight is the night that Lady Luck smiles kindly on me". Living with an abuser is like living with a slot machine.

> But the good times do come back, which make it all worthwhile. Here's the cycle: I am not worth more than a beating, I can take it anyway, if he didn't care so much he wouldn't beat me, and the silent bond is that 'we understand each other, we are a team, just you and me'.
>
> It is embarrassing to go home to a man who has hurt and humiliated you. It is even more embarrassing to want to and most of the time you do. It is impossible to explain to anyone what you don't understand yourself. There is a victim–abuser dance and you know that somehow and for some reason you are dancing despite your better judgement.

Philippa explained that it took her many years, many tears and lots of assistance to be able to explain it to herself. Her relationship with her father was paradoxical. On the one hand, he treated her like a princess and told her she was too good to work when her school friends got student jobs. He would play a game of saying, "Do you *need* it or *want* it?" She would laugh and say, "I *want* it" and with a flourish he would open his wallet. At other times, he would tell her what an ingrate she was, rolling his 'r' for effect. Her parents argued constantly and he would threaten to leave and start packing his bag. She would then set up a tray beautifully and present his dinner to him and try to keep him there, seduce him with food to stay.

Philippa lived with an impossible fracture in her relationship with her father. On the one hand, she was spoiled and adored and on the other hand she was an irritation and a target for his resentment. Begging a man to stay and seducing him with food was an old, familiar pain to which she had become attached. It was the face of love. Going back was like going home – where else do you go?

In this book we are going to ask you to take responsibility over and over again but we are not doing so because we blame you for the problem. We are not asking you to take responsibility for being abused.

It is not your fault. You are not the problem. You are, however, the solution.

Our recommendation is that if the relationship is a violent one you need to leave. We understand that leaving is not as simple as walking out of the door today and often that just isn't possible but you must begin the leaving process as opposed to trying to find a solution. The emotionally abused woman has more of an option to stay or to leave and we make no judgements on what decision you take. Many people and therapists have strong opinions on this decision. I don't. My position is a very clear one. Until you have healed yourself, you are likely to get involved with another abuser.

You will hear from Philippa's story that it took her three abusers until she understood that the healing had to be the healing of *herself* not the relationship. I know you can grow if you stay and I know you can grow if you leave and I don't mind which you do. If you choose to leave I suggest you do it only after you have extricated yourself emotionally. Leave emotionally before you leave physically. Until you have gained a measure of detachment you are likely to return and your confidence in yourself and your judgements will be compromised. You will only prove your worst fear, which is that you cannot live without him. The option you don't have is that you stay and do nothing differently because that will destroy you.

Staying or leaving is much less important right now than attending to the very complicated and diverse issues that got you into the relationship. There are issues that allowed you to ignore or not even hear the warning bells. Despite warning signs, you converted a damaging relationship into a marriage.

I suggest that you don't make a decision yet. Do the work on yourself and then you can make a well-informed decision.

Anna stayed and is happy with that decision. She says she likes the person it made her. She admits that she doesn't like her life and that quite simply the leopard has not changed his spots. She likes that the family has remained intact but she is painfully aware that her sons have been damaged by the abusive marriage. Anna has also taken pains to point out to me that society has evolved and what was unacceptable when she was much younger is much more acceptable now and the decision needs to be viewed in the light of that. Philippa left and she likes the person she is. Both of them have worked very hard on healing themselves. Of the original support group I only know of two who stayed and two who left and regretfully I don't know the fate of the others.

If you are at risk physically then your safety is of paramount importance and you must attend very seriously to your extrication. If not, you are at liberty to take your time in deciding.

Oscar Pistorius: The verdict is in!
14 September 2014 Blog post from
www.whenlovinghimhurts.com

Today Oscar Pistorius, the talented, disabled athlete was found guilty by a South African High Court of culpable homicide. The State was unable to prove, beyond reasonable doubt, that there was sufficient evidence to find him guilty of murder. The judge has sentenced Oscar to a five-year imprisonment of which he may serve as little as ten months. An idyllic romance turned into a crime scene on Valentine's Day. Despite the copious amounts of evidence, both forensic and from witnesses, we will never really know what happened on that tragic night. Reeva Steenkamp arrived at Oscar's elegant home, having tweeted her excited anticipation of a Valentine's night with her famous boyfriend and by morning she had been shot dead in his bathroom. She was fully clothed, locked in the bathroom and clutching her cell phone.

Samantha Taylor was his previous girlfriend and in her book, *An Accident Waiting to Happen*, Samantha's mother, Patricia describes a relationship in which her daughter was abandoned in his house for hours at a time. She describes a moody and angry troubled young man who, despite his considerable wealth, never paid for anything and more importantly appeared unable to tell the truth about anything. He 'punished' Samantha by pinching and biting her, he left the house saying he would be gone for an hour and returned a day later. Patricia says her daughter became reclusive and uncommunicative.

At this point the life of Oscar Pistorius hangs in the balance. News reports state that he is due for release on parole in August 2015 after serving only ten months in prison, and the conditions of the parole have not been specified. In a parallel development, the South African Supreme Court of Appeal has set a date in which the prosecutors will be given the opportunity to appeal the conviction for manslaughter. They remain hopeful that during the appeal Oscar could be found guilty of murder and not manslaughter.

Every abused woman is well aware of the struggle to manage this type of relationship and many suffer from anxiety and mood disorders as a result. They describe the relationship as fundamentally unpredictable and spend much of their time trying to create harmony without understanding the ground rules. What's a rule today is an offence tomorrow.

This section of the book helps in the day-to-day management of the relationship. Abused women need to acquire a new set of skills and habits, which take time and practice. This section deals with these immediate needs. The following section attends to the healing that is required to facilitate liberation from the abusive cycle.

The first skill we address is that of facing facts and refusing to allow yourself to live in denial or distortion of reality.

End Denial and Welcome the Ugly Truth
22 August 2014 Blog post from
www.whenlovinghimhurts.com

Most women who come for therapy are initially reluctant to discuss the marriage frankly for several reasons. In part, they feel disloyal and many express the fear that they will be perceived negatively for trying to lay the blame for their problems elsewhere. They are also embarrassed and ashamed of what they endure for reasons that they fail to understand. At a very basic level, not discussing the problem is a way of keeping it from being real. If it isn't spoken about then maybe it isn't true. Once a subject is brought to the surface it's more difficult to pretend it isn't there.

Discussions about abuse leak through slowly and are usually provoked by an incident. When the incident is on the table it's easier to discuss similar incidents and then patterns and finally the whole picture emerges.

Understanding the patterns of abuse is a process and not an event.

Let's understand the nature of denial. Denial is a coping mechanism that was first identified by Freud while working with recovering war veterans. It is the personality's way of avoiding information to feel more comfortable. However, the problem with denial is that it does the following:

- Other symptoms such as depression are created because this information needs to be processed.
- It prevents you from making constructive decisions. A decision made on scanty or distorted information is never a good one.
- It prevents you from developing the life skills necessary to assist you with your current predicament.

Denial takes many forms. Philippa tells me that she often 'forgot' dramatic incidents. She would find herself at physiotherapy or at the hospital but would be unable to recall the details of the assault event that got her there.

Excusing someone's behaviour is also a form of denial. Cynthia explains her husband's behaviour away and excuses it. She tells me that he works so hard and is so stressed and she understands that.

"Everybody attacks the people they love because that is the place they feel safest." There is a perverse pride hidden in that sentence. She is 'glad' to be the attacked person because it implies his sense of security lies solely with her. She wears her abuse as a badge of honour.

When any form of substance abuse is involved then, of course, it is the easiest thing to deny that the relationship is abusive by saying he had no idea what he was doing. Laying the blame at the feet of alcohol and drugs is easy.

Philippa was one of the women who denied abuse in the face of substance abuse.

I believed that he only hit me when he was drunk or drugged. One night I was lying in the guest room. The reason I was in there was that the previous night we had argued and he had hit me. I didn't want to share a room with him. When he came home he walked into the room and asked where his dinner was. From his walk and his face I knew that he was seething. I had made dinner but didn't want to tell him I had. Stone-cold sober he dragged me by my feet, kicking and screaming and shoved me onto the cold cement garage floor. He then locked it making it impossible for me to get into the house. That was the day I had to face the facts: He was sober; He had come home from an AA meeting; He had abused me anyway. What was I to do then with this information other than face it?

Why do women seek to deny the fact that they are being abused? There are several reasons. Firstly they feel ashamed. It is as though the abuse reflects poorly on the woman and not on the man. Mainly they are ashamed that they are still there. They are ashamed that they haven't left. They are ashamed that their husbands treat them shockingly and they lack the strength of character to leave.

Denial has a payoff – it allows you to stay where you are.

Many women sing the song of, "Better the devil you know tra, la, la, la, la." Now the shocking truth is this: You are an emotionally abused woman; and the worst thing you can do at this stage is leave.

Let me explain by way of a story.

Dalene married young because she was pregnant but also in love. For years she was neglected, insulted and ignored. She raised their child almost single-handedly and spent most of the early years of that marriage weeping. She was referred to me by her boss who liked her but was finding her emotional outbursts at work problematic. She worked very hard at trying to make her marriage work and when she finally gave up she was able to walk away knowing that she really had given her best.

Her marriage had never provided her with any financial assistance and he was far from being a hands-on dad. It took her years to leave. Initially she was adamant that she could endure anything he could throw at her. Finally she began to see that she deserved better. She began to see that her son's future was being compromised by a selfish, egocentric bully who brought nothing but tears into the home.

Dalene has contacted me again recently. She tells me that she has married and is very much in love. However, Dalene left counselling as soon as she left her husband, believing that she no longer required therapy and the problem was solved. Leaving an abusive relationship doesn't mean it has left you. She remained convinced that she had divorced the problem.

With her permission we have published her most recent letter to her new husband and as you will see from the contents of the letter, her new husband passes the bully barometer with flying colours. She finds herself once again being afraid to ask for much and beseeching him to treat her well.

Dear my love,

I am writing about last night. I had such a sick feeling in my stomach as you really don't understand when I communicate. Let's start with you first.

Yesterday at lunch I was wearing a revealing skirt which excited you along with my boobs. Yes, I was talking sexy, and yes you were really excited. The last couple of months lunch time hasn't been easy. Yesterday was a lot of fun for both of us. I discovered more about how to really excite you during lunch. I know you had an expectation of making love later in the evening. You also decided to/or should I say you expected to come home, eat, lie on the couch and watch TV.

My friend came to visit and those plans went sour. Later at 9.15pm you laid in bed, lights off, and with this huge expectation that the activities would begin. I really need you to understand some things about me. I really love you with all my heart. I have told you on numerous occasions that I want you and nobody else. I really want to repair our relationship. Repairing our relationship in my mind is NOT making love to take away all the PAIN. In my mind making LOVE is when the air is clear. I have so many things to discuss with you to make myself feel better. This is not something that can happen overnight. At the moment I have so much hurt to heal in my heart. I know I can get better but I really need you to understand and most importantly I need you to communicate with me.

I know you don't like talking. I need you to talk with me but before spitting out your anger and frustration I need you to think about what you say. If only you could feel the pain I feel you would understand more. I am trying my utmost best to let you know how I truly feel. I need you to tell me how you truly feel, when you agree with me, and when you disagree with me. This can be the start of our new chapter together. You have no idea how jealous I am of how open, for example, other couples are. They say what they want NICELY and they don't get into the silence mode like we do. This must stop! Do you agree?

This showed me how you were attracted to sexual visions. So many months have passed and you saw nothing. Your attitude of coming home for lunch consisted of:

A. *Bring your anger and frustrations though the door. Talking to me like dirt.*
B. *Looking for problems around the house and finding fault with chores I haven't done.*
C. *Showing me disrespect and clearly not understanding that I work from home when I am not at a client's.*
D. *Expecting lunch prepared for you. When you throw your toys out the cot and then still you make your own lunch and can't even think about me.*

Conclusion: I need you to think about this, talk to me about it or write back.

A general rule in life is never to expect anything, to avoid disappointment. Yes, there are many things I have never told you that I expected and yes I have been extremely disappointed. At the end of the day I LOVE YOU! That is more important than anything to me. Love has many wonderful ways of showing to another person, especially to me, your wife.

Don't ever expect me to serve you hand and foot. I work just as hard as you do. We both SHARE responsibilities at home and in life. I don't appreciate your reaction when you realised that your expectations were not going to materialise. There are many occasions that you have disappointed me, and I kept cool. With love comes hate. It is both our objectives to have more love than hate. You have done amazing things for me, and knowing this, I know how much you love me. Although, you have your own way of showing love, I accept this, don't argue with you. I appreciate everything you do for Cam and I. I need you to express love in your voice.

I really need you to talk or write to me with LOVE.

I have written my heart out to you. I will not expect a reply today or tomorrow. I expect nothing. I only ask for you to find a solution in the way you communicate with me, to think before you talk and to please think about a good moment to address our 'EASY TO SOLVE' problems. I am tired of ignoring the problems and trying to move on. This clearly hasn't worked for 3.5 years.

I LOVE YOU! YOURS ALWAYS, ME

The reason we decided to insert Dalene's love letter to her husband (with her permission) is that by default she describes the abusive relationship perfectly without having any idea that she is. Women have written notes, letters, faxes, emails and masterpieces – they are our begging bowls and we find ourselves with no more than a few coins as a result.

Women deny that they are abused because they are afraid to leave. There is now no reason to deny the abuse because the abuse is not a reflection of you, it's a reflection of him. You shouldn't even consider leaving for now. The last thing you want is to start or perpetuate the pendulum of leaving and returning. You lose credibility in your eyes and his. The leaving–returning trap is one that you need to avoid diligently. So, with the necessity for denial out of the way, let's welcome the ugly truth. You are an abused woman but you will find a way either to leave or to stay in a way which empowers. Face the truth. It is the first step to your recovery.

Reflection

Think about your own denial of abuse
Consider the following questions:

1. What was your original 'diagnosis' of your problem?
2. What were the first glimmers of realisation?
3. What was your first response to the words 'abused woman'?
4. What was the payoff in the denial?
5. How do you feel having faced the 'ugly truth'?

You can choose to write your answers down and share them with your counsellor at www.whenlovinghimhurts.com, or just answer them for yourself.

Do nothing: clinging and yearning

Healthy women would flee from an abusive relationship. Co-dependents have a different reaction. Their impulse is to work harder to make the relationship work. They cling. There really isn't another word to describe the desperation that motivates them. In this early onset of your recovery you have to know that you cannot trust yourself. Not a single thought or feeling. Your thoughts and your feelings are actually a reflection of your fear and pathology. They are not guidelines for the future. Having recognition that you're in an abusive relationship, the chances are that all your feelings will be amplified. For brief periods of time you will experience certainty and commitment. They will not be sustained. You cannot trust anything that you feel or think. Philippa describes what it felt like.

> I remember the day that I faced the fact that I was an abused woman. It was after seven years of abuse that I finally had the courage to lay the first assault charge against him. I escaped from Johannesburg, where we lived, to Cape Town in a desperate

attempt to find a little sanity. Almost in a trance I found myself in a bookshop desperately looking for stories on abuse. I bought several books and went to sit in a coffee shop, numb and helpless, soaking up every word in an effort to gain comfort. Forced to accept that I was an abused woman only made my situation worse. How was I ever going to stop yearning for him? How could I think of a life without him? How could I live with the fear of living with him, and how could I cope with the fear of being alone? None of the books I bought answered these questions. I felt more desperate than ever. I still wanted him to want me.

The worst thing an abused woman can do is rush headlong into her relationship or headlong out of it. Doing nothing sounds easy. In fact its one of the hardest things you can do well as a co-dependent. Co-dependency is symptomised by frantic doing. The idea is that as long as you do something there is a small chance that something will be fruitful. Doing nothing is what sobriety is to the alcoholic.

Most abused women are embattled in some form or another. They either fight constantly about everything and anything or they never fight at all. They stop fighting altogether when they know that whatever they say or do will be wrong.

Please do not under any circumstances enter a battle for which you are unprepared. All that will happen is you will prove your worst fear, which is that you are nothing without him.

Once women move past the denial and shame, they are either afraid or outraged. They always ask, "What must I do now?" Please don't do anything dramatic yet. There is a lot of work to be done but acting rashly is the worst action you can take.

- Unless you have fully understood the abusive relationship you are unprepared.
- Unless you understand why he chose you and why you chose him you are unprepared.
- Unless you have replenished your failing self-esteem you are unprepared.

Philippa said she felt like a pendulum swinging from one side to the other. In one moment her impulse was to leave, get into her car and drive away as fast as possible. A block later, the realisation that she might be single landed like a bomb and her impulse was to drive straight back.

> After one of the regular beatings I got into my car and roared off. Given that I had left so many times before I didn't want to go to my family. I felt stupid and ashamed. Here I was again with not even an overnight bag and no plan B. I drove straight back. In a block I had formulated a plan. I could never confess to him that I was scared and terrified of abandonment, so I decided to claim that the only reason I was there was that I needed a sleeping tablet. The potential added benefit to this fabulous plan was that he would understand that he had traumatised me and he would be sorry and take me in his arms and comfort me. He let me in. With hindsight I understand that my arrival was certainly no surprise to him. Like a dog with its tail between its legs I crawled into bed. The relief of being back in the bed overshadowed the fact that I had been physically assaulted. I lay in the bed with the welts around my neck, my body ached, my torn clothes were in the trash and all I could feel was relief.
>
> I have just been describing this to Sue, sitting at my dining room table in our pyjamas in the Berkshires. We have woken my dog, Osho, with our laughter. She's horrified and laughing because I'm laughing at how completely ludicrous my behaviour was. I have come such a long way. My laughter reminds me of just how recovered I actually am.
>
> In the past my laughter was like breaking glass. It was bitter and angry. I laughed at men and at love. Now my laughter is like petals that fall from the sky.

Avoiding the hook and bait

The following blog illustrates how to recognise the hooks and baits and how to avoid them.

Hook, bait and escape
8 September 2014 Blog post from
www.whenlovinghimhurts.com

Communication in an abusive relationship is a bit like running the gauntlet. One minute it's congenial and cosy, and, for no apparent reason, it switches. By now most of you will recognise the switch. It's a sneer or a change in his face. There is a tone or even a favourite sentence and then you know that this is no longer a cosy conversation. Everything that comes from that point onwards will be an onslaught of what you have done wrong or how awful you are.

Managing this relationship requires recognising the hooks and baits and not taking them. You are going to be drawn into an argument and then be abused. One of the signs of danger is the anxious feeling growing in your stomach – you are about to be hooked and then he is going to watch you flop around hopelessly trying to defend yourself or losing your temper or just being less than yourself in some way.

Negative labels are one of those hooks – you are called stupid, lazy, ignorant, opportunistic, unattractive and a bad mother.

The first habit you need to begin to develop (and remember that habits require persistence over time to become habits) is to ignore the negative labels. Don't entertain them. If he says you are too thin or too fat, don't walk around looking at other women to see if they are fatter or thinner. If he says you are stupid don't remind yourself that you did well at school or worry that you didn't. Simply don't entertain the labels. See these insults as hooks and don't take the bait. They are just ugly words and you don't have to swallow them. You are not a stupid fish taking the bait. You are a clever woman who sees the hook in the bait. Imagine yourself swimming away. Even if you are forced to stand there being berated, you are not there in your mind. You are a free clever fish who hasn't been caught. Swim away.

Make it a habit. See it, recognise it and whatever you do don't take the bait. Watch his mouth move and practise not hearing the words. Some women have used the image of the bubble. They are floating in the bubble that protects them and each insult bounces back to the person who delivers it. Some days you will do better than others. If you have a bad day it's fine. Tomorrow you will be better.

There are other hooks with attractive bait but they are equally dangerous, especially the one of reconciliation. "I am sorry", "I really didn't mean it", and "You drive me crazy" are different versions of the same bait that consoles you and takes you straight back into the arms of the abuser. Don't take that bait either. It will set new standards for you and him.

I was talking to Sue about the reconciliation hook and how beautiful some words sounded to me.

Sue, I remember when I felt truly liberated. It was the day the bait didn't even look attractive to me. I had become a clever fish who could swim away. I was sitting on the floor tearing up photographs of the two of us. Out of the corner of my eye I saw his boot. In the gentlest most seductive voice he said, 'You know I will always love you.' Now that was the bait that had been completely irresistible to me. I would have grabbed and gobbled it down without a moment's hesitation. I looked at him and carried on tearing. I was finally a free fish.

One of the defining characteristics of an abusive relationship is the constant criticism and bullying that is an almost daily challenge. It's worth remembering that communication is much more than what is said – it includes a mountain of non-verbal communication. Non-verbal communication includes body language that can be inviting or threatening. There is a tone of voice that leaves one under no illusions. The abuse is in his tone not his words. All relationships contain moments when one party is sharp or unreasonable and tempers can fray with the best of us. Unlike these occasional failures of judgement the abuser is consistently rude, abrasive, unreasonable and demeaning.

The issue here is not how unacceptable his behaviour is but how well you handle it. Abused women usually attempt to explain that the accusation is unreasonable and that some kind of misunderstanding has taken place. If you cast your mind back to the numerous times you have done that it becomes completely obvious that it's pointless. All it ever does is take you further down the road of conflict to the inevitable outburst that you are trying to avoid. The other option is to point out to him how unacceptable *his* behaviour is. Firstly, you are stating the obvious and if it isn't obvious to him, then this conversation is equally pointless. Philippa echoes this sentiment.

I have begged for my own redemption too many times. I have presented the evidence, defended myself and appealed my conviction. No matter what I do I have been found guilty too many times. Now I take the 5th.

You have attempted to defend and explain yourself to no avail. You have attempted to explain the error of his ways and you have apologised. Some of you have met him insult for insult in an attempt to redeem your failing self-confidence and I can guarantee that it ended badly for you. Your error of judgement here is that you have failed to recognise that this is not a conversation. This is a hook and bait and he is going to assault you verbally or physically. He is unhappy and you are about to become his victim. This is simply a fight waiting to happen. This is not a conversation – you are being toyed with.

The fact is that you can't change him but you can change your reaction to him. You may not be the problem here but you are definitely the solution. This game of cat-and-mouse can have no apparent reason.

"Hello, how was your day?"

"It was fine thanks and yours?"

"How could your day be anything but fine given that you have nothing to do and all day in which to do it? Mine was much less fine but I imagine more productive."

It has arrived – the hook with the bait. Sometimes they are less clear and you sense them before you hear them. It's in the body language or the tone of the silence or the hostile glare. The warning is in the walk or the way the glass gets banged down. Your insides feel chilled because you know that something has gone wrong and you know where this is going. You have been there often enough – you recognise this place.

Anna describes what typically happened at the dinner table when her sons still lived at home.

ANNA'S STORY

The family would be at the dinner table. He would have arrived home moody so we were all already nervous. Then there would be an exaggerated sigh and he would push his plate into the middle of the table and fold his arms. "What exactly did you do all day to justify this slop?" He would glare at me. It was worse than a glare – it was a look of complete contempt. Instead of recognising that he had already decided to have this fight and was not about to change his mind I would try to diffuse the situation.

"I'm sorry. It was the first time I tried this recipe and it hasn't

turned out as well as I had hoped. So I'm not applying for a job as a chef but I don't think it's shocking." (I'm trying for a light apology and a stab at light humour.)

No success.

"I am really sorry. I know you have had a difficult day and I should have been more careful." (My attempt at an earnest apology.)

No success.

I would storm off from the table or leave crying or sulking.

No success.

"Your mother is the worst cook on the planet and you eat her food without complaining."

No success.

"You are starting a fight for nothing. This is the same meal you had two weeks ago and you ate it without complaining." (My tough routine.)

No success.

Avoiding hooks is not easy because he is determined to take you down this road and hurt you in some way or another and the food is absolutely not the issue. It seems that food is a favourite hook and bait, possibly because we are so entwined with our role in this regard.

Philippa tells the hook, bait and caught story of her marriage.

I take pride in the food I create and am particularly attentive to the presentation. It's actually my hobby and my passion and one of the few places that I feel completely secure in my skills level. I took considerable effort in planning his meals. In the evening he claimed to be too tired to sit at the table and needed to watch TV to unwind. I brought him the food on a silver tray with a starched tray cloth. I set it down on his lap while he stared mindlessly at the TV. Most often he took one look and said, "Why did you dish up so much or so little?" I would run back to the kitchen to adjust the serving. He then demanded salt and I ran back and got it. Sometimes he wanted more so back to the kitchen I ran. This time I was delighted to be running – "He liked the food – yay." Well, that sense of wellbeing would inevitably be short-lived. I would then be told that I put too much on the plate. I tried really hard but I didn't recognise that I had no chance – he had landed the hook and baited it. It never occurred to me that I had not been given an opportunity to eat, with my food cooling on the plate. It didn't mean a thing and the ugly truth is that at the time I barely noticed. I was so intent on gaining his approval for what I had provided that I didn't notice. The best was the toast in the morning: "You never spread the butter to the edges." Do you know how careful I would be each morning to ensure that every crumb of toast was touched with butter?

Sue was somewhat stunned when I explained this.

"This is mind blowing. What on earth are you doing buttering his toast? Surely the CEO of a company is capable of attending to his own toast?"

This is why it is imperative to seek the guidance of a counsellor. At the time I felt proud of my type of loving.

Anna developed certain skills to survive this kind of hook-and-bait behaviour after decades of practice. A few months ago she gave her husband a lift to collect his car that had been in for repairs. He told her to be ready for 7am and when she was he was doing the Sudoku in the paper and made no signs to leave or to acknowledge that she was standing there waiting at 7am as agreed. She knew from that moment onwards what was coming. When they eventually left he began criticising her before they reached the end of the driveway and was shouting before they were around the block. She says he made her so nervous that she felt like she was turning into a menace on the roads and was more than relieved that they even arrived safely. When he got out of the car she said gently (despite the fact that he hadn't thanked her for the ride), "It's a pleasure and what a lovely way to start a day". She then drove off as calmly as she could making sure not to look in the rear-view mirror.

Ladies, that takes practice. As Anna explains: "They are bullies and a bully will continue to bully you for as long as it works. It's working if you are in a state. It's working if you are crying and most of all it's working if you are fighting back. It stops working when you stop reacting."

The outcome you are looking for here is for the game to not work. It needs to get useless and boring and then they will stop because they are getting nothing out of it. People get tired of playing a game that no longer feeds a need. Initially it will not stop. Remember that this game has worked so many times that he expects that it will continue to work and so it will be repeated. It's a bit like gambling. As long as you win sometimes you will continue to go back to the casino. Once you lose too often you start to lose interest. Initially the number of times the game is played increases because they are frustrated by the lack of success but with time it will diminish.

Please pay attention, however, to the fact that the incident on the way to collect his car took place only a few weeks ago. Of course, what that tells you is that after fifty years of marriage it is still being played, even if less often.

Anna says, "It happens less often and I am much better at handling it but it's still a part of my life. I have come to terms with the fact that, regretfully, I am not married to a man who will gently push aside a plate and say, 'It was fine, I am just not particularly hungry tonight.' I wish I was but I'm not and life is not a wish list."

Afterwards, when I asked her how she felt, she said, "The truth is that for about an hour or two I just wanted to cry and then I stopped feeling and started thinking. I know that I am married to a man who will seldom be congenial if he is inconvenienced and not having his own car was an inconvenience. There is nothing more to do. There have been hundreds of these incidents and they are unlikely to stop so I walk away and leave it behind. I would imagine myself putting down the incident and walking away."

Philippa makes an accurate observation. She says that avoiding hooks is really a beginning step. It is an important one because it will eliminate many incidents, but it does little to shift the dynamics in the relationship. One can easily be hooked by avoiding the hooks. It makes you hyper-vigilant with everything he says and the end goal is increasing detachment not hyper-vigilance. I agree with that but painful incidents are damaging and this skill is one of damage control which is why it exists here and not in the section on healing oneself.

When you see the hook and the bait, do whatever you can to swim past it. This is not a conversation to which you can make a contribution. This is not a conflict that lends itself to some kind of resolution. If you get caught, you are going to find yourself reeled in and you'll be flopping around gasping for air.

Let's go back to the example of Anna at the dinner table. How could you have avoided the bait? Tell him that when you and the children have finished dinner you will make him another dinner that doesn't take long to prepare. However, you can make use of your own non-verbal communication by doing the following:

- Make eye contact, but not aggressive eye contact – just enough for him to know that you aren't afraid of him. Calm eye contact allows him to know that you are undisturbed and in control; aggressive eye contact is a challenge to go into the fray.
- Keep your voice calm and congenial.
- Continue another conversation at the table as though this incident has not taken place.
- Do not clear his plate from the table until you clear the rest.

Create a solution but don't engage in the fight. The non-verbal communication is where you need to stay calm within. Many a battle can be won without ever having a fight. Sometimes you will succeed and when you do, imagine yourself swimming away and laughing.

However, some hooks are really difficult to avoid. One of my clients was telling me about the new house she and her husband had bought. He is immensely annoyed by her indifference to and failure to labour in the garden. In this new house a section has been allocated to her and she is expected to prove that she can in fact make a contribution in the garden. He has had it planted out and it is 'her job' to merely sustain it. Because I am an interested and envious gardener I asked to see it and she showed me the photos on her cell phone. Her section of the garden is north-facing in full sun and very exposed without tress or shrubbery around it. Everything that has been planted there is a shade-loving plant that is highly frost sensitive. They are, to the last, thirsty plants and most require the skills of an experienced gardener. She has no chance of keeping most of it alive and that which will live will never flourish. I am dumbfounded by all this trouble and effort to ensure her failure. This is a hook and bait that is almost impossible to avoid.

Cultivated indifference

---

*Silence can be your greatest weapon – keep quiet
and watch the other person fill the space with their
insecurities. Indifference, if used correctly, is the most
powerful weapon you will ever possess.*

There comes a point in any hurtful situation when we begin to hate the experience. You will begin to feel 'hatred' for your husband and your marriage, and frankly your life, as your abusive situation continues. I have heard the words, "Sue, I hate him" thousands of times in my office and I know and understand that the hatred stands alongside the love, yearning, fear, self-doubt and trepidation. The human heart is a complicated one and can hold many contradictory feelings simultaneously. I also know that feelings are like water. Feelings are not convictions – those are foundation stones that can be relied on to stay no matter what. Nonetheless, much of the quality of our lives is caught up with feelings and to deny those is to turn our faces from much that makes us human.

There are many utterly useless feelings that contribute hugely to our unhappiness but not at all to our growth or development. Some negative feelings have limited value. One of those is guilt. Guilt is a worthwhile feeling to a point. If we have conducted ourselves badly then we take responsibility for that and experience the guilt. From that place of guilt we are able to issue a sincere and heartfelt apology to the person to whom it is owed. Guilt allows us to examine our moral framework and pass an assessment. We can decide that what we did was incorrect and decide that in future we will not repeat the behaviour. We may understand why we did what we did but understanding is not the same as something being justifiable. In other words, we have learned our lesson and in so doing we have grown. From that point onwards staying immersed in guilt is pointless and self-destructive. Utilise your guilt to the point that it serves you and allows you to repair what has been damaged and then release it.

Hatred and resentment have no value whatsoever. They are a virus to the soul and the psyche, and these are the feelings that you need to guard against. There is a special section in Part 3 – 'Healing Yourself' that is designated to the release of resentment so I will not go into detail here.

Hatred is not the opposite of love. When you feel hatred you are as consumed as when you feel love – just negatively and miserably. There is no liberation in hatred. It will pre-occupy you and destroy your day but also you as a person.

The opposite of love is indifference.

Indifference will give you the liberation you are seeking. I call it 'cultivated indifference' because it is not an emotion that will come easily or naturally. You will have to manufacture or cultivate it simply because you need it.

Let us pay a little more careful attention to the opening quote – 'Indifference, if used correctly, will be your greatest weapon'. Note the part that says 'if used correctly'. Indifference is only valuable to you if you can use it selectively. If you become an indifferent person you will surely have lost some beautiful human qualities. Indifferent people are numb people. They fail to experience the nuances of life and are incapable of responding to a beautiful sunset. They never give the gift of enthusiasm or hope that we should and can so readily give to our friends, family and mankind in general.

You are not aiming to become a numb or indifferent personality.

You are aiming to own a supply of cultivated indifference as part of your artillery for life.

If the image of artillery is too masculine to sit easily with you, then imagine it as a warm coat that you wear when the weather demands. You own it and can put it on when you need it. It will protect you and when you no longer require it, you can take it off, hang it up and know that you have it for the next time you need it.

What does it mean to be indifferent? It means that you elect to not have an emotional response to this situation or this person despite the fact that the situation or person lends itself to a response of some sort. It is taking charge of your emotions and electing to refuse to react despite the provocation.

This is one of the skills that the women in the initial support group worked hard to achieve. During the first few weeks we examined the abusive relationship. We walked around and looked at it from different angles. We learned to know it cognitively not just emotionally. We understood the themes of abuse, similar to those in the Bully Barometer Checklist (see page 38) as:

- constant criticism and not being able to do anything right for a long time;
- name-calling and negative labels;
- no constructive conflict management;
- denial of the validity of your feelings;
- public humiliation even if done with humour;
- damage to support networks such as friends and family;
- using money to tip the power balance; and
- sexual humiliation, rejection or an insatiable need for immediate sexual gratification.

Through being part of a group these women no longer felt so alone and were not so confused about what was being done to them. They were no longer blaming themselves or diagnosing themselves to be the problem. They were no longer saying that the problem was that they were inadequate or depressed or suffering from anxiety. As a result of the confidence and clarity they had gained, they became extremely angry and it was at this point that I became increasingly concerned for their safety.

Their anger was understandable and even justifiable, but did it serve them well? In my opinion it put them at risk. This is like going into the ring with a heavy-weight champion. Quite simply you are going to get knocked senseless either physically or emotionally. The anger leaked through in uncontrolled ways. They had outbursts that seemed to come from nowhere and that they hadn't planned. Worse than that, they were acting out their anger. They were doing things like smashing items in the house, hurling dinner plates across the room. We needed to change it. Understandable or not, there is no victory in becoming like the abuser; there is no pride in losing control; and there is no appropriate role-modelling happening for the children.

Initially, the women were reluctant to set aside their anger. It was a more comfortable feeling than hurt, anxiety and despair. It seemed like the 'right' feeling once they could see the insidious damage that had been done to them. They wanted the anger. It made them bullish and more confident. It was bred in self-righteous indignation and it was difficult for me to ask them to set it aside.

Rampant feelings allowed to dictate our decisions are not healthy. Decisions based on careful thought and consideration with appropriate attention given to the likely consequences are good decisions. Uncontrolled impulses are going to take you to dangerous places.

"Frankly you look like an idiot and a drama queen." You and I understand that this outburst is the proverbial straw that broke the camel's back, but instead it looks like an amplified response to a single incident. You look as crazy as he has accused you of being. Destroying furniture and ornaments that you have lovingly collected and cleaned and dusted for years is, in time, going to leave you nursing your regret and sense of loss. Acts of revenge always backfire. When you dig a grave for another, you dig one for yourself.

In essence what I am saying is that you are right to be angry. It is understandable and justifiable. Anger comforts you because it replaces the hurt and pain that has consumed you. But you need to let it go because it fails to serve you well. What will serve you well in the place of rage is cultivated indifference. It has a quiet and dignified strength. It speaks volumes with few words. I know it's difficult but it's also valuable, and anything valuable is often difficult to achieve. Indifference is not being a doormat. It doesn't give permission for unacceptable behaviour.

Cultivated and selective indifference is the ultimate in self-control. It allows you to elect to respond to something or not and in the clarity of that moment you can choose a response instead of being mowed down by your own feelings. Cultivated indifference is the shield you own or your favourite warmest jacket when the cold winds blow. You will never acquire the skill until you can value it and understand and embrace why you need it. You have to want something before you can work hard for it, so please understand the value of indifference and let go of your bullish new-found confidence because you are going to find yourself playing well out of your league.

Indifference is an acquired skill. Authentic, cultivated indifference is powerful if used selectively and elegantly.

Having finally convinced the women in the support group of the need to change responses and develop new skills, the obvious question becomes *how*. How does one acquire this skill? There are a variety of ways and I suggest you practise all of them and then settle on what sits easiest with you.

Anna used a mantra. It was a saying she said over and over again to herself, especially when there had been an incident and she was sitting squarely back in her pain and devastation. Her mantra was: "I don't care to care. I don't care to care. I don't care to care." She had to say it over and over again.

When you repeat something often enough it creates a new neural pathway from your brain. It starts off feeling ridiculous – of course you care; otherwise there would be no need for a mantra. One could simply put down the ugly incident and the hurt feelings, the shame and the fear and keep walking. Once you say it often enough you will find that it begins to feel true. It takes time before it feels true. She says it works for her because when she is that upset she cannot think rationally and can only feel. The simplicity of the words was their key. "I don't care to care. I don't care to care". These words have become a part of her and when she's hurting she reminds herself of it and she finds that she can lay it down gently, like some sick wild bird that cannot be saved, and walk away. She lays it down gently because those are her feelings and she does not want to reject, with venom, any of her own feelings.

One of the other ladies in the group had an uncle who had a farm and as children they spent school holidays on the farm. They were happy times for her and she had a loving and safe relationship with her uncle and aunt. She used visualisation. She imagined that she was with her uncle and she was planting seeds and growing a crop of indifference. She understood from that visualisation that she would need to work hard on her crop to bring it to harvest and so she had to value it. She understood from the imagery that she would water her crop and protect it from harm. Most importantly, she understood that no crop arrives instantly. One prepares the soil by embracing the idea of cultivated indifference and then tending it while it grows. She put a photograph of her uncle at the bottom of her bed on a wooden chest and in the morning while she had her coffee she would look at her uncle and remind herself of what is required to bring a successful crop to fruition.

Another of the women also designed a visualisation for herself. She imagined that there was a type of keyboard in front of her husband and he would press start. She imagined that she had blocked the 'start' button. She could see him pushing the button over and over but it had been blocked – quite simply it no longer worked. She was safe because she could no longer be toyed with. It was her favourite visualisation because her husband had an aversion to technology and spent hours complaining about how things that were supposed to work never did. Things that were designed to make your life easier just didn't. He was a bit of a techno-klutz and could easily get frustrated with the TV remote, so it held a delicious irony for her that here was yet another appliance that was letting him down.

Each woman in the group designed a strategy that had some personal significance for her. An affirmation/mantra is very effective for people who are not inclined to be visual people. A visualisation is powerful because the brain takes to pictures very easily. However, having both a mantra and a visualisation would be doubly powerful and a reminder of the visualisation, such as the example of the photograph of her uncle, sustains the discipline that is required to develop a new skill. In order to take offence you have to reach out and take it.

Philippa was not a member of that original support group. She developed her own methods to slowly and painfully acquire her indifference. Initially she simply couldn't embrace the value of indifference.

Indifferent? I never wanted to become indifferent. If I became indifferent it meant that all my hard work was for nothing. I was far too invested to give it up. Indifference meant that it was over. 'Over' is like death to an abused woman. Who would I be without him? Nothing. When I first started cultivating indifference it was just another ploy in the game. I didn't really mean it. All he had to do was give a look, flirt or deliver a line in a seductive way, and I fell at his feet, grateful that he still wanted me.

This was part of the game of who wins. We don't even know we're playing it. All I wanted was to make him love me, acknowledge me and not abandon me. When I first considered the option of indifference it was excruciating because it meant the end was near. I could not imagine what or who I would be without him. I often pretended that I had mastered indifference, but it was just false bravado. THIS time I meant it. Ha ha, I never did. I only meant it long enough for him to think I had so he would capitulate and want me back. It's part of the dance of abuse – who wins, who can hold out the longest, who blinks first. You know how much satisfaction that gives an abused woman? That's a *feast* for a co-dependent.

When I was pretending to be indifferent I loved to tell and retell the story to anyone who was unfortunate enough to be around to listen. I would explain what he said and then what I said and how 'I won'. Cultivated indifference only became healing to me when I understood that it was what I needed for myself instead of winning points. I could only value indifference for myself when my self-loathing was such that I could no longer stand myself. Finally, it had value for me. When my false indifference failed me I needed to save myself because even I could no longer stomach what was going on.

Philippa explains her journey with indifference once she had recognised that her previous efforts were 'manipulation gift-wrapped as indifference', and then follows on with a saying to help her ignore the constant criticism.

Indifference is not the desert I imagined it to be. On the contrary, it is lush and quiet, deep and powerful.

There was a line I repeated often to myself. It was a line I heard at an Al-Anon meeting: In order to take offence, you had to reach out and take it. I stopped taking it. It was an incredibly powerful moment and thought to me. In the past my feeling was that being hurt and offended 'happened to me'. I had no idea that I had in some way participated. I had allowed and accepted it. I also used to tell myself that I can only become offended if someone I respect criticises me. I had zero respect for him and so his insults began to have less and less effect. I took fewer and fewer of them because his opinion held less and less weight and I understood that I didn't have to swallow the insult. I could step back and evaluate the comment and decide that it was untrue and so I was not participating in this conversation.

I also began to apply myself to being more discerning. He told me he was wonderful and I never really assessed that for myself. When he wasn't telling me how amazing he was he was telling me how depressed and needy he was and how much he needed me. I believed him on both counts despite the fact that every bit of information I was getting showed me that it was untrue. I wanted it to be true but it wasn't. Ignoring the truth was not going to make it go away. Believing the lies was not going to make them true. So I started seeing him in a different light. He was no longer the prize that I believed him to be. He was a weak, pathetic, disgusting man who began to repulse me. But know that I could only get there because the repulsion began with myself. I felt like a total failure. My sense of failure was what I was trying to avoid by believing the lies. The best I could get for myself was someone who beat me, lied to me, cheated on me, and humiliated me. I loathed myself for bringing this into my life and that of my children. It was a very painful time for me. There is a saying that the truth will set you free. It does but in the beginning it feels like it's going to kill you.

No skill is acquired overnight. You did not learn to play tennis in a day even though you decided to learn. This skill will also take time and practice. There will be times when you are sure that you will never get it right, but you will if you keep at it.

The value of indifference is that it allows you to manage your emotions instead of being compelled by them into actions that you will later regret. In any crisis, the wise approach is to stay rational without denying the emotional component. Cultivated indifference will give you an added benefit. Its energy is calm and controlled. It has a quiet dignity and I assure you that with time that dignity gains gravity. You will begin to respect yourself more and more and, believe it or not, you will gain the respect of others as well. It has a beautiful positive cycle that takes you up and up – as opposed to anger that will inevitably drag you down. The power of cultivated indifference is a skill that will serve you well all your life. However, we recall 'if used correctly' requires us to be relentlessly discerning with our responses. It is not always easy to discern when you should react and when indifference is what is required. I asked Philippa to talk about how she discerns the differences now after many years of healing herself.

There were two co-dependent behaviours that lingered for a long time. The first one was defending and apologising. If anything went wrong, as it does in the course of living, I was instantly on the defensive. I assumed that I would be attacked and criticised even before it started and am still often amazed when nothing of the sort transpires. Sue and I were on our way to a meeting, but despite having a GPS we managed to get lost. I expected her to be irritated in spite of the fact that our being lost had nothing to do with me. It made me aware of how gradual healing is and how stubborn pathologies are. My need was to defend myself even though there was not a hint of heaviness in the car. After all these years I remain anxious about being called stupid when there is a problem anywhere in sight, whether I have something to do with it or not. If I am attacked or criticised, it is difficult for me to be discerning.

Because I have spent a lot of time with Sue I have become painfully aware of the fact that I am still struggling with this part of my life. My impulse is to defend myself and apologise. If that doesn't work I want to dig up old bones and attack. I suppose I think that I won't be wrong all over again. In a recent incident I see that what I don't do is stay calm and assess the situation. I was criticised by a few people I love very dearly and was distraught. I spoke to Sue about it over a few days and she said very simply: "Phil, can't you see that what is being said is simply not true? This is not a fair criticism – it is a convenient one. Read your own emails carefully and you will see that it is simply not fair. Say so and point out the failure of logic here." I went home and read my response, which fortunately I had not yet sent. I had picked up every negative statement and attempted to justify myself and then because I felt so powerless, I had attacked everyone else and reminded them of every offence of the past. What I had been unable to do was glean the lie. I was unable to see through the mess to find the point. My inability is because I am instantly upset and therefore unable to be discerning.

The other behaviour that lingered is what Sue and I call 'Party Tricks', I am thankfully fully cured of this problem. This was a knee-jerk reaction I had towards men.

If a man gave me any attention I automatically went into work mode, even if I wasn't interested. A man's feelings were way more important than mine. So I performed. I giggled at his stupid jokes, humoured him as you would a buffoon on a sitcom and flirted as if he was attractive. All of this stemmed from gratitude because I was wanted and didn't want to hurt his feelings. Men's feelings were always more important than mine.

Habits are difficult to break and we are perversely attached to familiar pain. It will take time. Initially it will be something you do, and from time to time, forget to do. Then it will become a part of you. It transforms into inner strength, feeling unashamed, and inordinately proud. It really is worth the effort as Philippa says below.

When I was sick I made a noise. I was always laughing or giggling, swaggering and swooning. I talked a lot, laughed loudly and complained to everyone who would listen to me. I thought it was good that people noticed me – it made me proud. Now I am well and I am quiet. Finally I can see the people who saw me.

The nodding "no"

To be safe in the world every
woman requires a sacred "no".

All women struggle to say "no" firmly – it's our difficult word. It is as a result of what sociologists refer to as 'socialisation'. We are brought up in a context in society where we learn how to behave and, more frighteningly, how to feel about certain issues. Unlike boys, girls are encouraged to be cooperative. We are encouraged to be congenial and when other children offend us, we are encouraged to respond gently or not at all.

On a playground it would be perfectly acceptable for a boy to push another boy off a swing if he jumped the line. That same behaviour from a girl would be responded to differently. She would be expected to either let it go and play on the roundabout or tell her mother, who would then attend to it. Any attempt to attend to it herself would be regarded as unfeminine and discouraged. Nobody ever tells a boy to "just be nice".

Teenage girls are under no illusions about the fact that any assertiveness on their part would be deemed to be unattractive. She would be labelled as 'aggressive' and that's among the milder labels she would endure should she overtly defend herself or her rights too strongly. Were she to be put under duress she would be expected to cry and that behaviour would be considered to be an acceptable objection. Quite simply we have not been socialised to be comfortable with a firm "No". An uncertain and timid "no" would be acceptable but certainly not a firm one.

In the initial stages of a relationship we are all more inclined to not say anything about issues that bother us. We are enjoying the relationship and are disinclined to any kind of friction. It's very understandable, but the problem is that we allow the other person to believe that we find their behaviour acceptable.

Say No but act Yes
11 September 2014 Blog post from
www.whenlovinghimhurts.com

Do you have any idea of how often you say "no" but act "yes"? Philippa has this story to tell:

My husband and I went to Thailand on holiday. On the last morning we had an argument because I thought he had an inappropriately flirtatious relationship with a colleague who called him constantly. He hit me through the face so hard that I fell. I remember lying on the floor smelling the hotel carpet and crying. He stood at the door unrepentant and said over his shoulder, "I'm going to breakfast."

I was shocked and dazed. Then I made a special effort to look good and went down to the dining room. I sat at a different table and refused to look at him. I was taking a stand. After a while he apologised and begged for my forgiveness.

By the time we were on our way to the airport he had his arms around me and *promised* that he would never do it again. He was remorseful and I was so grateful. Him begging for forgiveness made me feel powerful and in control. I had taught him a lesson. It was okay to hit me.

What happened here was that I said "no" and acted "yes". The moment I arrived in that dining room my behaviour said okay. All that had actually happened was that I had taken one more step down the road to my own destruction.

*People learn how to treat you based on what you
accept from them.*

Women who have not been given the gift of a healthy self-esteem
are even more intent on receiving approval and affirmation from
the people around them. They are afraid that a firm "No" would
result in being rejected. Women have received the unfortunate
reputation of being manipulative because we struggle with a more
honest "No". I have often tried to encourage my clients to find a
firm "No" within themselves. Almost without fail they begin by
telling me that they just aren't like that. They are too nice. They
aren't a bitch. If I had money for every time a woman told me that
she was 'too nice' to assert herself I would be in the company of
Warren Buffet.

The result of being 'too nice' is that you will end up in a
relationship in which your needs are never met because they have
remained unclear. This will in turn make you resentful and not
particularly nice at all. Being too nice to say how you feel and what
is important to you is actually dishonest. As Philippa often explains:

> The men I chose were usually honest about themselves when
> I met them. I elected to ignore the information. I, on the other
> hand, was seldom honest about myself. I allowed them to think
> I was everything they wanted me to be and actually I tried to be
> all those things but I simply wasn't.

The other problem we have with a firm "No" is that the only
time we say no is when we are at the end of our rope and then the
"no" is not firm but hysterical. Our "no" is lost in all the garbage
that goes with losing one's temper and the result is that he heard
everything and nothing. He heard that you are furious and thinks
you will calm down and it is all over and forgotten.

A firm "No" requires clarity of thought. It is not an emotional
outburst. It's a refusal to accommodate behaviour that we deem to
be unacceptable and because we have reasons that we consider the
behaviour unacceptable.

We all know that communication between men and women can be a challenge at the best of times. Women like to explain detail and men like to be informed of the bottom line at the beginning. For women emotions hold more sway than they do for men. Men like to be convinced of something by the logic and not by the weight of the feeling. A firm "No" is backed by consideration and logic. Men understand that language – they live there. They initially may not like hearing it from us but they will more readily respect it than the raving and ranting and performing that we are inclined to do because we failed to make ourselves clear at the beginning.

Own a firm "No" – it doesn't mean you aren't nice. Not owning one is guaranteed to make you 'not nice' in the long run.

Once again I would like to mention the value of authenticity. I have had clients who have claimed to use the firm "No" to gift wrap what is simply unhelpful and unacceptable behaviour. Last week one of my clients had an argument with her husband and I would agree that his behaviour qualified as abusive. They are receiving couples counselling and the agreement was that he would refrain from name-calling and making reference to how much her monthly costs are. They were out for dinner and he called her names and once again made reference to how much she cost him every month. The next night she went out before he came home and took his credit card to a casino. As it so happens she won quite a lot of money and offered him a share of her winnings. Neither he nor I are remotely convinced of the merits of that firm "No" and trying to buy your way out of a predicament is just demeaning. Going to a casino is something that she likes to do frequently and using that opportunity to do so without restraint is certainly not a firm "No" – it's just a cheap shot.

From worrier to warrior

Worry has been my constant companion. We go shopping together, cook together and do the laundry. Worry is in my bed and on my chair, in the car and on my face. You would think by now I would have learnt to live with her more easily. I wonder with whom I will speak if she ever leaves.

I will spare you any opening statements other than the one above because you are all experts at worrying. What is required now is that you go from being a worrier to being a warrior. The term warrior is usually a masculine term that conjures up images of men at war. But, watch a lioness when her cubs are threatened and then tell me that we don't each have a warrior within us when something we love is being threatened.

What is being threatened is you, and it's important to find the warrior within you. Much credit for this idea must be given to John Kehoe and his recent book *Quantum Warrior: the Future of the Mind*. He echoes the work of many self-development authors who warn of the power of negative thinking to sustain our worry and prevent us from making the necessary changes to our lives.

Every negative thought damages your confidence and your day.

Often those negative thought patterns have been a part of your life for so long that they are difficult to even identify. Many of them were part of your childhood legacy. Some children were taught that work is a necessary evil and so they continue through life tired at the very thought of going to work and expecting nothing more than the tedium that is their job. Others were taught that work is a blessing and an opportunity. They go to work glad to be there and expecting the opportunities they often find or create. Some men believe that the family is a financial burden and others treasure the role of the breadwinner. For some women the home is an endless and mind-numbing ordeal and for others closing the curtains and switching on the lamps is nothing short of sacred. Behind all of these examples is a set of thoughts that will ultimately determine how your life feels and what you find and experience. Take out a mental cancel stamp and simply cancel the thought. List the thought patterns you wish to eliminate so that you can be on the lookout for them.

Philippa and I have been talking about the vigilance required around our thinking and how we need to stalk our thoughts. She has described with her usual remarkable insight how easy that sounds and how tricky it actually is.

The phrase 'stalking a thought' is a powerful trigger for me. Like Anna, I spent a considerable amount of time stalking my husband and just the word 'stalk' takes me back to a memory. One night I was so convinced that he was not actually working, as he said he was, that I drove to the office to find his car. I have a memory of myself standing there, in the dead of night, straining against the gate trying to catch a glimpse of his car. It wasn't the only time – just the first memory that sprang into my mind when I read the word 'stalk'. I was a forensic detective. I was a human bloodhound in search of the proof of my fears.

When I was a chronic co-dependent, I would have had huge difficulty with this guideline. Firstly, I was so obsessed with him that the thought of turning my attention to myself would have been a painful release. He was the 'old familiar pain' that I had become so attached to. Although thoughts about him hurt me, it was my place, my home, where I lived. I was obsessed with him and so watching my thoughts would mean breaking my own obsession.

Often I believed that he was lying and cheating and, of course, he was. Inside of me I always knew when he had begun to lie and it was always connected to other women. Once I had that in my head I couldn't rest for a second. I tracked the evidence, followed the leads, sifted through the conversations in my head looking for inconsistencies and my hurt was almost unbearable. It was never enough for me that I knew; I had to find proof and confront him. I had to have a verdict – he was guilty of adultery! Once I had the verdict there was nowhere for me to go. I still thought I loved him, I needed him to love me and I needed him to see that I was 'his real love'. There was always a moment of triumph when I had proved that I was right! For a brief moment I had the power of self-righteous indignation, I was able to threaten to leave or actually leave. I was in a position to demand his remorse. However, the terrible truth was that it was a pyrrhic victory. The proof of his infidelity just amplified my aching neediness and failing self-esteem. I talked about his infidelity as though it was a deal breaker. My actions, on the other hand, said, "please show me that you love me more than you love her" and "please see that you need me more than her". Need is what drove me. I needed him and just as badly needed him to need me.

Had I been able, with a measure of detachment, to track and assess my thoughts I would have seen that the root mistake for me was that love was need. We loved each other if we needed each other. If I had been able to tether that thought out from the mess in my mind, my other behaviour would have made sense. A co-dependent cannot distinguish between need and love. My total focus was to make him *need* me because I needed him. My narrative to myself allowed me to stay because I was so terrified of a future without him. I told myself that his infidelity was a symptom of his sickness and he needed me to fix it. If he would just give me a chance I could cure him of his need for other women.

So in essence I was an excellent stalker of him and of evidence. I was an expert. I stalked everything except myself. I was frantic all the time. I thought about nothing other than entrapment. I was going to catch him out. I was bereft, exhausted and on the hunt for exactly what I didn't need or want. The divine paradox that I have come to see is that of course I did need it. His cheating and lying was as much of a hook and bait as his seductions. I was a co-dependent who could only love with drama and tears. Love that was without anguish could not possibly be love.

If I had been able to step back and address the issues more calmly, I would have had a different conversation. The sane conversation/narrative would have to go something along the lines of: "There is no point in tracking down evidence because I will find it. I know that he is betraying me. Does it really matter what her name is and where he found her? No, the details are not the point. The real issue is whether or not adultery is a deal breaker for me and if it is, do I have the strength to walk my talk?"

Today my narrative would be very different to even that one. "Why would I want to be in a relationship with even a whiff of mistrust?" Healing has allowed me to have deal breakers that I can act on, not pay lip-service to.

If you had asked me to stalk my thoughts I would have told you that every thought was about him and what I was going to say and do to make him change. If I could have seen that at the time I guess I could also have, with time, been able to see that you cannot make an abuser love you enough, or at all, because they can't. You cannot make someone love you enough and you cannot change an abuser. I would have at least started down the road that said, "I may not be the problem but I am the solution".

Today I can 'stalk my thoughts'. When I am hurt and unhappy, I can apply a measure of detachment and watch myself almost slip into old habits and stop. I start with: "What do I believe that makes me react/feel this way?" I can look at another person's narrative and my own and understand that they feel real today but reality is a complicated and dynamic process. I always try to be what you call 'the enlightened observer' but the process of detachment is difficult and has taken years of practice.

Thought is grossly underestimated. It has the most remarkable ability to create opportunity and invite joy or worry. Do not let the power or thought slip by unnoticed.

Stand tall and proud

A warrior never fights unless there is good reason to do so but a worrier will fight often because she is tired and stressed. Whenever I am irritable and feel inclined to be argumentative for its own sake, I remind myself of my own transgressions. Whenever I am overcome by my own self-righteousness, I remind myself of how often I have misunderstood. Every situation must get a healthy dose of 'the milk of human kindness' and the benefit of doubt. This is not to say that there is never a reason to stand up for yourself. Of course there is but that reason, if it is a good one, will still be there after a night's sleep and another hour of contemplation.

Women have a reputation for being overly emotional, irrational and inclined to take offence when none was intended. It is possible that we have this reputation because we have earned it. A reputation can be changed when we constantly prove that we can behave differently. If it is our intention to carry the warrior within, we have to resolve to fight a good fight only. Our fight must come from the basis of integrity and principle – not worry and fatigue.

You are the artist of your character

I attended a *Bar Mitzvah* and watched a young man talk about the seven qualities he would like to acquire to be a man worthy of respect. Two of the qualities he spoke about were integrity (being a *mensch*) and honesty in the face of adversity. For each quality he had one of his friends light a candle and stand beside him on the stage. I watched that young man and his seven candles and was close to tears at how beautiful it looked, but more importantly at how seriously he had attended to the man he hoped to be. I remember making a wish that should I have a daughter she would be fortunate enough to marry a young man like this one.

I went home that night and thought long and hard about the character of the woman I wished to be. I found seven qualities and wrote them down in the back of my diary. Whenever I was on the phone or waiting for a client, I would read them and re-read them so that I knew who I was desiring to be. I thank that young man often for the gift of his speech.

Philippa talks about the ideas that spring to mind when she reads these words.

The word 'character' shocks me slightly. You see I never paid attention to character in myself or in him. I was attracted to looks and status. I thought that a good-looking man with status was automatically worth something. I didn't assess anything beyond that. Had I thought about character, I would never have married any of them. I don't think any one of my husbands married me because they thought I was 'worthy', outside of my usefulness. Our marriage had nothing to do with character. We were linked by our attractions and by our pathologies.

In those days I don't think I would even have been attracted to a man with a sound character. I would have found him boring. I needed someone who was sick and needy and moody and demanding and dishonest. I needed someone to *fix*. What on earth would the purpose of my life have been had I had a man who didn't need fixing?

When I came to the USA I was determined to never date a man who abused substances. I was still sure that the problem was substance abuse. When I met my third husband I was sure that I had cured myself because he was clean living. He didn't drink in excess and there was no hint of drug abuse. We shared a love of cooking and food and he was so romantic. That was the extent of my character assessment. I ignored his excessive neediness – no, that's not true – I loved it. He needed fixing. He was messed up by a divorce that, with hindsight, makes no sense. It was his messed-up-ness that was the ultimate attraction.

He was as ill as the others had been but this time the pathology lay in his sexual aberrations. He lived a secret life that made the lying of the others look like pre-schoolers. He had an entire life on the internet about which I knew nothing. "A man who is without honesty is a man without character" is what my rational mind would say. However, I was married to him so clearly my rational mind was not in charge of my life – my co-dependency was.

Now, I can honestly say that I could light seven candles to the qualities that I really respect in myself.

After years of abuse many women become what I call 'the walking apology'. Their posture is uncertain and lacks conviction. They speak as though they expect to be told to keep quiet or that they expect to be seen as stupid and wrong. They start sentences with "I probably don't know what I am talking about but ..." Otherwise they start with "My husband says ..." and go on to quote everything he says as though it were the gospel. Everything about their verbal and non-verbal behaviour says they think little or nothing of themselves. The world is a wonderful mimic – people think of you in the same way as you think of yourself. You cannot expect to be respected or even heard if this is your presentation of yourself to the world.

If you intend to find 'the warrior within' the first question to ask is: "What am I a warrior for?" The intention here is not to create an aggressive woman. A warrior appears fearless in the face of adversity but is not quarrelsome in day-to-day living. Before you argue, ask yourself these questions:

- Have you considered the other person's point of view?
- Do you have all the facts?
- Are you going to cause a problem for an innocent bystander?
- Was this information given to you in confidence and are you breaking that confidence?

Philippa talks about her inability to even catch a glimpse of the warrior within:

I had no idea how to be a warrior. I knew how to be victim, a martyr and a shrew. I felt like a victim because I was being accused of things that I knew I hadn't done or seemed trivial to me. Because I was a co-dependent I worked hard at all my relationships and none of those 'labours of love' seemed to count for anything. The abuser erases all that is done out of love and concern as though it is meaningless. I can't begin to describe to you how utterly defeated I felt during those times. I have come to understand, though, that I no longer blame them for dismissing my 'labours of love'. They were not labours of love but labours of neediness. It was just another method I used to manipulate acknowledgment. Ingratiation is irritating.

I spent my life feeling right and self-righteous. I felt wronged all the time and my life was about setting right the wrongs by exposing them. You talk about righteousness and I am not sure that I even know what you are saying because we are women who, by your own admission, are being wronged.

I agree with Philippa. She is being wronged much of the time but her fights are all fights about the wrong things.

You are fighting about what he said or didn't say. You are fighting about what happened yesterday. But are you fighting about anything fundamental in the situation? In that fight you take no responsibility for the fact that you allowed and forgave that behaviour a dozen times and that actually you don't respect your words one iota. You fight about his words and, in doing so, you are screaming obscenities and telling him how much he disgusts you. The way I see it you are doing exactly the same thing.

Let's go back to the last bitter and dreadful divorce. Philippa was reluctant to get divorced because she had invested so much time and effort and love in creating a home and she was heart sore to leave it. However, she admitted that she no longer loved him and found him repugnant. Then she fought with him because his behaviour was not loving and he was deceitful. But tell me how it is that she was not also deceitful? Did she actually tell him that she was staying because she loved the home and would have been incredibly pleased had he not been in it? She didn't. She told him she wasn't sure, but she was sure. She just wasn't ready to leave her lovely home. Not sure and not ready are not the same thing.

I remember Sue saying that to me at the time and I remember looking at my own deceit and owning that truth. It helped enormously in dealing with my rage and resentment. My deceit was no less shocking. I spent my whole life looking at what 'he' was doing and never took the time to examine what I was doing. Righteousness requires that we look at ourselves in any situation. I guess there is much to be said for the truism about not looking at the splinter in someone else's eye until you have addressed the log in your own. For a long time all I had in my possession by way of warrior strategy was a tantrum and that's what I used. I was so frantic and unable to stand outside of myself and observe my behaviour. I was in survival mode. In fact, my favourite shoes at the time were a pair of combat boots. I longed for a life of flowers and lace but had no idea how to achieve that. Today my home is full of flowers and there is lace everywhere – from clothes, to underwear and table mats. Every morning when I wake up I set my intentions for the day and one of them is 'live elegantly'. I don't mean elegance in the sense of status – I mean elegantly in that I never shout or throw a tantrum or do anything that may make me squirm tomorrow.

I encourage my clients to develop life skills that will attend to the issues and that will gain the respect of other people. These life skills allow you to enter a conflict that you have decided is worth entering in a manner befitting a warrior.

The first issue is to practise your assessment of the situation. Many people enter an argument at the point where the issue suits them. They report an incident without contextualising it. Joan will tell me that she has discovered that Jack has lied. She was on his computer and saw that he had a luncheon with Amanda and now she demands an apology and will not speak another word until such time that she gets one.

Consider acquiring some skills to equip you with more than a tantrum. The following are some guidelines for warrior training:

Take a long view and a wide one

Couples have understandings about how much invasion of privacy is acceptable. One couple may feel that complete access to each other's electronic gadgets is their understanding of transparency and trust and another couple may value more privacy and space than that. So, the first view must be a wide one. Have Joan and

Jack agreed with that level of transparency and is she behaving within the guidelines of that agreement or was she snooping? The long view must be that once Joan accuses Jack of withholding this information, she must expect that if she has been snooping that issue will be on the table and she will need to answer for it.

Before we pick a battle we need to be sure that we have evaluated our own morality and are prepared for the fact that the other person is unlikely to roll over and capitulate. The long, wide view allows us to prepare for the inevitability of this.

For many years I was the fighter in the family. People were careful around me and I was glad. Then they began to avoid me. Now I am older and I must wonder how many times I won the battle and lost the war.

Philippa phoned me – with only thinly disguised irritation:

Philippa: Sue, I don't think you understand. These men are liars and cheats and if we know he is cheating we have every right to snoop. If someone has nothing to hide then surely they have no objection to you going through their phone or emails – right?

Sue: No – not right. Firstly, I have nothing to hide from anyone but I object strongly to anyone going through my personal mail, messages and correspondence. It is a complete invasion of privacy and a disregard for boundaries that are required for any healthy relationship. Has it ever happened to you?

Philippa: Yes, now that you mention it. Eugene would open all my mail as though it had been addressed to him, and yes, I resented that even though there was nothing to hide. That doesn't count though if someone is doing something to me. Surely I have the right to find out what it is?

Sue: Phil, you already know what it is. If you are snooping on his phone or his computer you already know he is cheating otherwise you wouldn't be snooping. You tell yourself that you are snooping for confirmation. You aren't. It's a symptom of your obsession. You want to know her name, where he met her, what she looks like, what he said, what she said, when they met and how it is happening.

PhiliPPa: Yes, that's right and I have every right to know and I feel fine about snooping until I get it. I have sat with pieces of paper on the floor putting together puzzles of notes and emails that have been torn up.

Sue: Fabulous, and what did you do with that incontestable evidence that you had so carefully processed in the crime scene of your bedroom?

PhiliPPa: Well, I confronted him of course and told him how disgusting and reprehensible he was. I gave him all my evidence so that he couldn't lie and he would have to confess.

Sue: Yes, and then what did you do? Did you leave him? Was it a deal breaker now that you knew her name and the amount he spent on having dinner with her? Did he confess or did he keep lying and telling more ridiculous stories that you then attacked with the same vigilance? What exactly did you achieve from all that careful detective work?

PhiliPPa: Well I had the truth.

Sue: No, Phil. You already had the truth. What you got was the detail. What you needed was either the strength and readiness to leave him or the resources with which to do that. You didn't find either of those things in the phone, the briefcase or the computer. You didn't find anything you needed. You did, however, lose respect for yourself and you lost a strategic advantage.

PhiliPPa: What are you talking about? What strategic advantage?

Sue: Had you been a warrior you would have kept quiet about what you knew. You would have allowed him to underestimate you and get increasingly sloppy. You would have sought a counsellor to help you make this a deal breaker or you would have begun to feather a nest egg that would have given you the resources to leave. Had you been a warrior you would have waited patiently for an opportune moment to act instead of throwing what turned out to be nothing other than the proverbial tantrum.

Phil̄iᴘᴘa: Sue, in those days it was like an itch I had to scratch. I had to know, find out, confront him, act out my self-righteous rage, be right, and be the victim and then the martyr.

Sᴜᴇ: I understand the feeling. However, we are talking about warrior training and a warrior is not compelled to scratch an itch at the expense of a strategic advantage. That is not the behaviour of the warrior. The warrior skills would have been to allow him to underestimate you. Then you would have had the advantage of time to plan and prepare. That is the way of the warrior. Keep your mouth shut and your rational mind on high alert.

Doubt is valuable

Doubt makes you check yourself – but never let doubt be your master. If you are uncertain about your feelings about something or the facts, then go no further. I have learned to my detriment that what I am sure of today I may not be sure of tomorrow, particularly when I am angry and self-righteous. I have learned that whenever I feel self-righteous I need to stop and check myself. I encourage doubt in myself so that I don't act in haste and look like an idiot when a better perspective emerges in the morning. There have been incidents in my life when I have felt like I was choking on the amount of humble pie that I had eaten because I had failed to caution myself. However, one walks a fine line between caution and allowing oneself to be a cowered in which case you have allowed doubt to be the master.

Joan would need to be sure that Jack did not have a business meeting with Amanda before she can assume that he has, in fact, been deceitful about something that he should be obliged to reveal.

Philippa talks about her doubts about doubt and how it began as her master and evolved into a self-check system that became increasingly reliable as she learned the language of the sixth sense:

> To a healthy person the value of doubt is caution. Doubt is an instinct, it's that niggle, the feeling in the pit of your stomach that warns you. Instinct in an abused woman has lost its voice. If I felt that niggle telling me "no", I ignored it. In part it's a result of the constant criticism that I endured in my relationships. I had been called mad, paranoid, stupid and a liar, and as a result I could never trust my instincts.
>
> There was a wonderful description in *Women who Run with the Wolves* by Clarissa Pinkola Estés where she describes this as having your instincts deadened. That's exactly how it felt. When wolves are in crisis their instincts become deadened and as a result they do things that place the lives of the whole pack in danger. They, for example, take themselves into areas in which they will become locked in by snow and ice with no way out. When their instincts are deadened their lives are at risk. Need I say more?
>
> When I started to heal and began listening to my instincts, doubt was so terrifying that it paralysed me. I had no idea how to cope with it. Sue's description of doubt being my master was precisely what it was. You know that expression in AA – sick and tired of being sick and tired? Well that's how I felt about doubt incapacitating me. One of the challenges of working with your instincts is that it's like learning a new language. You get feelings of uneasiness and mistrust but you don't know if it's an instinct or if you are just more fearful today than usual. Hope and fear make understanding instincts all the more difficult. Hope can feel like 'having a good feeling' about something and fear can feel like the instinct that is warning you. It's a slow process, as is learning a new language – the language of the sixth sense.
>
> It taught me to question my doubts and not accept them at face value. You know how you describe how we need to

interrogate our thoughts? Well that's what I did with my doubts. I also discovered that having a doubt is one thing but the meaning I gave the doubt was what incapacitated me. It was the meaning I had to interrogate and that's what led me to The Work of Byron Katie (see www.thework.com).

Everybody in the world faces the challenge of doubt. We all have to embrace an uncertain future being cautiously optimistic. When I have nothing concrete to hold onto, I hold onto my belief that I can trust the Universe as my partner while I face and embrace my uncertain future. I love that line of Sue's – I can trust the Universe while I embrace an uncertain future. It gives me the same comfort as getting under the duvet with Osho at night. The only reason I can put a positive spin on it is because of your other line "you attract what you give out". I proved that one true over and over again.

Never underestimate your enemy

I like people to underestimate me.

Never underestimate your enemy but allow them to underestimate you. The sad truth is that there are occasions in our lives when we do have enemies and they are not a figment of our imagination or resentment. Our natural impulse when we feel under siege is to fight back. That impulse is natural but not strategic. A warrior would be inclined to be patient, have a small ego and wait for an opportunity instead of rushing headlong into the fray.

Patience is underrated and most people favour a dramatic confrontation that results in stories of what *she* said and *he* said and then *I* said, which is simply not as elegant as patience. Let people have loose tongues and treat you as though you are stupid. The opportunity will come when you can let them know that they are spectacularly wrong.

Trading places – an 'other person's' perspective

We have already talked about 'picking your battles' and not just going into the fray because you are angry and hurt. Before you pick a battle, stand in the position of the other person for a moment. Dalene blames her mother-in-law for the problems in her marriage and it sounds like she indeed fits the profile of the over-involved, enmeshed mother, like Clive's mother on page 66. If that is the case she has probably been very instrumental in creating this abuser. Now stand in her shoes and see that she has, in fact, already lost the battle. Her baby-boy who she intended to hang onto against all odds has left her for another. I am not suggesting that by standing in her shoes you forgive her, merely that you understand her. By understanding her you are more likely to be prepared for what will inevitably come from any confrontation.

Should Dalene confront her mother-in-law, she will need to be prepared for the very enmeshed relationship between mother and son and understand that her husband will experience enormous guilt should he stand up for his wife against his mother. That is the nature of the relationship. Even if he does support Dalene in her efforts to assert herself with her mother-in-law, she must expect severe backlash afterwards when his guilt is heavy for him. Remember that the profile of that abuser is that they cannot tolerate any discomfort and expect that the primary caregiver alleviate that discomfort the way his mother did. Dalene needs to understand the battle she has picked when she picks it in order to be fully prepared for what is almost inevitable.

Pay it forward

'Pay it forward' is a concept that most people are familiar with and it was made into a delightful film of the same title. The idea is that whatever you do now (good or bad) belongs to you and will return to you. If you give generously, you will receive generously in the future, and if your contribution to the world is a spiteful one, you can expect to be on the receiving end of someone else's spite. In its most simplistic version, 'our actions are our boomerangs'.

Life circumstances challenge this belief over and over and many women tell me that despite their ongoing kindness they receive only brutality and so they cannot subscribe to this belief. The film, *Pay it Forward* challenges the simplistic version of this belief in that the young boy who does pay it forward with his best intentions fails to produce the outcome he desires. At the end of the film he dies and is unaware of the real outcome of his actions with the fullness of time.

Pay it forward is not intended to be simplistic and is not intended as a way to manipulate your world. It is a belief system that becomes a way of life which, over time and in unpredictable ways, creates results. We often forget the times our behaviour was unacceptable and are quick to declare foul play when incidents don't appear to favour us. Sometimes we behave lovingly when actually we are trying to manipulate or are just responding to fear. Those behaviours don't qualify and won't return healthy loving despite our attempts to paint them pink. Pay it forward will not guarantee from where we receive the gifts of our contribution nor when they will arrive.

John Kehoe recommends a random act of kindness every day. I am recommending a lifestyle of kindness and generosity, an attitude of empathy and a willingness to help where you can. If you haven't worn something in a year, you don't need it and won't miss it. Give it to someone who does. Half the time our cupboards are groaning from excess – give it away. You are helping someone and that act of kindness belongs to you and is coming back to you. When you are mean, that act is coming back for you so check the ethics of how you live all the time. I make a point of living without excess and I am one of the luckiest people I know. Try it. I forgive easily and I am forgiven easily. I get things that I need because I give things away easily. I do favours and people arrive when I need them.

Keep your promises

Be as good as your word. When you make a promise you need to honour it. Respect your own words and other people will too. Make your words powerful and people will sense that.

I have had empty and cheap words. I kept telling my husband that I wanted a divorce and nothing changed. Eventually I realised that I had said "I want a divorce" so often it sounded like "how was your day?" I realised that I was expressing my unhappiness but was actually saying nothing and he was treating my words the same way as I did – meaninglessly.

Philippa recognised this habit.

I did exactly the same. I was always threatening to leave or get a divorce. I think we train men not to listen to us. They know that we will repeat ourselves *ad nauseam* and that we don't mean it. Whenever I would come for a session and tell Sue what he said and I said, her response was "words are cheap, they mean nothing" and that was exactly right. His words, promises and commitments meant nothing. And neither did mine.

When I visited an ashram I was advised to do an exercise on trust. It amazed me that my counsellor picked up on my trust issues without me saying anything about them. I kept putting it off and eventually I gave in and booked the session. It was in a pool with warm water. The counsellor who took the session said that the object of the exercise was to experience the same trust we have when we are born. She explained that I was to close my eyes, and she would gently sway me in the water. When she sensed I was ready, she would fold me into a foetal position and turn me over and over under water as if back in the womb. My initial reaction was panic. How would she know when I was ready, how long would I be under for and I was sure water would go up my nose. Her calm reassurance persuaded me. It was an astonishing experience. It was the first time I understood what trust meant. It sounds ridiculous but I really did not know what trust would feel like. I did not know what it felt like to trust someone or to trust myself. That experience in the water felt like the pure luxury of being able to rely on someone. I felt like she had my back.

It stands to reason that in an abusive relationship there is no trust. However, that experience allowed me to see not only what I didn't get from someone else but also that I wasn't giving it. It forced me to look at my own trustworthiness which was non-existent. I cheated on every man I was with, I lied, and if someone told me a secret I thought nothing of repeating it.

I also learned from Sue the value of words. In my abusive relationships words were fists. They never meant anything other than their capacity to hurt, and I developed a habit of doing the same. I said things that weren't true but I said them because they had the most capacity to hurt. It wasn't a conversation but a fist fight. I saw how carefully Sue chooses her words and I didn't want to fit her description of my words being cheap and meaningless. That's why today I have a 'zero tolerance for error' policy with myself on keeping my word no matter how trivial it may seem, from not breaking a coffee date to showing up when needed. If I can't keep a commitment to myself why should anyone else? If I am told a secret today I will take it to the grave. The effect of being trustworthy was probably the most rewarding part of healing. From feeling worthless for so long, proving that I was trustworthy went a long way to making me feel valuable.

Be wary of emulating your abuser

The abused woman lives with a man who is prepared and often eager to fight, and it is not attractive. I am not suggesting that you become a woman of war and the saddest sight for me is when I watch an abused woman become an abuser. I have seen abused women begin to emulate those characteristics. They speak to service providers like abusers.

I have seen them treat their children's teachers in a manner that is simply not befitting, to put it mildly – and I often don't feel mildly about it. One imagines that they have seen it so often that they become it. That has to be the ultimate failure.

If you impress me and I emulate you, I am growing.
If I become like you from osmosis
I have failed to be conscious.

Philippa recognises the risk of emulating the abuser.

I was slowly becoming one of those women. Ugly and unattractive. I walked around tense and ready for whatever came at me. Whether it was the hairdresser who didn't do my hair the way I wanted, the waiter who brought me coffee that was too strong or, heaven forbid, the teacher I thought was unfair to either of my boys. If I perceived a threat or an insult I went to war. What made my behaviour even uglier was that I didn't know I could be angry and not deliver the lines in an angry way. I didn't know how to articulate my pain without spitting anger. I thought my delivery had to meet my emotions. Not only is there no elegance in that, all meaning is lost as well. The one who raises her voice loses her words.

It was actually Jon Stewart, the host of the *Daily Show*, who showed me that if we disagree we don't have to be disagreeable. I never knew that. I also didn't know that an argument can be resolved in the same conversation and that every argument doesn't have to escalate into a fight resulting in packing up and leaving.

We tell ourselves lies based on
our fears and then react to
them as if they are real.

Be a woman who takes action

Women have become sanitised into our own ineptitude. We are afraid and our instincts for survival are deadened or faulty. We wait to be saved and protected, caged and handfed. We are taught a repertoire of words like parrots and we have forgotten who we are. The hag has not – she is timeless and trustworthy.

Hags for Halloween and beyond
17 October 2014 Blog post from
www.whenlovinghimhurts.com

On 31 October the spectres, ghosts, vampires, witches and wizards will be out to play. This ancient Celtic ritual designed to protect harvested crops from the 'underworld' is now a fun evening for children to dress up in their ghoulish best. Children will 'trick or treat' around the neighbourhoods festooned with pumpkin cut-outs. The candy is symbolic of the household's plea for the safety of their homes and crops. Halloween is the night 'the hag', with her blackened teeth, deep furrows and the hairy mole, replaces the princess. Out with the golden locks, blue eyes and dainty ways and in with the woman who takes action.

The witches in the opening scene of *Macbeth* predict his demise and are seen as having prophetic powers. Maybe they didn't need to have them. All they needed to know was that a man as ambitious and short-sighted as Macbeth could easily be helped to destroy himself. All they did was feed him his own ambition and allow him to feel secure enough to make the mistakes he made.

We challenge every woman who dresses her vampires and hands out sweets to the neighbouring ghouls to embrace the hag within. The hag is astute and she understands life. She is the one who knows that within each of us is a deadly weakness, that left unattended will be our demise. Tame the beast within or you will be overcome by that weakness. Hags understand that life is not pretty or pink – this is the 'wildness' to which mankind was banished.

In the same way that Clarissa Pinkola Estês (*Women who Run with the Wolves*) says that wolves get a bad rap and are in actual fact remarkable animals, who protect the pack, care for their young and show extraordinary prowess, so does the hag. Forget her blackened teeth and ugly mole. She is beautiful in her prowess and skill. She is untamed and feral, astute and powerful. The hag has the timeless knowledge of instincts. She is not afraid to feed you your own weakness on which you will choke or change. She will not be controlled by public opinion but only by her own. She is filled with good instincts for her survival and the survival of her clan. She knows and is unafraid.

Abused mothers feel themselves to be completely disempowered. They feel weak and useless. More often than not the complete opposite is true. Living with abuse takes an enormous amount of endurance and strength. Abused women live behind masks of congeniality and costumes of civility. They play trick or treat daily as Philippa describes so well.

Trick or treat

Skeletons, vampires, wizards, witches and the occasional Elvis Presley will soon be arriving at my doorstep calling "trick or treat, trick or treat". I have found my lanterns and spider webs, carved my pumpkins and will fill my bowls with candy. "Trick or treat". Candy for you.

Watching children at play brings me joy and sadness. It helps me remember.

There were so many beautiful moments when my sons were growing up – birthday cakes, halogen balloons, school plays and castles in the sand. I remember little boys in Superman pyjamas and mastering 'the bike'. But there are others.

Often those celebrations were trials of fire for me. I was consumed by my unhappiness and yearning. While I watched my little boys on stage and clapped wildly, the truth is that I just wanted to go home and have the conversation I'd rehearsed all day. I had my one-liners that I needed to deliver. I watched other couples in the audience and I envied every person that I saw. I was so sure that the whole world was happier than I was. My face was tired from smiling and every ounce of enthusiasm required that I dig deep into my reserves. Most of the time I just ached from unhappiness.

Now I can't help but scan the faces of the moms. They're always smiling, adjusting masks and re-inserting vampire teeth. Years ago I would have believed that they were all happy and cherished by their husbands and children – all of them except me. I alone was trapped in my misery and loneliness. Now I know better. It is not just the children who wear disguises and masks. We disguise our fear behind our brittle, bright smiles as we trail behind our children, wondering what we should do, when and how and if. We smile on. Eventually they will go to bed and we can too. We can curl up in a foetal position and cry or just not move.

I once read that when we look back at our tears we will laugh – I am still not laughing. It is not the raw powerful pain it was back then. Now it's just sadness for myself as I was then and for all the brave mothers who smile when they want to cry, who make costumes when they want to sleep the day away and who turn up no matter what. I will be looking for you behind the disguise.

All my life I wanted to be the Princess who would be saved from her own life. Today I hope for the love of a man who understands that the hag in me is far more interesting.

The sentence and the silence

To not surrender your dignity is easier said than done and in this book we aim to assist you to develop skills that uplift your dignity. There is an amusing saying that silence is often the best answer because it can't be misquoted. Silence is a bit like water. It stays the same but changes its impact. A gentle pond is a very different type of water from that of a raging wave but both are essentially of the same substance. In the abusive relationship you have been taught over and over again that silence can be the most powerful rejection. However, I doubt, despite this, that you have learnt the power of the selective and effective use of silence.

For any co-dependent the subtext of silence is rejection. Silence is a gaping hole that we fill with our fears and insecurities. When we are silent in retaliation, our silence is filled with hostility, fear and silent screams. Silence is torment. It is also often the calm before the storm and we live in fear of the storm breaking but the tension is so horrendous that the arrival of the storm is almost a relief.

Philippa explains the complexity of silence with the astonishing wisdom that one gains from hindsight.

My husband and I were going to India. I was seeking a spiritual reconciliation and intimacy that I was sure could be found somewhere outside of ourselves. The night before we left was hideous, which should have been predictable. I was excited about going and had high hopes for a spiritual reconciliation between us. If I was excited about anything he would make sure to target that with unerring accuracy. We went out for dinner and he spat a mouthful of fish into my face. In silence I left the restaurant and waited at the car, picking pieces of fish out of my hair. I was silent all night, intent on keeping things on track to give us the best opportunity to reconnect in India.

We travelled to Pune, which is an ugly industrial city that is an assault on the senses. It was noisy, dirty, chaotic and smelly, and I watched the scramble for survival going on through the car window. On the outside we were clean and elegant, sophisticated and in charge of our lives, but the silence between us was chaotic, busy, noisy with hostility and bursting with tension. I was scrambling for my survival no less than they were.

The ashram, by contrast, was beautiful. It had the most glorious gardens with water gently meandering over rocks into pools and ponds filled with lotus flowers. Through meditation I learned that we could watch the rush hour of our thoughts without being attached to them. I was not attached – I was consumed and I needed to meditate and truly grasp the idea of the transience of thought. At the ashram I was asked to think back to something that had been all important to me five years ago and recognise that today it holds no power over me. In the gardens of the ashram I fervently wished for the day that this heartache would be just a distant memory.

It took months of practice before my silences stopped being silent screams. With time silence became an opportunity for reflection. As my silence grew quieter my 'little voice', that I like to call my higher self, started to whisper. The quieter I became the louder that whisper became. I have struggled with silence for many years but finally my silence is filled with serenity. There is such a gift in a serene silence. My fervent wish made in the

gardens of the ashram has been granted – my heartache is a dim
and distant memory. In my silence is a song of gratitude.

When silences are silent screams

Silence is a vacuum and when we are faced with that gaping space
we fill it with fear and insecurity. Silence beckons us to fill it and
we do or we avoid it by asking for affirmation or begging to be
forgiven. If you were to create the silence it would also beckon to
be filled – but this time it is not you who will fill it.

There are guidelines to the use of silence. Firstly, it needs to be
used selectively and elegantly in order to avoid looking like sulking,
which begs to be ignored. Secondly, silence needs to be non-verbal
in action as well as simply not speaking. If you are not speaking
but you're banging the doors and slamming plates down on the
table instead of putting them there gently, you are actually speaking
volumes. Non-verbal anger or misery is not silence.

Often the elegant use of silence requires a sentence first. Let's
imagine the usual day in the life an abused woman. You have done
something or not done something that should be incidental but of
course it isn't. You have forgotten to buy the toothpaste or bought
the wrong one, for example. From there he will continue to inform
you of how hard he works and how little you do. You will be told
that you can never be relied on and you are an incompetent fool.
Many women find that simply keeping quiet will bring the barrage
of insults to an end sooner. I am, however, of the opinion that
'silence implies consent' so I prefer the 'one sentence followed by
silence' response. There are sentences that say almost nothing but
they do not concede the point. My favourite one is "Thank you
for the feedback".

Imagine that you have received the avalanche of negative
labels that you receive regularly and then you say, "Thank you
for the feedback", and continue to do whatever you were doing
but without any change in your non-verbal behaviour. He will, of
course, react, but from that sentence onwards you are to remain

silent except to repeat a version of it. "Yes, I heard you and thank you for your feedback."

Another wonderful sentence is "I will give that some thought" and then you go silent but with no expression of emotion through non-verbal behaviour. If that feels very stressful for you, then excuse yourself from the room. "Excuse me, but I am going to have a bath/make a phone call" or whatever would be appropriate. You then leave and stay away from him for as long as possible. If he speaks to you about something else, you can engage in the conversation, but coolly and with no relief that he has decided to speak to you.

Women are so grateful for the opportunity to end the conflict that as soon as the abuser speaks they engage with enthusiasm. That response says that you are desperate for his affection and that the outrageous loss of self-control and amplification of an incidental event is fine. Philippa has explained that the reason women are so eager to end the silence is that it is a raging and terrifying silence. She says that sometimes his silence would go on for weeks and then she would be 'almost grateful' for the beating because it would signal the end of the long, loud, rejecting, threatening silence.

Anna is one of the women who prefers to say nothing.

ANNA'S STORY

I say nothing. I just don't answer because even when I try he just interrupts me or tells me to shut up because I don't know what I am talking about. Sometimes it's just the usual rubbish – I was asleep when he arrived and that will be the end of the world despite the fact that it was after ten and I was waiting up for him to make sure he had eaten.

Other times, however, the issue is an important one. He has a huge problem with our sons and one in particular is very resentful of him. I would dearly love to have a decent conversation about this. If I so much as open my mouth he starts at me that this is all my fault and I have set our son up against his father and what kind of mother am I. The truth is that their relationship hurts me because I know it hurts them and all I want to do is talk it through so that we can have some way forward. I have stopped trying and

I just keep quiet. He is so used to it that he doesn't even notice that almost every conversation is a monologue. I suppose he likes it – that way he gets to hear the sound of his own voice often.

I am still of the opinion that a few useful sentences are worth having on the tip of your tongue. Their function is to diffuse the situation without conceding the point. They say nothing in themselves but keeping completely quiet looks surly.

- "Thank you for that feedback."
- "I will give the matter some thought."
- "I imagine there is a way to agree to disagree."

A sentence is not effective if you engage with the content of what he is saying. By not engaging with anything he has actually said you have very subtly dismissed it. At no point do you engage with the volume at which this was all delivered. You do not say, for example, that you are not deaf and so he need not shout.

Silence is, however, most effective when he is not actually there. If he phones you, don't take the call and only return it hours later. When you return the call apologise, give a reason and then say that you cannot actually talk now either because you must attend to this or that.

It is important to understand that every communication carries a sub-text. We all know very well that everybody has time to return a call even if only briefly to say that you will be unavailable until such and such a time. If we want to, we can. By not taking the call and not returning it for hours the sub-text of the communication is, "I have not been anxiously awaiting your call, which is why I missed it and didn't bother to check my phone. I also have matters to attend to that are far more important to me than what you have to say to me at this time." The sub-text of silence, on the other hand, says, "This conversation holds no value for me. I am not anxious to rectify the situation with you and I see no point in trying". The non-verbal failure to respond (not banging doors or crying) says,

"You are having very little impact on me because I no longer care what you think when you insult me like this". All conversations have a sub-text. Using the sub-text to convey a message is effective.

The effective use of silence sounds simple enough but it's not. Philippa explains that the effective use of silence requires inner work. It is not as simple as just not speaking. It requires a level of inner detachment and self-control, both of which are incredibly difficult for an abused woman who feels compelled to get his love and affirmation. It is her life's work and is part of every breath she takes. Philippa attempted to achieve a quieter silence by attending to detachment. In her silence she would repeat over and over "detach with love, detach with love". The other mantra she used is "I cannot control it, cause it or cure it". It was very helpful because abused women are often obsessed by what they did or didn't do to cause this terrible argument. While it is an AA saying, it has beautiful applicability here. You did not cause this dynamic, and you can't control it, but most importantly you cannot cure it. You can only cure yourself.

The important parts of this skill are:

1. Firstly that you understand that communication is far more than words, and non-verbal communication is very powerful.
2. The absence of communication should never be underestimated. This really is a case of 'less is more'.
3. Be aware that most of the time you and everyone else is responding to the sub-text of a conversation every bit as much as to the content.
4. Unavailability carries a very powerful sub-text and should only be used consciously and for effect.
5. Use the sub-text of communication with deliberation.
6. The aim of this skill is to retain your dignity because it belongs to you and you intend to keep it. Communication becomes more conscious and disciplined.

I would like to end this section with Philippa's insights on silence and serenity because they end any illusions of simplicity that I may inadvertently have implied in the skills development section of the selective and elegant use of silence.

I fumbled and stumbled along in my selective use of silence and got better even if my marriage didn't. My mantras helped me keep the silences quieter and they gave me the opportunity for reflections. Meditation helped me achieve that too. I like to refer to that voice of knowing deep inside me as 'my higher self'. As I quietened down inside my head it started as a whisper. The quieter I became the louder the whisper. The longer the silences the calmer I became instead of more frantic to end them, and the whisper got louder. One of the realisations I came to near the end of my marriage was that my serenity was too valuable to give away cheaply. At some stage anxiety and panic attacks had become a part of my life and I had forgotten what it was like to live without them. I realised that I was winning the battles but actually there was no way for me to win the war. The not-so-little voice in my head was telling me that I no longer needed or wanted anything from him.

I woke up one morning and watched him put his watch on – the final act before going to work. I remember it as though it were yesterday. We hadn't spoken in days. The thought suddenly arrived in my head – "How will you feel a year from now if you are still living with him?" The answer bellowed in my head and when I pushed back the duvet that morning I began to make arrangements to leave.

As Sue says, silence is indeed a strange baby. When I lived in my marriages, silence felt like rejection. Other times silence was just a silent scream. When I arrived in America all I wanted was silence. I couldn't even listen to music – it hurt my insides. Now silence is filled with serenity.

When the silence is hollow
your life is empty. When the silence
is hallowed your soul is full.

Change your attitude

Same issue, different outfit.

We have addressed the issue of cultivating indifference in the face of painful places and painful people. If it is possible to cultivate indifference, and it is, then it is possible to cultivate your attitude.

Be happy, it drives people crazy.

Be mindful of your attitude. It is one of the most powerful shifts you can make. There is a difference between an attitude and a mood. A mood is a reaction to something that has happened. An attitude, on the other hand, has constancy and leverage. It is a consistent but not rigid way of thinking and behaving that flavours every part of your life.

Philippa explained that she was so locked into reactions that she was unable to attend to her attitude.

My life of reactions took me on the wildest of goose chases. One day I was happy because he had phoned me and called me 'darling'. The next day I was furious because he was hiding his phone and taking calls in the garden. Then I was screaming at him and he was screaming at me and an hour later I was trying to get him to hold me and love me. I was dreading seeing him after a fight and yet couldn't wait for him to walk through the door and every minute he was late I was in agony.

Sue told me over and over again that the incident would recur unless I dealt with the issue. It would be the same story but a different day. The fight would be about something different but inherently it was just a reflection of the same issue with a different outfit.

A life of reactions is so pointless and so painful. With the wisdom of hindsight I wish I had spent less time on who said what to who and who did what to who and who won the round, and more time standing back and saying "What is actually going on and which attitude would serve me well?" An attitude is not a knee-jerk reaction. It is a selected response that becomes a way of life.

Mahatma Gandhi explains the stepping stones to building an attitude and thus a destiny:

> *Keep your thoughts positive because your thoughts*
> *become your words. Keep your words positive because*
> *your words become your behaviour.*
> *Keep your behaviour positive because your behaviour*
> *becomes your habits. Keep your habits positive because*
> *your habits become your values.*
> *Keep your values positive because your values*
> *become your destiny.*

What Gandhi makes clear in this quote is that an attitude doesn't happen to us. Our attitude is not someone else's fault. Other people didn't cause our attitude – we simply failed to select something different. We allowed ourselves to be caught by our knee-jerk reactions often enough for them to develop into an attitude. We developed an attitude by default.

The attitude that needs to be put on the table in the context of an abusive relationship is firstly a *positive versus negative attitude*. Developing a positive attitude has become trendy. My practice has its fair share of Polly-Annas. They are so determined to see the glass as half full that they refuse to complain about anything at all, including the weather or the traffic. Every problem is gift-wrapped with platitudes of sunshine and good cheer. It is enough to put an angel in a foul mood and it smacks of the most grotesque inauthenticity. It's the equivalent of making a doctor's appointment to tell him how well you are. Clearly that is not the situation because you are here. Putting a bow on a problem does not make it a gift.

With hindsight the majority of us can see that suffering is a great teacher and that our dark times are in fact gifts. However, it is virtually impossible to experience them as such at the time.

A positive attitude is not one in which we deny the reality of the situation. It is one in which we go eyeball to eyeball with the problem despite our fears, and choose to be willing to do the work required to change the situation or our attitude to the situation. It is rising to the challenge.

One of the reasons I am never exasperated with my clients is because they are here. The very act of turning up is the preparedness to do the work. These women are, in my opinion, braver than the millions who never turn up to examine their lives and seek solutions. The women who show up are willing to work harder than those who depend on their habits – good or bad – to get them through. Why would you not be willing to spend your days with the braver and more thoughtful? I feel privileged to do this work.

The first attitude to be cognisant of is positivity vs negativity. Building a positive attitude is more than seeing the glass as half full instead of half empty. A person is only brave if they feel fear and then act courageously. An adrenalin junkie is not brave. A person is not building a positive attitude unless they are crawling over fear and facing defeats and showing up anyway. It requires us to face up to challenges with commitment and dignity despite how we feel.

A reaction is because of how we feel and an attitude is despite how we feel.

*I understand that what you say is often not the
truth. It is the noise you are making to avoid
hearing the truth.*

The abuser lives in negativity. Basically he fears abandonment and breaks down and diminishes the person he loves to prevent her from leaving him. In his psyche the loss of love is inevitable and he labours to prevent his worst fear – and in so doing creates it.

The positive person will recognise that fear. She sifts through the archives of her memory to find the origin of the fear and has the courage to challenge its validity. She will overcome her impulse to be indispensable in an effort to trust that love can flourish without her management. As a person reading this book, you qualify as a positive person because you are doing the work. You are already a winner. Even if you are telling yourself that you can't do it, your behaviour says that you can. You are still reading and with every word that you read the chances of your recovery grow. Being positive is not light and fluffy – it's real.

The second attitude to be cognisant of is *respect vs disrespect*. The abuser is disrespectful in his words and in his behaviour. The co-dependent is disrespectful. She wants to believe that he can never cope without her. In her absence chaos would reign. Her appearance of love hides her desperate need to control a man she sees as basically inadequate. She isn't attracted to competent men because their competence threatens her role and grandeur as 'the saviour'. Like the abuser she is both inadequate and profoundly arrogant. The time has come to show some real respect. Most likely, had the abuser or co-dependent experienced a childhood imbued with respect neither would be in the predicament they find themselves.

Philippa tells a story about an incident in this regard.

I was having tea with my mother. My husband walked past and for no apparent reason, he hit me on the head – hard. Then he laughed. I was shocked. "Did he actually intend to hit me that hard? Was that supposed to be a joke?" I laughed along with him, mainly because I felt so humiliated but wanted to avoid a scene in front of my mother. She asked him why he hit me and his answer was, "Because I can". When she left I went mad. I called him a disgusting pig and before long we were screaming at each other. I was yelling that he had no idea how to behave and I don't even remember what he was shouting about but he was.

Instead of reacting like Philippa did – with confrontational yelling – what would a reaction with self-respect have looked like?

How about this: "I am going for a walk. We obviously have a huge problem but right now I am too shocked by what you did to address that properly. When I am calm I will make an appointment to see a therapist for advice on how to proceed from here. We clearly have many difficult conversations ahead of us but I am not interested in a brawl."

Many of my clients ask me why they should attend to their attitude when he doesn't attend to his. Once again I need to reiterate that you may not be the problem but you are the solution. Taking charge of our attitude is part of being the solution. Your attitude is understandable but if it doesn't serve you well, it is worth changing. An attitude is made up of how we think, how we feel and how we behave.

Let's attend first to how to we think. Are you aware that you run a narrative all day to yourself about what is going on in your life? If you are stuck in traffic you have a narrative that may be saying that your life is being wasted away by all the hours you spend going nowhere slowly. I am particularly poor at having a positive narrative around traffic so I will borrow my daughter's. Her narrative is that she likes her car and she likes listening to music which she has in her car so she doesn't care how long she sits there. She is fine and so is the traffic.

Test the power of words to create feelings. Close your eyes and check your reactions to certain words. Say the words – death, disaster, catastrophe, blood curdling, terror and Oh No. Say those words slowly and see how your insides begin to quiver and you feel like cowering. Just keep your eyes closed and keep saying terrible words and see how you react even though you know you are only reacting to a bunch of words and nothing real is happening. Try the same exercise but this time use different words such as challenging, obstacles, unfortunate and other words that suggest that life is less than easy. You will see that your reaction is completely different. Your stress reaction is directly linked to the language you use to talk to yourself about the problem.

In order to change your attitude you need to see that the narrative will create feelings that are helpful to you or not helpful to you. The more stressed and distressed you feel, the less in charge you are of how you react. Remember that to change your attitude you need to change how you think and then how you feel. To change how you feel requires that you attend to your language.

"He is a disgusting pig and I hate him. I hate being here and I wish I had never met him. I feel like dying."
Versus
"I have a serious problem with this relationship. I will need to stay calm because this situation is very provocative. Once I am calm I can begin by making sensible decisions."

To be a positive person requires that we practise a positive but truthful narrative. We distinguish the serious from not-so-serious and record the situation accurately but positively to ourselves.

What is a positive but real narrative about an abusive marriage?

"This marriage is hurting me and I feel damaged. I am, however, learning new skills that will serve me well throughout my life. I have options here. I can leave or stay but both routes require that I heal myself. Other women have done it and I can do the same. Nothing of value is learned in a day so I will continue to practise until these skills become a way of life for me. Then I can decide what I would like to do."

Once you have examined your thoughts and managed your feelings, the way you behave will automatically change. Your behaviour is the manifestation of what you think and feel. Once you have changed your thinking, feelings and behaviour, you are on the way to mastering a new attitude.

The ABCs of Life – Attitude, Belief and Choice
4 September 2014 Blog post from
www.whenlovinghimhurts.com

Last night I attended the final performance of a play called, "I Have Life", based on a book of the same name. This true-life story takes place in 1994 in South Africa. One night Alison was abducted by two men from outside her apartment in Port Elizabeth. They drove her to a deserted spot where she was raped. They decided to kill her to prevent her from identifying them. Her throat was slit, she was stabbed numerous times, disembowelled and then left for dead. But Alison was not dead. She described (with not a hint of bitterness or irony) the miracles that took place for her that night.

Firstly, it was uncharacteristically warm for that time of the year and so she didn't die of exposure. As these disgusting men left they threw her clothes out of the car. She was able to use her denim shirt to carry her intestines as she dragged herself and crawled towards the main road. The moon was particularly bright that night, which made it possible for her to find her way from this remote spot to the main road. Before they cut her throat, they had strangled her and in the process she had emptied her bowels. Had that not happened her intestines would have burst. Despite having her throat cut, her vocal chords were missed and so she could still speak and in the stabbing they 'accidentally' performed a tracheotomy which allowed her to keep breathing. Despite literally gutting her they missed all her vital organs – her heart, kidneys, liver and gall bladder. She lay in the middle of the road aware that she may be run over instead of saved. The car that stopped had in it a student who had just finished one year of veterinary science but he had the fundamentals of anatomy and was able to assist her. His friends phoned for an ambulance and they waited four hours for that ambulance to arrive. Shame on South Africa for that! However, when she arrived at the hospital a highly skilled thoracic surgeon was on duty and Alison is alive today.

Alison admits that in the early days of her recovery she struggled with a measure of self-pity and agonised over "why me?" She was clearly traumatised and struggled to make sense of the incident and her life. Today Alison is a well-known speaker on gender-based violence and abuse and a motivational speaker. She is married and has two wonderful children. Because it was the final night of the performance, Alison arrived in person. That was a treat.

Alison talks about the ABCs of her life. For her, Attitude, Belief and Choice are what define one's life. By the way, the two men who were responsible have been sentenced and hopefully will never find their way back to the streets – ever. The most outstanding sentence of the night for me was that if she had a choice to eliminate that incident from her life she would not choose to. She says the incident has given her life meaning and has amplified her love of life.

What can we learn from this remarkable woman? I have learned that I can choose my attitude and I have decided to choose an attitude of appreciation for all that I have and stop looking at all that I don't have. Choose an attitude and start to discipline yourself to perfect it.

Alison believes in miracles because she saw them happen all night. Her mother believed in miracles. When they got Alison to the hospital she had enough strength to write down her mother's phone number. When the hospital phoned, her mother phoned a friend and began a prayer group that grew to a thousand people strong in almost no time despite the fact that it was now at 4.30 in the morning. When her daughter had the power of prayer with her she left for the hospital. There was not a moment that Alison or her mother thought to reprimand God or have a crisis of faith. They had belief.

But Alison is not saying that only people who believe in God will find miracles. Alison is saying that every person needs to hold a set of beliefs. These are our foundation stones through a crisis – belief in something that is true to you and is the anchor in a troubled sea. She has spoken to international audiences who hold varying beliefs, of different religions, or no religions. A firm belief in something is a foundation stone around which you build a life.

I hold the belief that we need to do some of the hard work

ourselves first and then get the assistance we need. Alison crawled and dragged her gutted, bleeding body out of the bushes in search of her survival. Many of us feel that we don't get the help we need but I must ask if we do enough crawling and dragging to help ourselves first. Alison talks of her conscious choice to drag herself and crawl to the main road, grasping her intestines in her dirty denim shirt. She remembers leaving her body and looking at it and then choosing to go back because she felt her life was unfinished. Alison chose life. After she chose life, she chose to speak out against rape and help other women know they had nothing to be ashamed of. She chose to speak out against brutality and to help people find meaning in the most shocking circumstances.

Alison didn't say it was easy. She went back to that deserted spot over and over, seeking answers for why such a terrible thing had happened to a person who sought to have moral fibre as she had done. She feared that no other man would want her or that she would never be able to have a healthy sexual relationship. She suffered but today she is one of the world's angels and it seems likely that wings only grow from suffering with grace.

Let us all learn something from Alison who chose life. What are your ABCs?

Reflection

Your progress report

Think about the progress you are making as you make your way through this book. Also think about which areas require more attention or more time. Consider the following:

- What progress have you made in 'picking your battles' and the skill of 'cultivated indifference'.
- What warrior skills are you doing well with and which are you struggling with?
- What attitudes have you decided to develop and what progress are you making?
- What are your hurdles?
- What are your goals going forward?

If you wish to write your progress down and share it, you can submit it online to www.whenlovinghimhurts.com.

When I gave birth to a baby I went into labour.
To give birth to my own newness I must be prepared to
labour. It is the way of new beginnings.

Making a decision to stay or leave

It has to be said that the jury is still out on whether leaving or staying is the answer and it is likely to stay out.

Many women regret wasting a lifetime in what has felt like a corrosive marriage. I know one woman whose husband died and when she was asked if she would like to marry again her answer was, "No thank you. My days of slavery are done." Other women, like Anna, are pleased that they chose to stay and believe that for them this was the right option. Herein lies the profound truth. One woman's meat is another woman's poison. There is no answer that applies across the board.

However, there are guidelines that do apply across the board. You cannot live with one foot on either side of the fence.

If you have not left and are uncertain as to whether or not you should, you need to stay and attend to the marriage in the best way you know how. You will not be able to change him but you are able to change yourself and there are many happy people whose marriage is not the source of their happiness. They are happy because they have built lives that are meaningful. No meaningful life will grow from a failure to commit or an absence of diligent care. To be living in a marriage that you think you are leaving is to live in a no-man's land bereft of belonging or significance.

Women talk about leaving as though they are testing the idea on themselves and their husbands. It is as though they are tasting the idea and seeing if they like the flavour. The abuser is a man for whom abandonment is critical. Talk of leaving will amplify the abuse, not reduce it, even if in the initial few days he shows the necessary remorse you seek as re-assurance. Divorce talk will aggravate the symptoms.

Being divorced is not something you can practise or get used to. Talking about being pregnant won't prepare you for pregnancy. Talking about being a mother won't prepare you for being one. Talking about divorce won't help you be better at it and it will aggravate your marriage.

The worst part of living in a marriage that you aren't working at is that if you do get divorced you will never be sure that it was absolutely necessary. You risk having to live alongside the thought "what if I had tried harder?" If, on the other hand, you do live your commitment to your marriage and the idea that you may not be the problem but you are the solution, you will never have to ask yourself that question. If your best wasn't good enough then there is no room for remorse or regret. With conviction you can embrace a divorce knowing that you had nothing more to give.

A decision is not a life sentence.

If your decision is to stay then you have the option at a later stage to change your mind. It is better to decide to stay and live that decision than to stay betwixt and between. The decision to stay is not a decision for things to stay the same. If you stay you need to change – not because you are the problem but because you are the solution. Healing yourself will open up opportunities for you that you could never envisage, and in the fullness of time you will be a person with a new set of life skills that will change the lens through which you see your life. You will no longer view the world through the lens of the woman who is afraid and feeling inadequate. Your whole approach to divorce will appear different. You will no longer be escaping a horrible marriage but embracing a new future.

Many women leave a marriage with every intention of creating another one before the ink is dry on the last one. They catapult themselves out and rush headlong into the next one on the assumption that they are fine and he is not, in which case the simple solution is to swop him for a better model. That is a guaranteed disaster. A divorce has to percolate over time. Initially we know only who did what to who, when and where. With time the finer nuances come into focus and we are ready to look at why we chose him and why he chose us. With more time we see the contribution we each made to the mix that was 'us'. With even more time we become more resilient, more self-conscious in the best possible way and more attuned to our deepest fears and hopes. We are afforded the opportunity to know ourselves outside of the relationship arena. "I am" is no longer convoluted by "we are". Unless you are ready to take the time to heal, you are not ready to get divorced. A divorce is not to be underestimated in its ability to rock the foundations of your security no matter how difficult your marriage. Unless you are prepared to dig deep into your reserves without rushing into the arms of another man, your chances of a more successful second marriage are slim.

Some women have regretted a hasty divorce and others have regretted a life lived in survival mode. In my opinion neither divorce nor endurance is the answer. The answer lies in the journey of self-discovery. A life lived consciously, creatively and with appreciation is a life that will become beautiful because you made it so. Your decisions will grow into convictions and you will live the consequences of those decisions with the ease of a person who has come to know herself well.

Once upon a time I spent my life leaving and
returning, staying with relief and staying under
sufferance. Staying and leaving were my juggling
balls – up and down and around and around. Now
I have left without moving out of the room. No one
has noticed and I am glad and free.

Conclusion

The time has come to recognise that you are not a victim. This relationship is not an accident. You are contributing to the problem and you can contribute to the solution.

- Denial of the real nature of your relationship will keep you stuck in self-blame and feelings of neglect and defeat. Facing the truth is initially painful and finally liberating. Denial has a pay-off. What's yours?
- Choose your battles carefully. Being right is not enough – being wise is much better.
- Your words must reflect the truth. Do not use them as fists aimed to injure and cause chaos.
- Recognise the hooks and baits to avoid unnecessary conflict. Many hooks and baits will do nothing more than damage your self-esteem or create a blood bath and neither serves any purpose. Avoiding a hook and bait does not diminish you. You grow quietly by refusing to be played or manipulated.
- Cultivate indifference is the most elegant weapon you have. It is the conscious choice to not have a reaction to something that would previously have provoked you or diminished you. Your cultivated indifference allows you

to recognise the sub-text of the incident and understand its real meaning. Indifference is self-control, dignity and choice. It is not numbness or acquiescence. Create a visualisation that assists you in the creation of indifference.

- When you say "no" act "no". If you cannot respect your own "no", no one else can either. Your self-respect and credibility depend on it.

- Become a warrior the way women do. Negative thought patterns can be identified and transformed into positive beliefs which will create positive circumstances. Build your character the way an artist attends to a canvas – consciously, carefully and creatively. Take a long view. The best decision-makers are those aware of consequences. They can wait and watch. Entertain doubt to check yourself but never let doubt be your master. It should caution you but not immobilise you.

- Be underestimated. Ego is often very expensive.

- Pay it forward and be a person of your word. When your words are white noise or static – keep quiet.

- Use silence to your advantage – other people will fill the vacuum with their insecurities. Find peace in silence through managing your inner narrative about yourself and your life.

- Your attitude will determine your altitude. A negative hostile attitude will keep you in the swamp of your misery.

Part 3 looks at ways you can begin healing yourself.

PART 3
Healing yourself

Introduction

Growth only seeks the light after it has laid
down roots in the dark.

I understand that when you enter a marriage you want to give and receive. You expect to feel safer in the world and to gain a sense of belonging. You expect to feel loved and cherished and to build a life of mutual respect. If you are married to an abuser none of this will transpire. The abusive relationship has damaged you. His words have drawn blood. Financially, you have been toyed with or compromised significantly. Your sex life is, at best, confusing. More likely it is more destructive than 'confusing'. You feel like the proverbial sex object, or you have been rejected and insulted. He has had indiscretions or is a serial womaniser and you have been subjected to sexual acts with which you are uncomfortable or plain hurt and disgusted. Your friendships have deteriorated and your links with your family are tenuous. Despite your best efforts nothing you do is right for any length of time. You have found no strategy that works with respect to resolving your issues. Your feelings and opinions are ignored and dismissed and you are made to feel trivial. This is the profile of the abusive marriage.

The human heart is a complex one and it carries many different and contradictory emotions simultaneously. Sometimes that is a beautiful complexity that makes us glad to be human. Often it is a hideous, knotted ball that feels like it's tightening to the point that you will choke. That mess is made up of fear, betrayal, rage, hurt, devastation, love, need and yearning. There is also self-loathing. How can you yearn for the arms of a man whose words or fists have just hurt you so badly? What is wrong with you? Where is your self-respect? How can you get him to understand how he has wronged you? How can you get back *at* him? How can you get back *to* him? What do you need to do to regain his approval? This is the madness of the knot.

We are going to help you untangle that mess one thread at a time. You will find your way back to the complex human heart that looks like a canvas waiting for you to add more beauty.

> *"I am spiteful because I don't know what to do.*
> *I am silent because I don't know what to say.*
> *I am jealous because I am lonely.*
> *And all the while I smile and chat and pretend to you,*
> *my friends."*

Resentment: your daily poison

Of course you resent him. You expected him to love you and to allow you to love him. You resent him because you blame him for the sick feeling in your stomach. You resent the things he has said and done. You are right. His treatment of you is reprehensible. However, being right is not going to help you. Attending to your resentment is going to make every day more palatable for you. I understand that what you really want is for him to understand that you are right and he has treated you badly. You want his remorse and to hear that he loves you well after which you will be able to forgive him. Well, the bad news is that I want to look thirty again but it isn't going to happen. He isn't going to have an epiphany and bring you his insight, remorse, love and compassion. You are not going to have your resentment attended to by anyone but yourself.

Fact 1: You may be right but being wise will serve you well.
Fact 2: Your resentment hurts you the most so best you start attending to it yourself and as soon as possible.
Fact 3: Attending to resentment is a process, not an event. It requires changes in thinking, attitude and behaviour.

Don't waste your time on revenge – the Universe will
take care of matters way more creatively than you
could ever imagine.

Change your thinking: water the plants, not the weeds

You nourish an emotion every time you think about it. If the emotion is resentment, you nourish it with every resentful thought you have. The nature and origin of thought is a complicated issue and has been attended to (somewhat unsuccessfully) by psychologists, philosophers and writers. It is of no real consequence to us here. The bottom line is that you have no control over what thought pops into your mind. You do, however, have control over how much time you spend dwelling on it. You have developed a habit of dwelling and, therefore, growing your resentment.

Philippa explains:

Part of being a co-dependent is that we obsess and ruminate on every word, every incident and every action. We think about it, we talk about it and we are busy with it from the moment we open our eyes. Coping with our resentment requires us to cope with our pathology as well.

Do we really want to be rid of our resentment, anger and fear? Many of us cling to them because there is a distorted security in familiar pain. The familiar pain in the case of the co-dependent is obsession and rumination. We cling to that because it's all we know and supports the drama that is our life. Your first change in thinking is to commit yourself to the real desire to attend to and eliminate your resentment, not because it isn't well founded but because it fails to serve you well.

LEIGH'S STORY
After my divorce I was deeply resentful towards my ex-husband.
Every time I heard from him or about him or if someone even

mentioned his name, I would notice a burning sensation in the pit of my stomach. It was as though a hot coal began to glow in my insides and not a warm one – a damaging one. It was utterly pointless to continue to be angry, bitter and resentful but I was anyway. I decided to conduct a ritual, which consisted of the following steps:

Step 1: I decided to get over myself. Other women had successful marriages and mine was over. Well, that is how it was. I had regurgitated the ins and outs and why and wherefores so often I had made myself sick. It was enough.

Step 2: I had to clarify and label my resentments. Firstly, financially, I was much worse off and I deeply resented that. Secondly, our communication was terrible and I felt misunderstood and invisible as my time with him was unhappy and pointless. And thirdly, I felt he had wasted my precious time.

Step 3: I represented each of my resentments as something. There was a coin for the money, a blank piece of paper for the lack of communication and a plastic child's watch for the waste of time. I decided to bury them in a pot and plant a geranium on top.

Because gardening is 'my thing' it was a ritual that appealed to me. Geraniums are flowers that have cleansing qualities and so although they are not among my favourites it needed to be a geranium. I was still so full of resentment that I refused to buy the geranium (he had cost me enough already). Fortunately they grow from the snippet of another plant so I asked my neighbour for a piece of his red geranium. Red is also not my favourite colour as I associate it with anger and it was with deliberate irony that I requested the red one. My friend Jean arrived while I was busy with my pot and I told her what I was doing. She declared, "Now I am convinced that you are losing your mind."

My geranium flourished and I placed it at the front door so that I could see it daily when I came home. It was a daily reminder that I had decided to bury the past and my resentment. After a while I began to smile when I saw it and then it made me laugh as it grew sturdier and sturdier. Now I have no resentment at all. What I have in its place is a deeper understanding of both of us and a sincere wish for his wellbeing.

Make up any ritual you like. One of my clients is an artist and she painted hers. She said it allowed her to feel like she was getting it out of herself and onto a canvas. She painted the ugliness – not the ugliness of her marriage but the ugliness of her resentment. Anna wrote her resentment away. She wrote over and over again. She wrote all the things she couldn't say to her husband and wrote all her pain and hurt and anger and then she burnt it. She went to her favourite place and watched the ashes fly away. Philippa has recipes that she created to replace her resentment with creativity.

Rituals are valuable because they help make something real. They ground an event for us. There are weddings, funerals, christenings, engagements and birthdays because a ritual makes the event more significant. Create a ritual to let go of your resentment but keep your expectations reasonable. After the funeral of a loved one you don't expect your grief to evaporate instantly. When you get married you don't instantly feel united differently. A wedding is the ritual that makes it real but then the work still has to be done to make the marriage significant. The ritual consolidates the idea that you are no longer going to nurture your resentment. It is your commitment to letting it go.

Every garden has weeds. They grow more easily than
flowers. Just pluck them out and throw them away.
Do the same with the garden of your mind.

The 'cancel' stamp

An ugly thought is like an unwelcome guest. Don't invite it in. Don't make it a meal and don't invite it to stay. Your mind is your home. Keep it clean and safe and filled only with people and items you treasure and cherish.

So far you have committed yourself to a ritual to release the resentment. However, like a funeral, it will not in itself attend to the complexity of the grieving process. The next step is to manage your thoughts on a daily, hourly and sometimes minute-by-minute basis. As I said previously you cannot control what thought occurs to you but you can manage how much time you spend attending to that thought.

I have a CANCEL stamp in my mind's eye. When an angry, negative thought arrives in my mind I allow my mind's eye to cancel it, and when I am alone I say out loud – CANCEL THAT ONE! I control my mind's eye and so I see the cancel stamp across that thought and I don't ponder on it any longer. I have controlled the amount of time I have allocated to a negative thought that fails to serve me well.

I may not be in charge of what arrives but I am in charge of what I allow to stay. If I'm making this sound easy then I stand guilty of misrepresenting the truth. If there has been an ugly incident it will re-ignite the bitterness and resentment, which in the early stages of your recovery will hover just beneath the surface of your consciousness. An episode will usually leave us consumed with resentment and all the old feelings of fear and self-pity. On those days you will feel you have no control over your mind at all. There will be tidal waves of resentment and you will feel sure that you will never get this right. It's okay. It's a bad day and it will pass.

Think of yourself as a boxer (go on, I dare you to entertain that thought). You may have lost the round but it doesn't mean you have lost the fight. Tomorrow you will get up and manage your thoughts again and, like everything else, the more you practise the better you will become.

It is a life skill that will serve you well no matter what is going on in your life and anything that is valuable is difficult to master. Please don't give up.

Become a manager of your own toxic waste.

Replacements: fire resentment and hire gratitude

Appreciation, in my opinion, stands very close to grace. They hold hands, the way arrogance and stupidity do.

Resentment is about what has been done to you or taken from you. It is linked to the harm that has been done with words, actions or failures to act. Gratitude is the acknowledgement of what you do have and what has been given to you. It is the acknowledgement of what was done *for* you or not done *to* you.

Appreciation, in my opinion, stands very close to grace. They hold hands, the way arrogance and stupidity do. An arrogant person seldom learns anything because he thinks he knows everything and lacks the humility required for learning. In this way arrogance and stupidity have to be holding hands.

Appreciation is good for you and the people around you. It is good for the soul and as Meister Eckhart says: "If the only prayer you ever say in your entire life is '**thank you**', it will be enough." If you buy someone a gift or lend a hand or do a service and you feel sincerely appreciated you feel willing to do it again. More than willing – you want to. Appreciation is never too much to expect from anyone.

I always offer my clients tea or coffee or water when they arrive. I once had a client who had been coming to counselling for years and every week he had black tea. Once a week for years I would put his tea in front of him and he never acknowledged it. A smile or a nod is an acknowledgement. If he was having a bad day once in a while I would not have minded but for years he simply ignored the fact. One day and about a hundred cups of tea later I had had enough. I picked up the tea, opened the window and poured it out. There was a long silence and he said, "Was there something wrong with my tea?" "No," I said as gently as I could, "there is nothing wrong with your tea but I would like you to acknowledge in some way that I make you tea every week and you don't thank me. I am happy with a nod or a smile or a thanks but I get nothing. Let's start again. Would you like some tea?" I have to give him his due though – after this incident he was impressive and we had a great session about how he feels used and unappreciated by his family but also how he never acknowledged them either.

My guess is that much of your resentment is linked to feeling unappreciated. My questions to you are:

- How much appreciation do you feel or express to other people?
- How do you ask for appreciation?

I understand that problems preoccupy us. They take up so much of our existence that it is difficult to stand back and view life with a wider lens. However, you have to. When you view life through a wider lens you will see that you have much to be grateful for. I am at the stage in my life that I no longer need to take children to school and I work my own hours and so am able to get up slowly in the morning. Every morning I open my curtains and see the garden and watch the birds feed. By nature I am something of a sentinel.

My instinct is to walk around the perimeter of my life and check for holes and weak spots. I anticipate invasions and worry about at least a dozen things that probably won't happen. If I am having a particularly good time in my life I start worrying about 'the state of the nation'. While I accept that the 'state of the nation' concern is a South African hobby, I can have the country be on the brink of collapse by my second cup of coffee.

I have had to teach myself to begin my morning with gratitude. My dearest friend is dying of colon cancer. I send her well wishes and I'm grateful that I am not in pain and that my body will readily take me through the demands of my day. I spend at least forty-five minutes before my day begins with contemplations of all that I have to be grateful for. I don't tick them off like a grocery list anymore. Initially I told myself that I would not set a foot out of my bed until I had found five things for which to be grateful. Now I no longer list them. I contemplate them and feel the gratitude. I am grateful to this generous Universe for the abundant gifts I have been given. I am sincerely grateful and I believe that because I am, the Universe is more than happy to keep sending them.

I run a support group attended by a few women who are interested in self-development and growth and the company of other like-minded people. Last week we looked at a theme we called 'The Wealth of My Life'. We decided to expand the definition of wealth to include material wealth, opportunities and experiences.

We each chose a dead branch and three different coloured ribbons. Each colour was to represent material wealth, opportunity and experience. Each time one of us got an unexpected amount of material wealth (excluding one's salary) we were to tie a bow around the branch. Each person keeps track of the amount of money made, saved or gained through gifts that would be significant to them.

The plan is to bring back each participant's 'Wealth of my Life Tree' after a month to see what they look like. The purpose of this exercise is twofold:

- To expand the idea of wealth beyond a monetary figure; and

- To remain aware of how many wonderful opportunities we get and experiences we have that contribute to the wealth of a life.

Appreciation and gratitude must become a part of our psyche. Philippa now has her American citizenship and when we spent time together she told me how much she enjoys Thanksgiving because the idea is such a beautiful one.

After my divorce I became the sole breadwinner in my family and it was difficult. It was a role I failed to prepare for because I had never anticipated having it. I didn't want it and it was an enormous burden – despite that it has given me some inkling into a man's life and I am grateful for that perspective. I had a small family to take care of and was made aware of the much larger burden some men carry, having had fewer opportunities than me for a good education and how they do it without complaint. They often leave the house early and get back late and barely get to see the home they provide for their family. The financial burden is usually theirs and my family was small so I imagine that for many their bones are groaning under that burden. I know that abusive men play games around money because money is power and power and abuse are bedfellows.

It is also true that many of them feel like walking wallets and when they complain about working hard for everyone they are telling you that they feel unappreciated. Many of you are not breadwinners although you provide the back-up income. The financial burden still does not feel like it rests on your shoulders. When last did you thank him for that? Do you attend to your own car insurance and, if not, when last did you thank him for that? Have you become so focused on what he doesn't do that you have lost sight of what he does do? I can hear you thinking that because you do nothing right in his eyes and he never acknowledges you, why should you? Because you set your own standards of behaviour that has nothing to do with his.

Other reasons are:

- Like begets like. When you immerse yourself in appreciation for everything you have you will find yourself receiving that appreciation from places where you hadn't even known you were making a difference.
- Be the change you want to see.
- When you feel grateful it makes you happier.
- The Universe is abundant and it will give to you when you are sincerely grateful for what you have already been given.
- This is the wide lens and your problems will look smaller, not bigger.
- Grace is beautiful and no one can resist a beautiful woman.
- It is easier to ask for something that you have already given.

Firstly, you must give appreciation sincerely before you ask for it. Please be careful of paying lip service to appreciation. Gratitude is more than saying "please" and "thank you" in an obligatory way. In the same way that you have been immersed in anger you can be immersed in appreciation. If you feel it, the feeling has power.

Not everyone has the luxury of having a slow start to their day but we all have time during the day to attend consciously to gratitude. A feeling of gratitude is a contemplation of what we have and the blessings in our life, and with time, practice and sincerity it is the perfect replacement for resentment.

With respect to asking for it you must first know that you have the right to feel appreciated. It is never too much to expect. You cannot successfully ask to be treated differently if you are a walking apology. You have the right to be appreciated. Feel clear about that.

*My psyche is cluttered with old dreams and false
hopes. It is also full of 'possibility' from which I will
grow new dreams and clear-eyed hope. From the
ashes of my mother's sentences will come mine. Like
a Phoenix, we will rise again, moulded by fire and
despair to dream new dreams and forge new hope.*

Philippa organised a surprise birthday party for her husband. She worked very hard to keep it a surprise and organised it with the flair that she is so well known for. Her cooking and baking are outstanding and her table settings have always managed to take my breath away. She gave him good wishes for his birthday and publicly thanked him for their life together. He kept his back to her for most of the time that she was speaking. I was there and I remember that my opinion of him went into the sewer that night. His behaviour was appalling but hers was impeccable. I remember wanting to salute her for the style and grace with which she conducted herself. She didn't get his appreciation despite the fact that she deserved it. However, it still rightfully belongs to her and it will come from somewhere else and from someone else. No one can steal what rightfully belongs to you. I imagine I was not the only guest who lost considerable respect for him that night and gained considerable respect for her.

Ask quietly. Ask simply. Be the change you want to see. There is no guarantee he will give you the appreciation that you deserve and yearn for but if you live with a feeling of gratitude the happiness will belong to you.

*No one can steal what
rightfully belongs to you.*

Reflection

Resentment and gratitude

Healing yourself is a lengthy and exciting journey and you can return to these questions over and over again to explore the growth and change that will take place over time.

Resentment:

What you resent initially will change with time and there is merit in repeating this exercise.

1. Clarify exactly what you feel resentful about.
2. Write down an explanation of your resentment in about one page.
3. Think about a ritual you could design similar to the ones in the section you have just read, and write down why you have selected to do it the way you have.

Gratitude:

1. Write a letter to yourself in which you explain what you have to be grateful for.
2. Please don't write the letter until you have spent at least ten days thinking about gratitude.
3. Find at least one quote that strikes a chord with you regarding gratitude. If you can't find a suitable one, write your own.

If you wish, you can submit your answers online at www.whenlovinghimhurts.com or do it yourself.

Reclaiming your self-esteem

Would it surprise you to learn that both men and women use their relationships to distort their self-portrait?

From Hero to Zero
31 August 2014 Blog post from
www.whenlovinghimhurts.com

When I was in the USA spending time with Philippa, we visited the Norman Rockwell gallery. If any of you are passing by or are close to Stockbridge please don't miss it. What a treasure! There is a painting of Norman Rockwell doing a self-portrait using a mirror. This is such an accurate rendition of a self-portrait.

Would it surprise you to learn that both men and women use their relationships to distort their self-portrait?

"Beauty is in the eye of the beholder."

It is for this reason that falling in love is one of the most compelling experiences we have. It is why we are often reckless and undiscerning when falling in love. When a woman meets a man who is excited by her she feels beautiful, sensual, young and blessed. When a man meets a woman who is excited by him he feels powerful and bullish. We love the reflection of ourselves through the eyes of the other. It is their gift to us and ours to them – to see ourselves beautifully.

Philosophers always say that romantic love is the poorest, lowest form of human love because it is essentially self-centred instead of being other-centred which love should be. We love the other because of what it is doing for us. Those early stages are typically referred to as the honeymoon phase – those balmy days when we feel perfect, when we can do nothing wrong, when nothing other than each other feels real. We feel almost divine – no wonder we are compelled down often dangerous paths.

Philippa talked about how this typified each of her destructive marriages. "They hung onto my every word. I felt clever, insightful and, above all, indispensable. I loved it."

Well, who wouldn't? Her second husband needed help with his substance abuse and it was she who convinced him to attend AA meetings. It was her solace, tender, loving care and exquisite meals that coaxed him past his depression. The beginning of her last marriage was almost identical. He was recovering from his divorce when she met him. He depended on her to guide him, counsel him and love him back to his mental and emotional health. She recalls that one day early in their relationship he spent almost the entire day talking to her on the telephone from work. At that stage she was still a co-dependent and so she loved it. This behaviour should have set off alarm bells. Why was he so insatiable? Why wasn't he attending to his work? Why wasn't he giving her space to attend to hers? Instead of entertaining these discerning questions she was immersed in feeling clever, special and blessed by his vision of her.

Even women who are not co-dependents love the reflection of themselves through the eyes of the men who love them. As the abuse becomes more entrenched into the relationship, that reflection changes. It becomes negative and increasingly dismissive. The woman who was told how beautiful she was is now being told she is overweight or underweight. The woman who was sexy is now being called a tramp and a whore. The dignified woman is now being called boring. The abusive man is seldom realistic or mature. He often expects his wife to look like she would if they were going on a date every day when he gets back from work. They cannot accept that their partners may have flu and feel awful. If she feels bad he feels angry. They will not accept that she may be pre-occupied with family issues or work problems. If the focus shifts away from him and onto any aspect of her life other than him, he is angry. Her work, friends, family or her own self reflections are all threats to him. They threaten to remove him as the focus of attention and any threat must be destroyed.

Constant criticism is one of the characteristics of an abusive relationship. Instead of feeling like a goddess she begins to feel inadequate, unworthy and unattractive. Instead of feeling charming, funny, trustworthy and insightful she feels stupid, boring and hysterical. Whereas she used to be trusted she is now accused constantly of being opportunistic and unfaithful.

Seeing ourselves through the eyes of another is potentially a gift, but cannot be depended on to anchor our self-esteem:

- Falling in love is a beautiful time in your life and seeing yourself through his eyes is a gift.
- That gift is a work in progress and so it must change.
- In some cases it will become mature and realistic.
- In other cases it will become negative and destructive.
- Enjoy the gift but value realism – it is more sustainable.
- Reject abusive labels – they are distortions of reality.
- Be careful of men who blame their partner exclusively for the failure of their last relationship.
- If you feel indispensable he is too needy to have a healthy relationship.

Please don't look at yourself in the mirror and tell yourself you are gorgeous! Hold your realistic self-esteem quietly, deep inside you and protect it from dangerous men.

"How can you say that women shouldn't look in the mirror and tell themselves they are gorgeous?" Philippa asked me with incredulity. "It's exactly what we've been told we should do."

"I know women are told to do that and I think it's ridiculous. It was written tongue-in-cheek. Some women simply aren't and a self-esteem must be much more grounded than thinking you are gorgeous. I wrote it precisely because it's beyond silly and unhelpful."

Own a self-esteem that is rooted in reality and not in the perception of the other.

Reclaiming your self-esteem is one of the skills that an abused woman needs to acquire. The painting at the Norman Rockwell gallery shows an artist depicting himself accurately from his reflection in the mirror. Unfortunately, much of the time we see ourselves mirrored through the eyes of the people we love. The abuser's constant criticism will diminish you in your own eyes. The challenge is to own a self-esteem that is rooted in reality and not in the perception of the other.

Begin by asking yourself what you like best about yourself and make a list of those qualities. You need to be sure that every quality you write down is true. I, for example, like the fact that I am a hard worker. I know that to be true and I respect it in both myself and other people. But I have had someone call me lazy. Because I know that label is untrue of me, I can watch that negative label land like a seed on tarmac. It simply cannot take root because I know the truth about myself.

One has to be 'a discerning viewer' in this exercise of making the list. There are things about which I am less certain, like "Am I a good mother?" I definitely pass because I know I was dedicated and reliable and tried really hard. However, I was also often very preoccupied with financial concerns that rendered me less than present. That is the truth. Once I know the truth someone else's perception cannot be given more weight than my own. To do that would assume that they know me better than I do. Once you have made a list of the qualities you know to be true, ask people whose opinion you trust and value to give you an assessment of yourself. Beseech them for their honesty and explain that their opinion is valued and will only be helpful if given honestly. This exercise allows you to see if how you see yourself is being accurately revealed in the world. Do they see you as you see yourself? Do they see and value other qualities that you don't see in yourself? Ask them and ask yourself which are the qualities you like least in yourself. If you accept the feedback and agree, then you know where you can begin to work on yourself. If you don't agree with the perception of you that is held by other people, you need to attend to the impression you are giving to the world. You are now in a position to begin to cherish what you like about yourself and change what you don't.

When I see myself through the eyes of someone
who loves me I have a swagger. When I see myself
through the eyes of my enemies I cringe. When I look
in the mirror I can see who I was but today
I can decide who I will be.

A positive self-esteem rooted in reality is a work in progress. Years ago I noticed that people failed to remember me when they had met me in social settings. I remembered them but they seldom remembered me. I used to call myself the 'invisible person'. When I watch people who are remembered I see why. They pay attention to people's names and use them often. They are interested and ask searching questions and engage with other people's lives. They enjoy the social experience and the people and as a result they are seen and remembered. If I would like to be remembered I need to show up for the occasion instead of acting like the silent observer.

The most valuable point to this exploration is not to end up with a list of your positive and negative qualities. That would be pointless because we are supposed to evolve and change with time and circumstances, internally and externally. The real point is to reclaim yourself as the mirror. You will no longer see yourself through the eyes of the beholder. Yours are the eyes. People's negative labels will no longer hold the power to diminish you in your own eyes because you have taken back control. The very act of exploration is the reclaiming of your power. You will decide which qualities require work and attention and you will attend to them because they are qualities that you don't like and not qualities that someone else has set for you to aspire towards.

Philippa explained that for many years she could never have been her own mirror. Eventually she felt so broken that she was just the last criticism that had been thrown her way. For years she felt like she had been given oxygen if there was a problem for which she wasn't being blamed.

Reflection

Reclaiming your self-esteem

1. Make a list of five qualities you like about yourself and explain why you respect these qualities in your life.
2. After discussing your list with people you trust, was there any discrepancy between how people see you and how you see yourself and if so what behaviour is causing the social misunderstanding?
3. Consider the qualities you plan to attend to and how you will go about it.

If you wish to share your list and the outcomes of your discussion, you can submit them to www.whenlovinghimhurts.com.

Creativity heals

Understanding creativity

Most people associate creativity with fine art. They are quick to assure me that they aren't artistic and cannot possibly attend to creativity. The field of psychology avoids dogmatism and has lived more or less comfortably in the shades of grey we know to be our profession, but with uncharacteristic dogmatism I will state categorically that creativity heals. We all know that a wound of the body will heal more easily when it is kept clean and allowed to rest. We don't need to know how cells regenerate. They just do when we care for the wound. In the same way I cannot tell you how or why creativity attends to the wounds of the soul but it does.

An expanded sense of creativity in our lives requires that we see the opportunities for creativity in everything we see as ordinary. Every time you get dressed you have an opportunity for creativity. You can take the T-shirt that's at the top of the pile or you can be more careful and design what you would like to say that day in the way you choose to dress. You can rush out of the door without so much as a backward glance or stay a while and pick a scarf or slip on a bracelet. When you do the latter you have embraced, just for a few minutes, an expanded sense of your own creativity.

So, if creativity is a healing force, why are so few of us doing it? Negative thoughts produce negative narratives.

- "I don't have time." You really don't have five or ten minutes while you are getting dressed?
- "I am not creative." Can you be anything without practice?
- "It never works – I don't like the things I create." Can someone help you? How often do you try?

You are not expected to produce a screen play, write a book or paint a masterpiece. We are talking about the quietest embrace of creativity in your everyday life. Every time you set the table you have an opportunity to embrace creativity. When you bake a cake, make a meal, arrange a bowl of flowers or write a message in a birthday card you can do it thoughtlessly or creatively. If you do it creatively you are beginning to heal.

This journey is not without its frustrations because if our lives have been hopelessly lacking in creativity we will struggle. You may not be able to produce something that you enjoy because you have had no practice. You have expended no energy in accomplishing this project. Nobody has ever accomplished anything without labour and practice. Creativity is the same. It requires attention, time and practice. Our society has taught us that some people 'are' creative while others 'are not'. If your early efforts have been disappointing you have probably told yourself that you 'are not' creative and any further efforts have been abandoned.

I can speak from experience here. My favourite place is the garden and fortunately my mother was an accomplished gardener as was her father. As a result I have abundant knowledge of gardening and a quick phone call will provide me the information I need. If I phone my mother and tell her the parsley looks terrible she tells me that parsley needs more shade than that spot provides. My first tiny little garden was my classroom and I made many mistakes. I had to learn that you can't plant thirsty plants in the same bed as plants that will only flower when they are deprived of water. Sometimes I walk around the nursery and I can see the inexperienced gardener from what they have on the cart. I know what's going to happen. They have bought beautiful plants because they are in full bloom and in all their glory – and at a reduced price at that. They are at that price because they are finished for the season. They will plant them and within weeks they will all be over and then they will declare that they are 'useless gardeners' and give up.

Despite my love of gardening, a flower arrangement was a frustration for me. For some reason I failed to be able to buy a combination of flowers that ever satisfied me. The flower shop was a miserable place for me because eventually I couldn't make a decision having failed so often and then made impulsive, clumsy/incorrect decisions that confirmed my narrative of "You are useless with flowers". Julia Cameron has a beautiful sentence: "Art is born in attention, its midwife is detail." Instead of giving up I began to pay attention to other people's flowers that I liked and ask myself why and how they were better than mine. I began to understand my errors. I asked my friends who arranged flowers well. I learnt because I wanted to.

I have seen many abused women make a virtue out of the deprivation of their creativity. They tell me that they are not interested in what they look like as though their morality does not allow them such superficiality. The implication is that attention to your appearance is tantamount to vanity and they cannot see themselves as vain. They place virtue on their neglect of their appearance. They neglect to pay attention to their homes and the virtuous statements around this are numerous. Firstly, they claim that the home must be a place to kick off your shoes and not worry about where they are. The idea is that mess and comfort are one and the same thing. They claim to have no time to attend to the finer details of the home because the burden of running it is too onerous. They buy cakes because it's quicker and cheaper than making them. Flowers are a waste of money and wrapping presents can be done at the shop from which they were purchased. Each of these were opportunities to embrace your creativity and they have been lost in a narrative that places no value on a creative lifestyle.

Here is a story from Tamlyn about how she made a virtue out of deprivation of her creativity and how developing it helped her heal.

TAMLYN'S STORY

When I first began seeing Sue I was recovering from a serious car accident and was very depressed. I failed to tell the doctors but admitted to Sue that the accident was actually a crazy 'almost suicide attempt'. I wasn't trying to kill myself. I was trying to hurt myself badly enough to stop him from leaving me. I knew my husband wanted to leave me and I was so panic stricken that I almost killed myself to keep him. I really believed that I had no chance in life without him. I survived and he stayed with me because his family would never have accepted that he leave an initially bedridden and then quite damaged wife. He stayed under sufferance for a few years but his rejection of me was total. He slept in another room and almost never invited me to go anywhere with him. I made myself a prisoner in the house and in the marriage that was in any event a nightmare.

A few years later he left me anyway and remarried quickly. His new wife was very attractive and younger and was everything I wasn't. I say that as though I was threatened by her but I wasn't (or so I thought). The story I told myself went like this: Anyone who has to go to so much trouble with her appearance has to be very insecure and I know she is because I know what he's like. She clearly doesn't have much to do if she has all that time to titivate. I, on the other hand, have a business to run and children to attend to and am much too busy in my important pursuits to attend to such trivia.

When I was married I was nervous every time he came home that the house would be a mess and he would be furious. Now that I was no longer married to him, I no longer needed to be stressed about those things and the children and I could relax and enjoy our home. The place was a mess and I became more and more used to that mess. I was pleased with what I saw as my rebellion.

My ex-husband became more and more successful and secretly I was bitter because we had struggled so much. I pretended I was pleased for him. His new wife fell pregnant and I was delighted. I was so sure that she would become matronly and messy but she didn't. For years I waited for their marriage to disintegrate as ours had done because he was selfish and she was superficial but it didn't.

Our son moved out and went to university away from home and I pretended I wasn't angry that he had a beautiful girlfriend. My success was rooted in vengeance and rage.

A few years ago I needed to see Sue again. I had never remarried and in my opinion I had grown into a self-sufficient and competent woman. However, I was always too busy, always stressed, always losing my cool, feeling strung out and feeling very intimidated by my staff. I suspected that I had an abuser among the staff and it had resurrected many of my old fears and insecurities. Sue suggested I fire him and then asked why that solution hadn't been obvious, which took us back to the abusive marriage and my story about how 'pitiful' his new wife was (in my opinion).

It took Sue a while to tell me but she did. My narrative was a lie. My appearance was a mess and it was not an absence of vanity that was the issue here. I was so self-satisfied with my absence of vanity idea that I hadn't given it any thought. I had shut down not healed. I had been teaching my daughters that only superficial, horrible women paid attention to their appearance and we would never be like that. We all treated my son as though his attraction to lovely-looking women was a pathology. I had mentioned that I wanted to lose a bit of weight but I thought I needed to lose a small amount. Even that Sue confronted and told me that for my size and height ideally the weight loss should be significant not minor. She told me that she didn't mind if I lost the weight or not but the time had come to stop lying and stop pretending that I was fine when I wasn't. The important part was that I was to take a long and honest look at myself and the time for change had arrived.

I was so turned off from my femininity that I had no idea where to start. (That came after promising myself that I would never see that 'wretched woman' again.) We started with the small stuff – what is my favourite colour? I had no idea. I realised that I was a middle-aged Goth with nothing in my wardrobe other than black. I started off by buying a yellow handbag. It was the colour of my jaundice.

I had a business selling pension protection packages. Sue came to one of my talks on financial management and afterwards she told me to "clean up the house and lose the mess". Once again I swore that I was through with 'that woman' but then I began to see it through her eyes and that she was right. Nothing in the house was relaxed. It was horrible. We were always looking for things and losing things and it was chaos not relaxation. My home said nothing about me. When I looked at her office it said everything about her and suddenly I wanted a home that was a reflection of who I was and not a bitter reminder of a marriage long gone but clearly not over for me.

It was years after my divorce but I began to realise that I had closed down on my creativity and my femininity. I had no idea. I told myself that I was better than other people. I definitely made a virtue out of shutting off my creative self. Today I have a tidy house, I buy sunflowers, I keep the grey out of my hair, and I have lost weight and feel wonderful. I have tried my hand at doll-making and pottery. Finally I found 'my thing' – its dressmaking and I absolutely adore making clothes for my daughters, my friends' daughters and finally my daughter-in-law has asked me to make her wedding dress.

Create a collage

We all know the saying: "a picture is worth a thousand words". The brain loves pictures and processes them easily. John Kehoe has written very helpful books on harnessing the power of the subconscious mind. His book, *Mind Power in the 21st Century,* speaks about the power of energy to create reality. There is a basic quantum physics assumption that energy creates form. What is energy as it pertains to those of us trying to heal and grow? A thought has energy and so negative thinking will create a consequence and positive thinking will create a better consequence. Speech has an even greater energy and action has more energy than anything. Everything we think, feel, say and do creates itself in a physical form. To harness the power of speech we use an affirmation, which is a short sentence or phrase we repeat several times a day for weeks. The repetition will create a neural pathway and the sub-conscious mind begins to accept and create the sentence as a reality. Some examples of affirmations are:

"I am happy, healthy and wealthy."

"Every day, in every way, I get better and better."

"I am calm and content."

The key to an affirmation is not to use a negative word in the affirmation. You would not say for example "I am no longer angry" because the mind will focus on the word 'angry'. Instead one uses positive words like 'calm' and 'content'. The other key is never to state the affirmation in the future, for example, "I will be calm and content". This tells the mind that you aren't calm and content but you will be there – one day in the future but never now. An affirmation is always stated in the present tense and always with the use of positive words.

Because the brain loves pictures, visualisation is another technique used to re-programme the mind from negativity to positivity. Herein lies the power of the collage to help heal your life. You are giving your brain a positive picture – the same positive picture – every day for weeks.

John Kehoe's book teaches the power of affirmation (something you say over and over again) to programme the mind to accept and create. Kehoe teaches the power of visualisation. The brain likes pictures and so will be easily programmed by a picture and herein lies the power of the collage to heal your life. You are giving your brain a picture – the same picture – every day and it will begin to re-programme your sub-conscious mind.

Some of us are better at visualisation than others. I for one struggle to hold an image in my mind for any length of time, let alone imbue it with detail. So if I am to train my sub-conscious mind to create with the use of a visualisation, I need the visualisation to be sustained and constant. For this I use the collage.

To make a collage, stick two pieces of A4 paper together to give you sufficient space to be creative. Give your collage a heading and a date at the back. Call it something like 'Creator of Dreams' or 'The Dream Maker'. Then go through a pile of magazines and pull out pictures that depict the life you would like to have. I always recommend a photograph of yourself in the middle, but only if seeing yourself doesn't set off anxieties about how you look and stress about your weight or wrinkles. Make a pile of pictures and cut them out. Cut out words too – Happiness, What a fantastic opportunity, Beautiful Day. Cut out any phrase that forms part of your dream life and place that across or underneath the picture.

I have a few personal favourites. When I make a collage I always cut out an eye and place it somewhere on my collage because it means wisdom and insight to me. Every dream life requires both of those. I don't use a photograph of myself because I am never crazy about how I look in photographs but I always have at least one picture of a flower, which is my signature for myself. I also always put in a saying that is meaningful to me at the time. It is important that there are no white spaces between the pictures. They can overlap or be placed right up against each other but no spaces on the page. It must be processed holistically.

Design your collage, glue it down and then put it under your bed. Just before you turn the light out each night, take it out and stare at it for a minute or two or three. It should be the last thing your mind's eye sees before you turn out the light. In this way you are creatively conditioning your sub-conscious mind to create the reality in that picture. Ironically, you will find that, even though you created it, for the first week or two it will surprise you every time you look at it. It means that the brain has not remembered or processed it yet. Every time you look at it you empower the subconscious mind to create it.

My daughter grew up watching me create collages when I had a problem and needed to change my mind-set about something. One day she sat on the bed and said, "Does this mean that things are not good again?" I remember that I laughed and said, "It means that they could be better and are about to be." She makes beautiful collages today and I always ask her to keep them because they really are pieces of art. She has seen many made and has become an expert herself now, although she was really dubious about their merits when she was much younger. I once put onto one of my collages a picture of a bus in London. About a year later we were in London together and a bus drove past. She stood dead still and I remember her saying, "No way! There is that stupid bus you put on the collage!"

Every great piece of art
started off in imagination.

I reiterate that there is no need to paint a masterpiece or write a book but there is a need to embrace a more creative lifestyle. There is a need to see that the Universe is a remarkable creation and to take the time to see and appreciate that. Don't just glance at a tree or a flower, but take the time to really look at its details. You will never really appreciate the magnificent Universe in which we live unless you give it your attention. I walk my dogs and sometimes I pick up acorns and put them in my pocket to remind myself of how amazing it is that a magnificent oak tree has such humble beginnings. I always keep an acorn somewhere in my house in a place higher than my head to remind me that my dreams are bigger than where I currently am. I like to look at seed pods on plants and fruit and trees because it reminds me that the Universe is abundant and not scarce and that scarcity thinking is untrue thinking.

Protect the artist within by being kind about your creations. Nobody became masterful at anything without attention, practice and effort. When a woman begins to create I know she is beginning to heal. The other day a client's husband made an appointment to see me. He told me somewhat irritably that his wife had found a bead shop and was making 'rubbish jewellery'. I smile to myself because now I know she is beginning to heal. It's always a good sign.

Healing yourself requires that you live a more authentic life and a creative life is a more authentic life because you are the product of creativity. Not everything will be of interest to you. Some people like to sew and others to dance. Some plant and others sing, some write and others cook. I promise you there will be something that you cherish and if you don't know what it is, start looking.

In the meantime don't give up opportunities for creativity in the smallest ways. Wrap your presents with care and find a poem for a birthday wish. Put flowers on the table and when there is no money for flowers there are leaves from branches and creepers that do well. I know because I've done them. Attend to your Christmas tree with love, create invitations for your child's birthday party, cook your Thanksgiving dinner or other special dinners with thanks and live consciously of the wonderful world of which we are a part.

It was during my divorce when one of my clients said, "What is wrong with you these days?" I must admit I got a fright. I wondered if I had given the impression of not paying attention or if my unhappiness was leaking through into my work. "What do you mean what's wrong with me?" I asked.

"Well," she said, "Ever since I arrived here there have always been flowers in this office. You haven't had a bowl of flowers here for three months so I think there is something wrong with you." There was indeed something wrong with me and it was showing.

Don't walk past a single opportunity to do something more beautifully.

Whenever life was particularly difficult for Philippa, she sought to create beauty. She had no idea why. She didn't know that creativity was a pathway to healing – she just followed her instincts. She creates napkin holders and table settings that are much more than that. Each one is a victory over depression, anxiety and self-doubt. I have many of her creations on my table and people often comment on how unusual and beautiful they are. Whenever I lay my table with them I know that women can overcome mountains with flowers, feathers, lace and fruit. Only a woman can pull that off.

When I see a working windmill in Holland I understand the greatness of men. They use the windmill to reclaim the land from the sea and I am in awe of their courage and audacity. When I see a mud hut in the middle of nowhere in KwaZulu-Natal and there are patterns on the wall, I know a woman is home. I am in awe of her willingness to beautify all that she has, no matter how humble. If only men and women cherished all that is remarkable in each other.

Belief systems

Do you believe that anybody is better than nobody?

We all have a worldview and we inherited that from the people who raised us. Our parents held views on life and the world and they taught those to us – sometimes by spelling them out many times and sometimes just by the way they behaved. We imbibe these views by a kind of psychological osmosis called social conditioning. During adolescence we rebel against some of these, which is why this period is often such a tumultuous one. If it's any consolation to parents who have endured those trying times, it's a healthy developmental period and the more compliant teenagers will find it more difficult to forge a more authentic independence as adults. We emerge from adolescence and early adulthood thinking that we have gained financial and intellectual/emotional independence.

We all know that even as well-established adults we struggle to shrug off parental disapproval. It is a burden even though we know we are fully within our rights to make independent decisions. Some adults are more able than others to manage the weight of parental disapproval but few will deny that it exists even when they act like it doesn't.

For the most part that sense of independence is a delusion and we enter our adult lives with a 'borrowed belief system'. Some of these beliefs are so subliminal that we have to unearth them before we can attend to them. Believe it or not your belief system has formed the foundation of the house of your life without you even realising it. It shaped it and dictated it.

It is your obligation as an adult to examine your worldview. Your recovery will depend on your growing awareness of it. You owe it to yourself to dig around in the undergrowth and find the belief that has allowed you or forbidden you to lead a life that has served you well. I am not suggesting for a minute that you toss out every belief system that you got from your parents. On examination you are likely to find much of value there and that is what you need to cherish and keep. Other belief systems will prove to be wrong and unkind or judgemental. Maybe unworthy prejudices have been passed from parent to child and have remained unexamined and thus in existence. Your role in this stage of your recovery is to unearth the belief systems that you inherited in your childhood and failed to place under scrutiny. You need to change the belief systems that are incorrect, untrue and have failed to serve you well.

I am also not suggesting that you blame your parents for failing to prepare you adequately for an adult life. Firstly, like all dynamic organisms, society evolves and what may have been true fifty years ago often no longer is. What may have served your grandmother well will not serve you well in a different society. Secondly, your parents were also not assisted to scrutinise what they were taught from their parents and they too have been victims of ideas that didn't belong to them. Your task is to become aware of your belief system instead of living habitually. Scrutinise it for value and accuracy, and then release those values that are incorrect and that fail to serve you well. I am repeating the words 'serve you well' with intention and if you bear with me you will come to see why.

Belief systems that fail

Here are some examples of belief systems that have failed to serve you well.

"I am nothing without a man."
Here is Philippa's story about belief systems that fail:

My father taught me to believe that a woman needed a man to look after her and by that he meant financially. "Women are not capable of looking after themselves," he would say. I never considered the possibility of financial independence. Making my own money was never an option. Knowing nothing about money except how to spend it seemed feminine and glamorous to me. This is not to say I was not aware of how important money was. I knew that, but what I didn't know was how to make it and I had no intention of ever making that my challenge. My father's behaviour taught me that getting money and feeling loved were somehow intertwined. Becoming financially independent has been one of the most frightening challenges of my new life.

My mother's worldview was no more helpful or accurate than my father's. "Single women have no status," she would announce dogmatically and with such certainty that I never thought to question it. She made it sound like a fact and I assumed it was.

So I got married with the idea that marriage would afford me unending financial security and the proverbial 'open wallet' and that my marriage would give me all the status any woman could ask for. I grew up with these ideas and never interrogated them for their legitimacy in my life. I believed them and I felt sorry for unmarried women – they had no status in my eyes either. I felt sorry for women who needed to work and I didn't envy them their financial independence. My father had taught me that this independence was not mine to pursue and so I didn't.

When I met my first husband I was barely out of school and despite my youth and lack of life experience they encouraged me to get married. His family was wealthy and he was well qualified as a professional. My father was satisfied that my financial wellbeing was being taken care of and I could continue to live in the manner to which I had been taught to be accustomed. His family was well established and so my mother's link between status and marriage had been satisfied too.

Neither of my parents entertained any misgivings about my age. No attention was paid to how emotionally healthy our relationship was and it clearly wasn't from the very early stage. They were not remotely concerned about the constant friction between us and so neither was I. With my parents' blessing I simply sailed forth and directed my attention onto a wedding because I had no real understanding of the demands of a marriage and no one thought to assist me in understanding the gravity of this decision. Sadly, it took many years of pain and humiliation and having my life in ruins before I was able to unpack these ideas with sufficient clarity. For me a good marriage was one in which I could spend with gay abandon and in which I was given the status I thought went with being married to 'a man of means'. The truth is that I found myself married to the meanest of men who gave me heaps of money.

What should have been relevant was not the size of his wallet or his standing in society but the quality of our relationship. Through therapy I have learned that there were other important questions that should have been asked.

- How well do we communicate?
- How well do we make decisions together?
- How well do we resolve conflict?
- How healthy is the balance of power in our relationship?
- How compatible are we?
- What qualities does he have that I cherish?
- How reasonable are our expectations of each other?
- Do I trust and respect him?
- Do I feel loved and respected by him?

Had I run any one of my relationships through this list of questions none of them would have justified a marriage. They all passed my money/status test but all failed to flourish and in my case they failed to even survive. I know I sound like a gold digger. However,

I was only very subliminally aware of these mental associations. It is with the value of hindsight that I have come to understand why I married men who never respected me or valued me sufficiently even before we were married.

I have been single for years now. When I was in therapy with Sue she would encourage me to spend at least six months not being in a relationship. She said I needed to explore myself and could never do that because I was constantly caught up with trying to manage a relationship. At the time I could never see the importance of that. I could never see that I had any value outside of a relationship and never gave myself the time to even recognise that. I am not saying that I don't want a relationship. I am not bitter about love. I welcome the opportunity to go into a relationship not consumed by need.

When all looked lost, I found myself.

"I am unworthy."

Many children are brought up by neglectful, egocentric parents who never tell them that they are unique, special and deeply loved. The saying "Children should be seen and not heard" reveals a belief system that children's opinions are unimportant and that they should be minimally invasive and inconvenient to the parents.

Some parents did that publicly because it was a widely held parenting style, but privately they were attentive and loving parents, and the children grew up with a healthy self-esteem and suffered little or no damage from their lack of public appreciation. Other parents managed to leave their children with the belief that they are unworthy and unlovable.

I am going to take you back to Anna's story by way of an example to show you how it directly affected her decision to marry an abusive man. Anna's mother was hysterical and emotionally unstable. She had no time for her children and was completely preoccupied with her own emotional state. She neglected her children and had them believe that her feelings were important and theirs weren't. Then she had her third child and for reasons that we don't know, she adored him. So there were two neglected children and one that made her sun rise in the morning. This had to lead the children to believe that she was capable of being loving and that if they had been 'better' or more lovable then they too could have been the recipients of her love.

Anna went into adulthood with the subliminal belief that she was not good enough. She was in some way deficient and unlovable. When the man that she married was cruel and neglectful it failed to set off any alarm bells for her. Why would it? This was, after all, what she was accustomed to. When his feelings were important and hers were dismissed, she coped very well. Why wouldn't she? This was after all what her life had been all about. She was the perfect candidate for an abusive marriage because she was used to it. She was accustomed to attending to other people's feelings as she had attended to her mother's and never expected any attention in return.

Anna's recovery was in many ways accidental. Her husband was less generous than Philippa's had been, despite the fact that he too was a man of means. It is my honest belief that she felt so unworthy that she found it difficult to make any financial demands and so found herself in need of additional finances. She began to work and she was, of course, very obliging – her childhood had taught her to do that well. As a result she was well liked and began to do very well at work. Frankly no one was more surprised than Anna herself. She had never believed herself worthy of success. Her self-esteem began to grow with her growing success. However, her husband was completely dismissive of her success and, in fact, downright resentful. Anna's belief that she was unworthy and unlovable allowed her to marry a man who treated her as unworthy and unlovable.

"That's just the way men are."

Women who grow up in healthy domestic situations have clear expectations of the role that a husband and father should play. Abused women often grow up in unhealthy domestic situations or with absent fathers and they have no idea what they can expect from their partners. Many women stay in denial about the nature of the relationship by saying, "That's just how men are". The abusive relationship doesn't allow space for both parties to negotiate their expectations – or even discuss them. It's his way or the highway.

Every healthy couple will clash over the failure to meet each other's expectations. Those clashes, if handled properly, are part and parcel of a healthy relationship. But when one party has no voice the relationship is abusive.

Philippa describes a common pattern in all her abusive relationships.

Whenever I tried to explain how I felt I would be screamed at and the remarkable thing was that he told me I didn't feel that way. At the end of being yelled at I would then be told, "No one will ever love you like I do." It's a tiny piece of insanity. First you are disrespected and then you are told how loved you are. I had no idea what to do with those conversations. I grew up in a household where on the face of it my father was treated like a king. The table was set perfectly for him every night and the subtext was that he makes the money so he makes the rules. On another level he was completely disrespected but it remained as mere subtext and was never out in the open. By the time I got married I had no idea how to conduct a marriage outside of creating a perfect meal and presenting myself dressed to the nines. The worse my marriages got, the more main dishes I produced as though the variety would somehow cure that revolting relationship.

I actually had no idea what I could expect from a man. When I first got divorced I tried talking to my family about why. With hindsight I see I could not articulate my powerlessness, voicelessness or confusion. Their response was to tell me that "men are just like this. It's not so bad and certainly not reason enough to leave." For years those words kept me from identifying the real dragon on my path, which was that I was a co-dependent likely to relive the abusive cycle until I could heal myself.

"I am not enough."

Another faulty belief system is "I am not enough", which encourages abused women to fill up the emotional emptiness with things and habits. I asked Philippa to write about her way of feeding the need, which in her case was through shopping.

I called shopping 'retail therapy' and Sue reminded me of how I used to talk light-heartedly about loving beautiful packets with exquisite things in them. She explained that many abused co-dependents shop excessively and compulsively. I was a compulsive shopper – every day, all the time and in ways that consumed me. A shopping outing was followed by hours of mixing and matching, then re-mixing and re-matching and thoughts of when and where I could show off my new outfits. I would try on shoes and attend to bags with shoes and on it would go – for hours.

Why? If I were to be kind to myself, I could say that I have a finely tuned sense of aesthetics and I value excellence in things (if not men). I really do appreciate anything that is beautifully crafted, balanced and executed well. But ruefully I must admit that it was more than that – much more.

On reflection my life was ugly, my thoughts painful and my fears often overwhelming. I pushed them aside by giving myself a place to go in my mind that pleased me instead of hurt me. The forlorn truth was that I didn't feel like I was enough. I had to be ultra-glamorous and the epitome of well-groomed because I was trying to get his attention.

I was trying to make myself feel more valuable than I actually felt. If other people were impressed I could 'earn points' with him. I used the attention to constantly prop up an ailing self-esteem. I was also trying to fill an emotional emptiness with beautiful things that made me happy. In the short-term I was filled by the beauty of my purchases but as with all 'substitutes for the real need' my satisfaction was short-lived. The next day the shops beckoned and I followed. The true picture of my life was temporarily blurred and out of focus when it looked beautiful from the outside. For a while I could borrow the eyes of the onlooker and be impressed by what it looked like – but wasn't.

In my mother's house everything always looked perfect. Furniture was taken out and dusted and vacuumed regularly. The table was set with silver, and presentation was everything. In contrast every single cupboard was in a state of total disorganisation and that never bothered her in the least. All that mattered was that it looked perfect from the outside.

In a society like ours 'things' have a subtext and we all understand it. A Rolex is not just a superb watch. It is a loud, indisputable statement that you have arrived where few others have, and that you are somehow better than them. I understood that sub-text. If I had beautiful things then surely I was worth something? Surely this proved that I wasn't really that broken needy woman seducing my husband, who I had no respect for, with food and glamour and affirmations he didn't deserve? Those elegant packets were my lie to myself and the rest of the world. They said "You have arrived!" The truth is that I had arrived nowhere except in another hauntingly terrible marriage with another power-hungry man who didn't know the difference between strength and brutality. The truth is that I wasn't sure why or what I had done wrong – again. Once again I felt unloved and empty. Once again I was fighting, pleading, making up and busting up. Once again I was shopping and at no point in all that time did it even occur to me to question why I needed to shop so often.

Reflections and insights do not come in exquisite packets and the contents are often not beautiful but I have come to value those far more than any designer dress in an elegant packet. Now it is easy for me to walk past a boutique boasting magnificent clothes without feeling the need to go in. I am no longer a living, breathing mannequin made up of empty spaces on the inside.

Finally, I know that I am enough and the shops no longer beckon to me.

Men bought me trinkets when I yearned for love. They took me on holiday but never shared my journey. They dressed me and fed me but I was cold and hungry. I looked outwards when I needed to go in and came in when I should have stayed out. They were confusing times.

"I need him = I love him."

> *Both the abuser and co-dependent are dependent on the inadequacy of the other to feel safe.*

Fairy tales have encouraged young girls to believe that love means being saved from a life of hardship. Prince Charming saved Cinderella from a life of slavery to her stepmother and ugly stepsisters; Snow White from being a servant to the seven dwarves; Sleeping Beauty from endless sleep; and Rapunzel from the witch's tower. The myth tells women that being saved is the equivalent of love. Love and dependency becomes so intertwined that they appear to be the same thing. Young women who grow up with healthy role models and self-esteem mature in their perceptions of relationships. For the co-dependent there remains no difference between love and need. They need and want to be saved.

The abuser and the co-dependent have exactly the same problem. Both of them have low self-esteem. Neither of them have any belief that love is sustainable through trust, affection, respect and labour. Neither of them believe that they are lovable in an ongoing way through the ebb and flow of life with all its challenges. They have to ensnare and enslave 'the beloved' to force them to stay.

An abusive man damages the woman he thinks he loves to prevent her from leaving him. He makes her pathetic, needy and anxious to ensure that she feels unable to survive without him. His fear of loss makes him brutal, demeaning and savage. Then he loses respect for her because she becomes what he created. The co-dependent tries to make him need her as much as she needs him – for the same reason. His dependency makes him a prisoner in the relationship in the same way that the abuser makes her a prisoner in the relationship. The abuser needs her weakness and the co-dependent needs his weakness. Both are dependent on the inadequacy of the other to feel safe. Both believe that without that weakness they are destined to be deserted.

The abuser acts like the beast and the co-dependent acts like the saint. She will run around him, feed him, serve him, adore him, forgive him, obsess about him and applaud him. The co-dependent feels sick when he isn't around. She craves him and yearns for him – surely that means she loves him? She tells herself that even if he doesn't know it yet, he needs her. One day he will realise that. If he needs her and stays with her, surely that means he loves her?

Both are destined to bring into being the very thing they fear most – abandonment. The abuser is angry and mistrusting. He assumes that she is lying and cheating and using and abusing him. Everything she does will be viewed through the eyes of a man who knows that women are untrustworthy. Love is untrustworthy. The co-dependent does the same but differently. She cannot be attracted to a man who doesn't need her or who is stable. What will she do? How will she create sufficient need to ensure that she is indispensable? How do you prop up a man who is steady on his own feet? Without his need she cannot feel safe. Without the drama she cannot be sure that love is alive and well. If she was secure she wouldn't crave his attention or feel adrift in his absence. How then would she be sure that she loved him?

There is a formula. Dependency breeds fear. Fear breeds resentment. Resentment is love's enemy.

The co-dependent will inevitably live a life of resentment, no less than the abuser will. The abuser will create dependency and thus fear and with the fear comes the corrosion of love. He will inadvertently create the very thing he fears most – the loss of her love. The co-dependent is already afraid of loss. Her fear will create resentment. She resents him for not loving her enough because he doesn't need her enough. The very instability that first drew her to him will result in his pathological behaviour that will feed her fear and her resentment. She loves and hates his weakness. She loves and hates the selfishness that she created by not setting standards. She loves and hates the drama she created. She loves and hates his contempt for her. It makes her work harder and keeps her driven and she hates how he makes her feel. She is deep in the trap of 'fear breeds resentment and resentment is love's enemy'.

Both the abuser and the co-dependent share a common belief system. Love is not real.

"I loved you the most when I knew you the least."
Anonymous

When loving him hurts – The passion paradox
21 January 2015 Blog post from
www.whenlovinghimhurts.com

Falling in love is about excitement, yearning, desire and passion. Describing a relationship as falling in lust would be equally appropriate for men as it is often lust that drives men into relationships. Women on the other hand tend to call it love. It is the lace and lavender of lust.

Love or lust, it makes no difference. When the earth moves we feel compelled to go with it, engage and hopefully commit to it. Loving/lusting is usually referred to as the 'honeymoon phase' – usually well over by the time the honeymoon comes around. Years into their relationship, people yearn for the balmy days of butterflies, when lipstick made a difference and men think longingly of the days when they were young stags. Date nights, new lingerie, Botox, and no TV in the bedroom are often attempts to reclaim those early days. Viagra, horny-goats weed and pornography ... another man, another woman and another marriage bites the dust. Passion rules.

The sad truth is that the co-dependent often doesn't suffer from this problem. Why? She believes that it's because what she feels is real love. Not so. Passion is fuelled by fear and insecurity. The passion of beginnings allows the relationship to be consolidated into something firmer and more reliable. The co-dependent woman never feels secure. She is never safe in the love and respect of her partner. She is constantly working to be better, to prove her love and loyalty and to perfect the art of being his partner. When she fails, even briefly, he rejects her, leaves her, or threatens to withdraw his love or replace her with someone more worthy. She is devastated, shocked and fundamentally insecure. The perfect recipe to keeping passion safe and flourishing.

Being kissed and touched is proof of his forgiveness. Even a wink is devastatingly sexy and alluring when any sign will do. A wink suggests that making love will follow and once again she can feel like 'the one'. Maybe if they make love two nights in a row she can begin to feel safe again – even if only briefly. Sex stays exciting because it signals the end of the rejection. It signals that he loves her again and she has proven herself to him yet again. She hopes, she yearns, she prays for the days when she will feel safe and indispensable and without knowing it those days erode the passion on which she is so dependent.

The passion dilemma is that once people begin to feel safe they are able to attend to life and demands outside of each other. Life doesn't facilitate passion. It serves the ends of raising a family, pursuing a career and meeting our responsibilities to the people around us and the greater community. Those demands are often tedious, relentless and unforgiving. They are the demands of a healthy adult life and are often noble and growth-producing. They, however, do not encourage and breed passion.

Passion is not designed to define our lives or our relationships. It is designed to be a stepping stone to a healthy long-term relationship or to die out before that mistake becomes a longstanding one. Passion's blue print is that it transforms into a quiet and persistent, but not demanding, attraction for each other. It doesn't keep demanding our attention. It no longer says, "look at me, look at me". It just is.

Where did the passion go?

Nowhere – it just grew out of its own fear which sustained it. It isn't gone – it's just no longer the same rowdy, demanding, all-consuming two-year-old it once was.

"My brand of loving is noble and superior."

Co-dependent women often have no idea that their pathologies are rampant in their lives. They fail to recognise that the brutality in their relationship is not an opportunity to prove their devotion. They have an unfortunate narrative that keeps them working harder for approval instead of their own self-esteem. Philippa talks about what she thought was noble patience. With hindsight she acknowledges that her pathology was rampant, insatiable martyrdom.

Co-dependents could be called patient because we can wait – for hours and years. When I look back my life feels like a waiting room. I waited for him to stop being angry with me. I waited for him to love me again and to recognise my worth. I worked at getting it and waited for the time to arrive when he would finally acknowledge me. I waited for him to come home and see the labours of my day. I waited for the time that he would stop lying to me and stop taking calls in the garden. What I wanted above all else was that he would see that my particular kind of loving was superior to all others.

My love was superior because I could sit vigil and wait for him – even when he was angry, drunk, or just plain missing. I could get over anything and forgive anything. Who else would love him enough to do that? I could understand his needs and anticipate them. I had no idea how unhealthy I actually was. I could see that intellectually but emotionally I felt my love was noble and superior and with time he would see that – and so I waited for that time. Today I understand that the particular kind of loving of the co-dependent is not noble but the ultimate paradox.

On the one hand my self-esteem was so shattered that I could be sworn at and beaten, dismissed and lied to constantly but I would still go back. I would accept an apology as though it was the first time I had heard it – with relief not reservation. I didn't think enough of myself to refuse to accept that treatment. I didn't fall out of love and I didn't re-evaluate respect for myself or him. I was a complete victim and lived at his mercy. On the other hand I was a martyr. My love was not self-serving the way other people loved. Mine was self-sacrificing and noble. My forgiveness did not have limits the way other people's did – it was endless. Only I could understand his depression that led to his brutality and I was strong enough to endure the scars of his childhood. I was the one who would prove to him that love is strong and that no matter what he did to me I would be there – loving and forgiving and willing to help him. I was the cure to his past disappointments and I was the woman who would not leave him as the others had done. When I felt like the martyr my sense of self was at an all-time high. I was strong enough for both of us and I was his crutch and person he loved enough to abuse. I was the only person he could be totally honest with. It was so perverse that his beatings were the secret we shared for a long time. The payoff here was only obvious to me with hindsight. When I was the martyr I felt like I had a purpose and I hid behind that purpose. He was my purpose and I could hide safely in that role and not attend to the challenges of my own life.

As the victim/martyr I sat in the waiting room of my life waiting for the recognition and appreciation that I thought I deserved. My noble self-righteousness prevented me from seeing that I was nothing more than an abused wife. While I was being bludgeoned on the head, I was patting myself on the back for enduring this.

I am very relieved that the misogynist is a mean-spirited beast. Had I been given just enough acknowledgement and appreciation I might still be there thinking that my particular brand of loving was superior to all else. Fortunately they lack the generosity of spirit to give just the little bit more I needed to keep me stuck in the waiting room of my life.

These are just some of the examples of the belief systems that have allowed women to get into and stay in abusive relationship. They were not conscious beliefs. They were gently tethered out of memories, hindsight and careful evaluation of events. They were, however, the belief systems that were directly responsible for many of the unhealthy decisions and painful consequences.

Those belief systems will need to be stalked with the prowess of the warrior. We need to see them in operation and stop them. However, they also need to be replaced with belief systems that do serve us well.

For the purposes of this book I want to distinguish faith from belief. To have faith means to believe in something about which we have dubious or no evidence. Faith provides the gift of confidence in the unknown and that which is unfathomable. Faith, although inherently beautiful, is often referred to as blind – we must step into the great unknown with confidence that does not stem from evidence or comprehension. Often the words 'belief' and 'faith' are used interchangeably. We are distinguishing faith from belief and we are removing belief from the religious or spiritual arena – those matters exist far from the realms of what we are addressing here.

In order to hold a belief about something you must be willing to challenge it and interrogate it. You are no longer a child and so you must own a belief system that you have spent time reflecting upon by yourself. It is equally important that you accept that other people hold different belief systems that are also worthy of respect. We hold many beliefs that have nothing to do with spirituality.

Belief in anything has come grudgingly to me. I think of myself as rational and logical but maybe I am just a suspicious person. Even a simple statement like "You get what you pay for" will be subjected to considerable scrutiny from me. For months and sometimes years I will buy the same product, like mascara for example, from the bottom of the range to the top and decide if the price difference is justified by the end result. I do the same with the purchasing of fruit and vegetables. Over time my belief is that the sentence "You get what you pay for" is not true across the board. It holds true for certain things but not others.

My beliefs have arrived as epiphanies or have evolved slowly over time. They have been subjected to close scrutiny and diligent experimentation. At times they have been challenged by my life experiences and then re-instated with the benefit of hindsight. Time has proved them right or faulty. These beliefs have become the bedrock of my life. When I feel hopeless, depressed or defeated I turn to them over and over again. I make life decisions that are congruent with those beliefs, and when I am uncertain they point me in the right direction. Quite simply, I own a firm, resolute set of beliefs that have kept me anchored in the wild waters of my life.

A belief will never be able to anchor you until you have walked around it and looked at it from different angles. Until you have tested it and watched it and tried to do it differently, you will never be able to trust it. I am going to give you examples of several of my firmly held beliefs. Until you have tested them and defied them yourself, you are unlikely to embrace them or trust them fully.

Belief systems that work

The following is a list of some of my own beliefs, as an example.

"I believe that money that rightfully belongs to me will come to me and if I come by money by foul means I will not keep it."

> *The Universe keeps a perfect set of books –*
> *and she charges interest.*

This does not mean that I neglect to send out my invoices nor that I fail to follow up on outstanding fees due to me. It does not mean that I have a careless relationship with money because carelessness in any relationship will damage it. It does mean, however, that I will not become bitter and twisted when I don't feel that I have been given a square and fair deal. My attitude is that I have owed in ways that I have ignored or not remembered and so it is payback time and I am glad to be out of a debt. Bad financial deals or circumstances may well be no more than the debt collector for the transgressions we ignored or forgot about. Failing which, if the money does ethically belong to me, it will find its way to me when I need it and in the most unexpected ways. It saves me from the poison of feeling cheated.

I have seen this over and over again in my life. Once I bought a rug and the shop assistant rolled up two by mistake and I only paid for one. I attempted to justify this by telling myself that it is not my problem if they don't employ competent staff. To further justify myself I gave one of the rugs away but the other was ruined when a pot of paint was dropped on it. I suspect the cost of that dishonesty on my part would be more than the fact that I didn't have any rug at all at the end of it. I suspect that the debt from that behaviour would have continued in ways that I had no way to track but must accept responsibility for nonetheless.

There are millions of financial transactions that go on in a lifetime but I know that I must be scrupulously honest and fair and always broker a win–win deal and then I am safe. It helps me pay with a smile and when events seem to hurt financially I accept that I might not have the ledger but the Universe runs a perfect set of books – and charges interest.

"I believe that the truth may hurt but it never causes damage in the long term. Lies may land softly but they always cause injury."

You have the right to speak your truth but an obligation to do so gently.

I know from personal experience that the truth can hurt very badly. However, I am also aware that somewhere beneath the shock and horror of the information a small part of me is relieved. It feels like some sub-conscious part of me already knew and is glad the truth is finally on the table. I have also been lied to often, particularly when I was married. While I was listening to the lies I was relieved that my suspicions were not being confirmed. On the surface I was glad to hear the lies but again I was aware of that part of me that remained uneasy, dissatisfied and strung out.

I have also lied. Sometimes I wanted to get out of trouble and sometimes I couldn't face hurting the other person. I am not talking about the 'white lies' about a bad haircut. I call those fibs not lies. I know now that when I lie I diminish both myself and the other person. I am not sparing them the hurt. There is a part of them that knows I am lying. I am keeping that part of them suspicious and hurt and uneasy. I am also unlikely to keep this information from them forever so all I am doing is avoiding the inevitable. I know that I cannot protect someone with a lie. The best I can provide is the gentle truth so that they can begin the healing process once the shock and despair has abated. The best I can do for myself is take responsibility and own my failure or betrayal or neglect.

I don't expect to be forgiven for telling the truth. I don't expect to be thanked and I don't expect that there will no consequences. Many children have been brought up on the doctrine that if they tell the truth it will be fine and so they do so in an effort to avoid consequences. The truth is not a way out of consequences but it is the first step in the healing process. Go back along memory lane and you will see that when you were hurt with the truth it was easy to forgive later. I respect and forgive people who hurt me with the truth. Those who lied to me I would frankly prefer not to see again. There remains a sour aftertaste that is not readily forgotten.

"I believe that I cannot make anyone love me but I can make them respect me by the way I conduct myself."

The heart beats to its own drum and follows its own path.

Of course there have been times in my life when I have wanted a man to be in love with me as I felt I was with him. Frankly I wasn't that interested in his respect, but I wanted his love and passion. I know that I cannot manage or manipulate these feelings. The heart follows its own path and beats to its own drum. I can manipulate him into feeling guilty about leaving me. I can manage to make myself indispensable and I can be easy-going and not provoke an argument, but the truth is that I cannot make him love me. The heart of another person falls outside of our managerial capabilities. I have watched my own ineptitude often enough to know this to be true.

I also know that there is no point in blaming him or myself for this. He cannot make himself love me even if he wanted to. We anticipate that being passionately in love will go off the boil and a more steadfast, comfortable loving will take its place. Sometimes a relationship just sours.

Many issues in a relationship can be resolved and managed.

Couples can learn conflict management, expectations can be modified and habits changed but love cannot be forced into anyone's heart. I accept this with regret. However I can make someone respect me by the way I conduct myself. I am in charge of my behaviour, my skill, my diligence, and my respect and appreciation for other people. I value respect so I behave in such a way that I earn it. I cherish it and do nothing to compromise it.

I once loved a man very much and for him the lights simply went out. Instead of addressing the issue honestly he simply became more and more unavailable. His behaviour was the unspoken lie. It was not his business demands that kept him away more and more often; it was the fact that he simply had no desire to be with me anymore.

Once I began to pay attention to my 'inner voice' I was able to stop pretending to be pleased about his growing success. With deep sadness I was able to stop trying and stop being ridiculous. I stopped buying clothes I thought he would like as though an outfit could possibly resurrect a relationship. I stopped choking down my disappointment and acting upbeat with yet another last-minute cancellation. I was able to speak the truth and just go away.

My foundational belief allowed me to salvage my dignity and release him from his guilt. After several years the after-taste is that he didn't have enough respect for himself or me to be honest instead of behaving badly. It is easy to stop doing the impossible once you pay attention to the truth. I was able to accept the truth without feeling insulted or inadequate.

I was once engaged to a wonderful man. On paper he was everything I would have chosen for myself. However, he made me feel tired. I wished I could love him and believed that I would have a good life as his wife. My heart would not support that decision.

Sometimes I think about him when my life is difficult and I lament that I didn't marry him but it would not have been true love. When someone does not love me enough I know that it's not necessarily because he doesn't think enough of me. I respect that as my heart will not succumb to the instructions of my mind, maybe his is the same. He may want to love me but cannot.

"I believe that no matter how unhappy and desperate I am today the time will come that I will be happy again."

I clearly remember the first time I wished I was dead. I was at school and I just knew that I would never ever be able to do long division. No matter how often I tried or practised I seemed to be the only person in the world who could not work it out. The second time was when I accidentally killed my pet mouse. I had found this baby mouse and had hand-reared it with a dropper every few hours. My grandfather had declared her to be 'vermin' and the consequence of that was that she was no longer allowed to stay in my room with me. I would set my alarm and every few hours through the night I would go outside into the playroom and feed her with a dropper with warm milk. For whatever reason that day I decided it was time for solids and she choked to death as I watched in horror. For some reason I still remember those two incidents well.

Since then I have seen that big black hole with many of my clients. We have circled it together, very aware of the dangers that lie therein. I know very few adults who have not wished they were dead many times – myself included. They aren't necessarily suicidal. They simply don't want to be here because it's too difficult, too painful, too scary or too pointless. When I feel that way I often remember that I can do long division now and even if I couldn't it hardly seems worth dying for.

Once I sat in the garden at the hospital after being told I had ovarian cancer and that I must expect to receive radiation and/or chemotherapy. I no longer have cancer, didn't need any of those treatments and instead I am deeply grateful for the days that I do have and the life that is now safely mine – for now. I remember sitting in that sad little hospital garden and actually thinking that if nothing else I would die knowing how to do long division despite the fact that there is no necessity for such a skill anymore.

The day I found out I had cancer my dear friend Pat insisted on coming with me to see the surgeon. On the way to the hospital she said, "I know that you are bad at talking about things when they are actually going on and you prefer to talk later [what a blessing to have friends who know you well], but please tell me

227

what you are thinking." The truth was exactly as I told her. "Pat, I know that when I tell you what I am thinking you are going to think I am in denial. The truth is that I feel as though someone has made a mistake. I saw the scan and I have seen the ultrasound but I still feel as though there has been an error. I can't explain it better than that." That reliable 'inner voice' did not let me down. There had indeed been no mistake. However, the tumour was an encapsulated one and with one surgery I was fully recovered. Part of my contemplations of the day was that this time maybe there would not be a spring after the winter. Maybe this was to be my last winter but somehow it just didn't feel like it was.

Of course the time will come when there will be no more spring here so this belief is not absolute – I know that. However, I am deeply comforted by the ebb and flow of life. I know that all things change and seasons come and go and so will the unhappiness – and the happiness. It is the rhythm of life and I have come to cherish it as it is.

Reflection

Re-examination of your belief systems
This reflection challenges you to re-examine the belief systems that have failed to serve you well. Please consider at least two belief systems that have failed to serve you well.

- Where did they come from?
- In what way are they incorrect?
- In what way did they support unhealthy life decisions?
- What adjustments have you made to them?

If you wish, you can submit your answers to the website www.whenlovinghimhurts.com.

Reflections on reflections

By now you have begun to understand that you have allowed your self-confidence to be compromised. Remember that your dignity can be vandalised and assaulted but it is only lost when you have surrendered it. You are responsible for the loss and more positively you are responsible for its re-creation. You are responsible for how you appear to the world and responsible for your inner health and wellbeing. Your inner self is like a secret garden that you tend within yourself and it will either leak through or glow through depending on what you do.

One day one of my very dear clients arrived for her appointment.

"Morning Mary, how are you?"

"I have had a lousy week. Dean reversed the car into the gate motor. I think he is losing his sight and not telling me. Then the family came for lunch and as usual Dean and Erik were at each other's throats. I think they are so alike and neither of them can see that. But never mind all that. I want to tell you about my real life."

It was an extraordinary sentence. "What is your real life, Mary?"

"It's the life inside of me. When that's right the rest is easy."

After some time in therapy Mary had begun to understand that her inner world required forgiveness. She had to forgive her mother for staying with her stepfather. She had to forgive herself for abandoning her mother for making that decision. She had to forgive herself for allowing her mother to die alone and dirty in an abusive marriage. Mary had never been able to forgive herself or her mother and as a result her life was one of grudges. She could recall every mean or insensitive sentence her husband ever said to her and they weren't frequent. She harboured every careless action of her neighbours. She ruminated on every insult and every unreturned favour. I had already been 'fired' twice by her for some imagined insult or betrayal for not 'taking her side'. She would make and cancel appointments for a few weeks and then I would have to phone and make good my offensive behaviour. Finally Mary faced the fact that she had a problem with forgiveness and was burdened by grudges that made her sick and unhappy. Mary was furious when I told her that in my opinion she was not in an abusive relationship. She had been unable to forgive herself and as a result was unreasonably unforgiving towards others.

Requirements for reflection

Mary had discovered the art of reflection. To reflect means to consider at length, to ponder and to contemplate. Before we can reflect we need humility. Before you begin the process of reflection, you must at least be able to entertain the idea that you may be wrong, short-sighted, self-centred or suffering from tunnel vision. Contemplation asks us to see something from the point of view of other people. We have to ask ourselves if, just maybe, they have a point. It requires that we examine our basic assumptions and accept that the other person may hold different but not incorrect assumptions. None of us like to change our mind, particularly when we have fought hard to defend our position. Reflection is impossible without humility. To be humble is to be prepared to be aware of our shortcomings.

I can hear the collective sigh of the abused women across the world. Indeed you have been told of your shortcomings constantly. They are delivered to you often at considerable volume or via stony silence. Often they have come with slaps and punches. You live with self-doubt and self-blame and you apologise more in a week than other people apologise in a year. That is not humility – it's being downtrodden or beaten down. Humility is not fundamentally about admitting to being wrong. It is about suspending belief and taking a wide and long view. It asks you to empty yourself out of old views, prejudices and stale opinions, and cherry pick a new insight and perspective.

Once you have nailed down humility, you need courage. Reflection asks you to think about painful times in your life and go back to drawers and cupboards that have been packed away and locked. Many spiritual gurus say that there is no time but the present. There is no value in the past or in the future – only in the now. Reflection asks you to go back in time but to go back as you are now.

Mary was much younger when her mother died. Her husband was not abusive but he had been brought up in a very conservative family and was a judgemental man. Mary had learned to be judgemental simply because she had never thought long and hard about the value of compassion. Many years later her son was a problem teenager and she was victim of the 'judgemental' crowd in her church and her community. Today she understands the value of compassion.

The Mary of today needs to go back to the time she terminated all contact with her mother because she couldn't understand why her mother was unable to break out of her abusive marriage when Mary and her husband had generously offered her a place to live with them. Today she accepts that she had not really contemplated her mother's life or the real implications of her 'just leaving'. Mary needed to revisit the day she got the call that her mother had died and the condition in which she found her when she got there. She was ashamed of her mother and ashamed of herself for the condition her mother was in.

These are not comfortable memories filled with self-righteous indignation. This trip down memory lane requires courage. The value of unearthing these memories is that Mary is no longer the same young woman she was then. Today she can see who she was then and why her world-view made it possible for her to make and live with the decisions she made then. She was different in those days. She knew and understood less. Once Mary had found humility and the courage, she needed to name the problem. It was guilt. Mary was guilty and could not forgive herself. As she could not forgive herself she could forgive no one else either. The same lack of compassion she showed for that confused and impressionable young woman she once was, she had for everyone.

How does one reflect? You walk around the territory thoughtfully. Mary blamed her husband and his family for 'making' her judgemental. She blamed herself for being a failure as a daughter and blamed her stepfather for allowing her mother to die without dignity. Then she just kept on blaming everyone for everything. She needed to look back at herself more gently, to look at guilt itself, at forgiveness and regret. She needed to remember who was compassionate with her when she needed it and why others weren't. She needed to think about compassion and to practise it. She needed to catch herself not being compassionate and to try again. Mary thought about guilt and compassion while she shopped, while she watched a movie and when she read. She watched and listened to compassionate people and made a study of compassion. She wrote notes and asked questions and practised forgiveness when she was annoyed. Slowly but surely she was weeding her inner world of bitterness, regret and failures to forgive.

The point of my story is that Mary was initially hurt and upset and reluctant to revisit this material but she became excited by her inner life. She was busy changing an angry, bitter woman into an interested, curious, compassionate one. When she found the compassion for herself she could find it for others. She could change because she took charge of that inner self. The journey had begun to excite her and therefore the sentence, "Never mind all that. Let me tell you about my life".

Guidelines for reflection

Reflection is for the psyche what gym is for the body. Exercising your body will always be good for you but there are any number of ways to achieve that. You can gym, walk, run, do yoga, cycle, play tennis, swim, hike, dance – in fact as long as you show up and move consistently you will be doing exercise. I always recommend that you do what you like because it's more sustainable.

Reflection is much the same. There are dozens of ways to think deeply and to explore the self and your ideas. Choose anything that works for you and do it consistently. Many of us will claim that we are unable to do exercise because there is no time. Well there is – you can walk to the shops instead of drive, you can take the stairs and not the lift or you can walk briskly instead of at an amble. The same can be said for reflection. It is true that it takes time but we have to make time to do it. Mostly we spend our reflection time having imaginary conversations with people who have angered us. We fret about poor service delivery and worry that when retirement comes around we will be insufficiently prepared. All of that is wasted reflection time.

Here are a few reflection warm-ups that I have been taught by special people around me.

1. My friend Pat has a game she calls, "What was the sentence of the evening?" or "What was the sentence of the day?" We would be having dinner and suddenly she would announce, "Okay that was the sentence of the night." Initially I paid very little attention but one day I asked her about it. She tells me that whenever she goes out or spends time with people, she likes to find the sentence that was the most enlightening or the most ridiculous. The first obvious advantage is that you begin to pay proper attention to what people are saying and you are thoughtful about the conversation. It implies that you are weighing up what people say instead of allowing conversation to pass you by without noticing. Suddenly you have become a good listener. You are assuming that there will be a sentence of the night and so you

are on the hunt for the treasure. I was beginning to understand why she is such a popular person – it's because she pays attention to what is being said and applies her mind. People sense that and like it and she likes to feel that, at the end of an evening, she has a little treasure of illumination. Now we both do it and when we attend functions together we discuss what we each thought the sentence of the night was. I assure you that it is a huge improvement on the gossip post-mortem that follows most social engagements.

2. She also taught me to go in search of the 'special scene' in a movie. When she has finished watching a movie she always asks herself which scene she liked most and then tries to work out why. If a scene resonates with us it speaks to some part in us. If I think back to movies that I have particularly liked I can do that on reflection. There was a scene in the movie *The Last Samurai* in which a man comes out of the darkness and through the trees in a terrifying mask. It lasts only for a few seconds but I can still recall the scene. I know it speaks to me of my own fearfulness, which is why I live like a sentinel, checking the fences and posts of my life for weakness. In one of my favourite movies on domestic violence, called *Once were Warriors,* there is a scene where the abuser and his wife sing a love song to each other. I loved the irony of the scene – she could sing her love to him with a black-eye and I knew he would beat her again before the night was over. However, it was that scene that helped me understand the terrible dance of love and brutality. Don't just turn off the TV or walk to your car – do so with thought and reflection. Why did you like the scene? What did you learn? What part of you did it resonate with?

3. Write a list of 15 qualities you have. For example, tolerant, tidy, energetic, shy, hard-working, loyal, boring, reliable, conservative, and so on until you have 15 qualities, and then put that piece of paper away. Tomorrow take another piece of paper and use your non-writing hand and write a sentence "I am now writing

with my left hand". Then allow your mind to go blank and using your non-writing hand write down 15 qualities that come to mind. You are now accessing the other side of your brain and you may be interested to find the qualities you are hiding from yourself and others. Keep a notebook with you and write down a note here or there when an interesting thought occurs to you. When you have time go through your notebook, see what is there and ponder.

4. Change the conversations that you are having. Gossiping must go. It is unkind and is just another way to prop up a failing self-esteem. If you are gossiping about people, they will be gossiping about you. Instead start to tell people about a movie and ask them why they thought that scene was important. Ask their opinion on movies you have both seen or books you have both read. Teach people to explore themselves through the events that are going on around us. Each event holds opportunities to learn and we waste them all. Pat is an English teacher and I remember the exact sentence that made me sure I wanted her as a friend. She said, "How do you teach *Gatsby* to an 18-year-old? I am so exasperated at the expectation that these teenagers can be expected to really grasp that material." This was a person I wanted to spend time with.

5. Pay attention and ask questions and you will be amazed at what you learn. My friend Mary-Ann and I went out for dinner one evening. The restaurant was decorated with slices of tree trunks. Suddenly she said, "You have touched that thing twice since we sat down. Why?" Well, it was obviously done recently because I could still smell the fresh timber. My father was a carpenter and when I was a child I would sit on his lap when he came home from work and I could always smell the sawdust in his hair. Ever since, the smell of cut timber finds a tender place inside of me. Then I was able to ask her about her father and her favourite memory of him. These are all instances that contribute to intimacy. The human soul craves intimacy, and conversations

about other people and what they wore and what they said are not intimate. They feed nothing except our ego. A conversation that comes from deep within the memory banks of another person is an intimate one. Compare how you feel at the end of an evening of gossiping versus one of intimate conversation. This will tell you all about the needs of the human soul.

6. Be mindful of what you are doing. When you are gardening be mindful of the garden and you will find immense wisdom. I once wrote 'something' in one of my notebooks and have dug it out by way of an example:

A gardener's notes
I don't have the answers, not even the questions – just some thoughts. In many of my darkest moments I took to the garden and have learned about life through the gardens that I tended with love. I grew my gardens from my heart and this is what I learned.

There is no winter that will not become a spring. No matter how arduous and cold, no matter how bitter the wind and dark the day – it will give way. This winter may numb you to the core of your being but it will not be forever. Spring comes softly and unnoticeably to the undiscerning. You will miss the beginning unless you are looking. Things that looked dead will live again because there is warmth and because the time comes. Death and dormancy often look the same. That which was dormant will spring to life and that which is dead must go. I do not keep dead things in my garden. With regret and sorrow they must go.

The weeds will come. Not to you but to every garden. They are not personal and don't take it personally. They are part of gardens and for reasons that I fail to understand they will flourish more easily than flowers. They are not your fault. They are not a result of what you did or didn't do. They are just a part of a garden. Don't allow the existence of weeds to make gardening a thankless task. Just pull them out, throw them away and move on.

That which is, is. An oak tree will never give you a cherry blossom. You must cherish the acorn and accept it for what it is – it will never be different. Don't miss the magic of the acorn while you are searching for the cherry blossom. It is not for you to decide what it will be. It will be what it is.

Love is not enough. I may love my rose bush but if I don't understand it and know what it needs it will never flourish. It may live but it will never flourish in all its glory. Sometimes I don't have what my plant needs. The protea needs wind. I simply don't have it to give and no amount of effort on my part is going to change that. Better that I give up and apply myself elsewhere much as I may want the protea in my garden. That you care will not be enough.

Cutting and pruning looks savage and unkind but it is not. Deadwood will drain the life from a plant and a brutal pruning may save it. Identify the deadwood and cut it away.

Be generous with your garden. There is so much and the garden will do well when the plants are divided and separated. Often they grow too close and beg for space to be all they can be. Give away the cutting and the excess. You don't need it. The garden needs space and you will see that you don't have less when you have given away.

There are so many ways for a garden to be beautiful. Don't resist change – welcome it. See the beauty in other people's gardens that are not like yours.

Above all else know that the garden will not stay beautiful unless you work and tend to it. Maintain and change, fix and feed, weed and water and tend to it with love.

You have a choice. You can be in the garden and fretting about how lazy and ungrateful the children are or you can be in the garden and be mindful about what the garden has to teach you.

I have asked my clients who have different hobbies if the same exercise can be done and they have shown that indeed it can. One of my clients was a rock climber and he did the most wonderful commentary on rock climbing. The summit was the goal. He talked about finding direction, about decisions linked to risk and about the value of teamwork. He talked about being able to depend on equipment and the habit of perseverance. He told me about savouring the moment on the summit and the climbs that needed to be abandoned and why.

Cooking provides you with the same opportunity. You can cook and be annoyed and rehash a conversation you had last night. You can imagine that tonight you are going to say this or do that. You are going to live in the tumble dryer of your mind or decide more creatively. You can elect to look at your beautiful ingredients and see how perfect they are and marvel at the creation of our Universe. You can think about what it means to cook with love and wonder if it makes a difference. You can be thankful that you have a meal on your table tonight because many don't. You can decide to enjoy your creation even if it's scoffed down without thanks or appreciation. You can think about flavours and colours and presentation, or you can slap it on the table. Just know one thing – I once had a client who told me that his grandmother cooked for him 'with love'. I am not sure if she ever knew he thought that but ten years after her death he said it.

Philippa will tell you how cooking was her salvation over and over again as gardening was mine.

Reflections from the kitchen

In the same way that Sue heads for the garden and Tamlyn to the sewing machine, I make a beeline to the kitchen.

I have a long history of combining food, men and love. Initially I used food to urge my father not to leave us. The moment he began to eat I knew he would stay. Ever since I really believe that I fed men to get them and keep them. I was a walking testimony to the old adage "the quickest way to a man's heart is through his stomach". As always real life is more complicated, as was my love affair with cooking.

Cooking appeals to me for two primary reasons. Firstly, I do like to nurture people. Women often do. Feeding people is a form of nurturing, a way of loving and the way I show that I care. I never want to become an embittered woman who refuses to love 'in case I am hurt'. Without compunction I applaud that part of myself that likes to nurture with food and will continue to do so. I think that is why, no matter how hurt I was, and how often food failed to gain his love or retain his commitment, I continued to cook. Secondly, cooking appeals to me because it resonates profoundly with the aesthetics junkie in me. The world of cooking holds endless possibilities for creativity. One creates with colour, texture, balance and, most of all, flavour.

The kitchen was the place my mind stopped hurting me. If I lay under the duvet I ruminated about what he said and why, what I said and what I should have said. My mind was a mess of painful ideas and images. In the kitchen I was the master of my own mind. I could set it to work on balance and flavour. Here my wayward mind became my servant and worked with me instead of against me. I knew I was competent in the kitchen and so when I stepped back from my delicious creation I was no longer worthless, stupid or crazy. It was the proof I needed to move forward with my life. Alchemy is always possible in the kitchen.

My feelings and my moods were often torment to me. A lot of women I know write when they feel like that. It is their way of 'getting it out and onto the page'. I cooked mine out. I had food for moods. When I was immensely sad I cooked certain meals and when I was mad I cooked other meals. Moods and flavours were my therapy.

Much later I began to see the ways in which my relationships had failed to nurture and sustain me. I can associate men with food types and flavours. One serious relationship I called 'Hamburger' because he could fill you up quickly but not with anything of substance or imagination. One of my husbands I called 'Icicle' because everything about him was so chilling, brutal and unrelenting.

Being a chef never kept me the men I fed with such devotion but I remain a devoted cook. I still cherish my ingredients and the smell of fresh bread baking in my oven. I still believe that food is so much more than fuel for the body – it is my labour of love. It still gives me enormous pride to present a plate of food that is beautiful to the eye, sustenance to the body and poetry to the taste buds."

The point that is being made here is that we can elect to live mindfully and with care and attention to detail and when you do that you start to change. Often my clients ask me how that happens and my answer is always the same: "I don't know. I don't know how meditation reduces stress or why being in nature makes us feel better. I don't know how toddlers learn language but I do know that if you talk to them, one day they talk back. We don't need to know how the psyche regenerates itself, but we do need to believe that it does."

When I was a teenager my father would often say in exasperation: "Nobody can tell you anything, can they?" Well actually they could and I was happy to listen. I have always loved listening. However, what he couldn't do was convince me that it was correct. For that I needed my own life. It was my laboratory. My life was the place that I could test ideas. I could only find my own truth through my own life. I know that I still have more work to do on belief systems that do not serve me well. I have a belief system about relationships that needs attending to.

Contrary to expecting a happy ending, my parents' marriage taught me to expect a miserable end. That belief system allowed me to choose a husband who was almost certain to produce that and he didn't let me down. In order to attend to it I had to first look at it, find out where it came from and watch myself not repeat it. I had to watch people who had successful marriages and I saw that they actually existed. I had to converse with them and celebrate their success and ask questions about their success. I had to be prepared to be wrong and wanted to be. I needed to revisit love and embrace it as a notion with realism and respect.

Attending to a belief system is a process not an event, and I welcome any belief system that serves me well, provided I am sure that it has merit. Remember that every adult has the responsibility to be discerning.

To see clearly is to be free from agony. The co-dependent spends her life in a self-made agony of her obsession of chaos and drama. Unintentionally and subconsciously she perpetuates her own misery. That misery is the lens that we talked about in Part 1. In the absence of these anxious ruminations, they can begin to see through an entirely different lens. The following story shows how Philippa's memories of Africa were so closely linked to the unhappiness of her life. Through the eyes of someone else she can begin to see that South Africa holds promise that she had never previously imagined.

Out of Africa

"I once had a farm in Africa" is the opening line of Karen Blixen's book *Out of Africa*. She then describes in almost excruciating detail where her farm was (in Kenya) and what it looked like. She describes the plateau and the grasses, the wideness of the sky and the layout of the land.

I once had a life in South Africa and I think I barely noticed it at all. I am going back soon. Sue loves South Africa and she has been reminding me about the colours of Africa. They are the clay orange of the earth, the bright red of ripe tomatoes and spilled blood and the yellow of sunflowers and saffron. These are the colours of Africa. South Africa has adopted a philosophy called *Ubuntu*. Its direct translation is humaneness but she says that if you have *Ubuntu* you have jazz in your soul. It is about the soul. She reminds me that the sun is hot and the Highveld lightning storms are like witnessing the wrath of God. There is Table Mountain and vast strips of white sand and a sea so cold it can take your breath away. There is nothing gentle about Africa except the Africans themselves who will smile the widest, whitest smile at your arrival.

For me it was so different. The struggle of South Africa was so like my own. It was about being abused and brutalised for no reason except that you were there. It was about being treated badly for no reason except that they could. The struggle was a long and bloody one and the casualties were high. There were lies and hidden agendas, allies and enemies and the fight was bitter to the end.

Ironically, Africa and I have both found our liberation after years of struggle and labour. South Africa has made so many efforts to heal the scars of the past. The Truth and Reconciliation Commission demanded that the whole truth was made public. Victims of abuse were allowed the opportunity to tell their stories and be heard this time. The Constitution of South Africa has demanded compliance with human rights and finally all the people of South Africa have a free and democratic country to call their own.

Recovery is a messy business and not a straight or easy path but the intention to heal goes a long way to helping the healing process. Sue tells a different story of South Africa. It is not a story of poverty and corruption. It is not the story of poor service delivery and rioting. It is a story of healing with all the setbacks and mistakes that take place along that path.

It is a good time for me to go back and visit the country of my birth. This time I too can pay attention to the colour of the grass and the vastness of the sky. I too can walk along the beach in Cape Town and see the moods of the sea that Sue has told me about. I too am free to look at the country that was my torment and my hell and see that much has changed for it and for me.

To see clearly is to be free from agony. When Sue was with me in the Berkshires I watched her see things around her. She watched the trees and the humming birds, and the plants that aren't in South Africa and colours that aren't their colours. I was too unhappy to see much. I look forward to going back ... without going back to the places and the memories.

Reflection 4

On Reflection

Write an essay of approximately five typed pages entitled "On reflection" and detail what insights you have gained from a period of reflection. If you wish you can submit it to www.whenlovinghimhurts.com.

It can be anything from reflections on your relationship to reflections on the changes you are experiencing in your life or psyche. It can be reflections on the areas where you experience no change or movement.

If you elect not to submit it to the website, we suggest that you begin to keep a journal for reflections that you keep but do not reread for a few weeks. Reflections gain clarity from being written down.

Closing comments

We draw to ourselves that which we can imagine.

It's difficult to find a way to end a book about a journey of self-discovery, which has no ending. Maybe the way is to tell another story about stories?

If I trace the threads of my life, stories have always played a part in some way or another. When we were children my father told us stories about witches who lived in certain houses. Whenever we drove past those houses we crouched down on the car floor for fear of being turned into toads by those witches who disliked even the sight of children. Some afternoons he came into the house bellowing: "Fee-fi-fo-fum"; I smell the blood of an Englishman; Be he alive or be he dead; I'll grind his bones to make my bread", like the giant from *Jack and the Beanstalk*. This was the sign that the giant was home and we scampered around the house looking for hiding places from him. The giant made all the sound effects like banging on the cupboard doors to signal his approach. My childhood was filled with witches and wizards, faraway trees and wishing chairs.

Then I became a young social worker and the stories were different. People asked me over and over how I did this job. They wanted to know why I never found it pointless or depressing. The reason is actually quite simple. Life is not depressing and people's life stories are filled with beauty and redemption, despite the hardships and toil. In every story was a pearl of wisdom and in each were sparks of hope and the indomitable human spirit. At that stage I worked at an out-patient clinic for alcoholics and drug abusers. Every person and every story was another opportunity to beat a dreadful disease. On the surface the situation often looked dire, but inside it wasn't. In my office magic happened and every day I was happy to go to work. That was 35 years ago and to this day I wonder what happened to people I remember. I think of them often and their stories are as important to me today as they were then. From the well-heeled to the homeless, they all counted.

Then I became a mother and started a private practice to be more available to my daughter. She was, in my opinion, quite an anxious little girl and I began to tell her stories in which she could recognise herself as the hero of the story. I thought it might encourage her to find the courage for life that she seemed not to think she had. She loved them and it started a habit of storytelling in our family. "Tell me a story, Mom" was the sentence I heard all the time. Some of the stories I knew from my childhood, some I borrowed and some I made up. Those just grew as I was telling them.

Her friend, Lolo, was the real lover of stories. She would be in the car less than two minutes when she would say, "Sue, please tell us the story about …" Her favourite was David and Goliath. I would explain how poor David, the young shepherd boy, felt when he saw the giant, Goliath. The sun glinted off Goliath's armour in the morning sun. (I had no idea if armour existed then but in my story Goliath had it and David had none.) I described the dust cloud as Goliath hit the desert sand and how the crowd roared, "Yah David, what a man!" She jumped up and down in the car with glee. "What did David say, Sue? Was he happy?" Then I explained very seriously that David was humble and aware that he alone had not slain the giant. At times we would have arrived at our destination and they wouldn't get out of the car until the story was done. We went to the zoo and I told them that seals once sung a seal song but it had been taken from them because of what they did. Those two children arrived at school with a mountain of nonsense about singing seals but they loved the stories of their childhood.

In private practice people continued to tell their stories – often painfully and slowly. It was while I was in private practice that I developed a 'special interest' in abusive relationships for no reason other than that they kept arriving. Who knows why but this world works in strange ways. There was no specific intention on my part but clearly intention was at play. Often my clients suggested that I write a book. I had never intended to do that. I saw myself as the secret-keeper. It was my job to hold those stories close, guard the secret and honour the sacred space in which they were told. How on earth would it be possible for me to write a book and guard the secrets?

When I bumped into Anna in 2014 she told me that the stories of the other women she had met in the support group had helped her feel less lonely and inadequate. The women who wrote the letters after the radio talkshow were telling their stories because they needed to. She convinced me that women didn't want their stories to be kept as secrets that would turn to dust. They needed their stories to be told and they wanted to read other women's stories. It's the only way they really understand that they are not in this alone. They become convinced that there are other women who live the hopeless pendulum that is an abusive relationship. I have come to understand that stories are therapy – both in the telling and in the hearing.

The truth is that I was uncharacteristically unprepared for this project. I just began to write and vaguely intended to employ someone to attend to the social media aspect of this. My daughter was wholly unconvinced. "Teaching you to copy and paste has been a challenge. I have seen you when people talk about cyberspace – you look like they're talking Japanese." Undeterred I continued to write.

In the interim my uncle passed away and left me some money and no sooner had that been paid than I received a call from Philippa who had recently moved to the Berkshires. That made it possible for me to take a trip to the USA. Within three days of talking I knew that I had found my new partner. She too was willing to tell her story publicly, and her honesty and self-examination was incisive and insightful. Over and above that, she was experienced in publishing, having written her own book and published a recipe book. Philippa has boundless energy and commitment to her projects and from the balcony of her home we launched this project properly.

Anna had stayed in her marriage and Philippa had left and both were doing well. I was able to write a book without breaking any confidences and I had found a way to keep Anna from 'mentioning' the plight of abused women every time she clapped eyes on me.

Every day I am in awe of the circumstances that made this possible. Even the time differences between South Africa and the USA has worked for us. While she sleeps I write and while I sleep she writes. When we wake up our computers are full of the thoughts and ideas that were born during our days. Had you asked me if I thought this possible I would have told you that it was not. My job as a therapist is to keep sacred all that is said to me and so it must be. Secret-keepers don't write books about other people's stories.

My deepest wish now is that, having reached this part of the book, you are already wiser, more self-controlled and braver than you were when you started. Like a faithful member of AA I ask that you go back again and again to the information in this book. It is not a book to read and put away. It requires practice and re-reading. Alcoholics go back to AA because each week they learn something new. You will find something new that resonates with you every time you read it. Act it until you become it and I promise you that if you work at your recovery, you will have it.

ANNA'S STORY

I want our readers to know that they are not alone – there are hundreds of thousands of us. When I was a much younger woman I experienced the most excruciating loneliness and shame and so I told no one about what was actually going on in my home. That first support group gave me such comfort. I sat and listened to women telling my story and for the first time I really understood that the shame was his and not mine – even if he didn't feel it. Finally I didn't feel it either.

It's so difficult to work out what my parting comments are because much of importance has already been said. I must rely on my own story at the end. It's fitting.

I wake up every morning of my life and despite anything that may have happened last night or last week, I decide that today I will do three acts of human kindness. This commitment to acts of kindness are expressions of my gratitude for the life I have been blessed with. For many years my greatest challenge was self-pity. I was so hurt and felt so short-changed by this horrible marriage despite my best efforts. Self-pity was my narrative. That has changed completely and today my narrative is one of immense gratitude and appreciation for the life I have. I express my gratitude with those acts of human kindness. I feel very blessed and as a result I want to give to others constantly.

The second huge shift for me was to release fears about what people thought and felt about me. I had spent so much time grovelling for approval that it had become a way of life. Now I can honestly say that I no longer care what people think of me or how they feel about me. I care what I think and feel. I check my own behaviour against my own standards and I pass or fail. If I fail, I commit myself to improve but mine are the only standards that I will live by.

My final comment is on listening and possibly that is a symptom of my marriage. Being married to a narcissist means that I have spent a great deal of time listening to him on every subject imaginable – from greenhouse gas to my appalling housekeeping. I listen to the story of his aching finger and the in-house favourite – that last night's dinner has given him a stomach ache! I listen to him on how wonderful he is. All these years of listening has made me an expert and again I am grateful for the skill.

I have learned that if you listen very carefully you hear what is actually being told to you instead of merely what is being said. They are seldom the same thing. I am the success I am today because I know how to listen. My clients tell me much more than they say and I can keep quiet long enough to hear. People are so keen to express their opinions on things that they miss the symphony of truth that you will hear when you really listen. I hear what is not said and what is said so defensively that I know it's a lie. I hear the yearning to tell the truth and the fear of really being seen. I know that abused women are told to "shut up" constantly. I actually did that and as a result I can hear because I know how to be quiet. While you are shutting up you might well be learning what no one else will hear.

My parting words are to wish you all well, to urge you to put down the shame that does not belong to you and pick up your game. Be smart, be subtle and learn to keep your own counsel.

Philippa closes with the following wise comments:

Like Sue, I too am going to start this off with a story. When I sat in a Grade 11 history class, the teacher described the Latin expression *"deus ex machina"* in relation to some event that occurred in the past. I can't remember what it was but the words resonated so profoundly I never forgot them. He explained it by way of an example of Superman: when a woman is about to fall to her death from a high bridge, Superman sweeps in to save her just before she hits the ground. I recognise that, despite Sue's best efforts, only I could slowly and painstakingly resolve my problems. However, when I have felt on the brink of my own destruction, I have felt saved by Sue. In that way, Sue has been my *"deus ex machina"* for the past 22 years. Now she can be yours.

I mentioned in the book that one of the many lessons I learned from Sue was how careful she is with her words. It was my first lesson in discernment. As an abused woman the word *'value'* had no place in my vocabulary. Words had no value, the relationship had no value, trust had no value, respect had no value, and neither did self-respect. It makes sense then that the expression applied to learning new healthy patterns of behaviour is likened to 'learning a new language'. Sue was my new language.

I am going to attempt to explain how I learned to value Sue's words. Unlike a lot of therapists, Sue offers opinions. They are actually more than opinions; more like prophesies as each one came true. Over the years I collected notes from my conversations with her. Each word landed so perfectly for every crisis that I needed them to comfort me long after the phone was down or a therapy session was over.

When I was with my first alcoholic, drug-addict boyfriend, I took him to see Sue. He insisted on leaving for Europe the day after I returned from a cooking trip to Thailand. "There comes a time in everyone's life when they reach a crossroad," Sue explained to him. "They are given the choice of taking the healthy path or the destructive one. You are being offered this choice. We both know that you want to get away for two reasons. Firstly, you are still angry that Phil went on the trip and childishly want to punish her. Secondly, you are in the initial stages of your latest binge. As long as Phil is around it's difficult for you to drug and drink." He insisted on going and sadly he died a few months later. I think of this conversation every time I reach a crossroad in my life.

With my second husband she implored me not to marry him. I was still sceptical of her theories in those days and ignored her warnings. When he took an overdose of sleeping pills one afternoon I called Sue hysterically. "Don't worry," she said calmly, "he loves himself too much to kill himself." Of course she was right. She asked me to call the paramedics. They took one look at him and said he hadn't taken enough to warrant a trip to the hospital. After seven years of abuse I ran back to Sue to pick up the pieces. Not once did she throw in an "I told you so" or judge me. I lived for my weekly or sometimes twice weekly sessions. It was my only link to sanity.

When I met my third husband I introduced him to Sue before I married him. She declared him an inane wimp. Still not certain that I could trust her instincts or predictions I went ahead anyway. During that divorce, I called her often from Los Angeles. This is an example of one of the magical conversations I had with her: "I am so angry with him for what he did to Jamie and the lies he told that I am consumed with ways of exacting revenge," I complained to Sue over the miles of static.

"Why would you want to do it yourself when the Universe does it better? Watch it play out brilliantly as it's done. Look at what's happened already. His being thrown out of his house highlights the 'circles within circles'. His kids drove you out; yours drove him out. What he did to Jamie he did to himself. Jamie was homeless; *he's* now homeless. He made Jamie insecure about his future; now he's insecure. He did the same to you. He allowed you to think that everything was fine when he sent the letter describing how much he loved you and then threatened divorce two days later. He now has a suitcase in his hand, exactly what he wanted for you. He wanted to give you a court order; he got a court order. When you start to see the links, it leaves you amazed. He's booking his lies for the future, and the Universe will take care of him way more creatively than you can. The best partner in the world is the Universe because it's a partnership with infinite intelligence."

This conversation had a profound effect on me. Revenge is a waste of time because with every abusive relationship, the Universe did take care of them way more creatively than I could ever imagine. What this also taught me was to live a life of integrity. "We attract what we give out," Sue often reminds me. She showed me this by way of a drawing. She drew a circle and then explained how bits of the circle get knocked off by life experiences. We then land up as a funny shape. We go out and look for a relationship with a funnier shape to fit our funny shape. A relationship built on this can only fail. She taught me through the value of words how to re-build my funny shape into a perfect circle.

I love the concept of 'circles within circles' and am always on high alert in recognising them. It's fitting that the last circle on words and language was drawn here in the Berkshires. When Sue arrived to visit and asked me to work on this book with her, initially I was too stunned to respond. I was overcome with emotion. If ever I needed confirmation on how far I have come it arrived with her offer.

The day before we submitted our final re-write to the editor somebody said the words, "Philippa, you are safe." The word 'safe' brought tears to my eyes. Sue and I have just been talking about how this word has not featured in this book. It is fitting and serendipitous that it should arrive at the end as the perfect conclusion.

Working on this project has been a gift of a lifetime. It is a privilege to work with Sue and an honour to offer my experiences to other women who live with challenges similar to mine. Unlike Anna, I had to leave. Had I remained in my second marriage he would have killed me. Thankfully by my third marriage I had placed enough value on myself to know I deserved better. Having said this, I know how terrifying it is to leave. Sue often reminded me that all I would get if I remained in the marriage was brain damage. At least when I left there was an end to it. When the brain damage ended and the healing began, a way of life opened up that I never even dreamed of. Had I known, I would have left sooner. We don't need to know all the answers when we first leave. When I dwelt on that I became overwhelmed with the impossibility of it all. I learned to take one day at a time and some days I could only do minutes. The days added up and each day of healing brought me closer to a life absent of abuse. For me, that is the only life worth living.

If you remain silent the shame is yours.
If you speak out the shame is his.
Shout out as loud as you can.

The end of this book is not 'The End'. To see clearly is to be free from agony. Abused women live under the radar, unheard and voiceless. We aim to change that and have created a support network for abused women around the world on our Facebook page: When Loving Him Hurts. Join us and share your thoughts, fears and victories. You can also email us at: whenlovinghimhurts@gmail.com.

Recommended reading list

Here is a list of books that we found inspirational in the writing of this book. Many of these are classics and there are several editions available in addition to those we mention here.

Cameron, Julia, *The Artist's Way: A Spiritual Path to Higher Creativity*, published in 1992 by Souvenir Press.

Eckhart, Meister, *Selected Writings*, published in 1995 by Penguin Classics.

Pinkola Estés, Dr Clarissa, *Women who Run with the Wolves*, republished in 1994 by Random House.

Forward, Dr Susan, *Men who Hate Women and the Women Who Love Them*, republished in 1986 by Bantam Books.

Gold, Taro, *Open Your Mind, Open Your Life: A Book of Eastern Wisdom*, published in 2002 by Lionstead Press.

Kehoe, John P., *Mind Power into the 21st Century*, published in 1997 by Sterling Publishers.

Kehoe, John P., *Quantum Warrior: The Future of the Mind*, published in 2011 by Zoetic, Incorporated.

Thamm, Marianne, *I have Life: Alison's Story*, published in 1998 by Penguin Books.

Williams, Margery, *The Velveteen Rabbit*, republished in 2010 by HarperCollins.

31702911R00157

Made in the USA
Middletown, DE
02 January 2019